Praise for *Behold, America*

newspapers to novels is a marvel. But it is more than a history lesson. She's constructing the case for how the US elected Donald Trump, a catastrophe many of us struggle to understand' *Prospect*

'A richly engaging account' Dominic Sandbrook, *Sunday Times*

'Churchwell takes us on a whirlwind tour of the first decades of the twentieth century ... We hear the discordant voices of American reformers, immigrants, reactionaries and nativists, satirists and polemicists, Ku Klux Klansmen and ersatz Hitlers ... Churchwell is well attuned to the nuances of the national conversation' *Literary Review*

'Both brilliant and painfully timely' Alex Preston, *Observer Summer Reads*

'*Behold, America* explores how these two underpinning catch-phrases have more complicated histories than Trump would ever acknowledge ... As Churchwell persuasively and painstakingly demonstrates, the "American dream" meant something quite different then ... Impressive' *Tablet*

'Timely and instructive' *Economist*

'[An] enlightening new cultural history ... The shadow of the 45th President hangs over all 300 pages of *Behold, America*, a book designed expressly to demonstrate just how that history rhymes with the present ... While it is indeed a history of two phrases, *Behold, America* is also a history of the people who used them ... An American in the UK, [Churchwell] has the benefit of an outside perspective on the country of her birth, which is prone to national self-delusions just as grand as Britain's, if not more so. *Behold, America* punctures many of them' *i*

'*Behold, America* is rooted in an acute sensitivity to language. Churchwell's primary concern is to unpack, from a trawl of the press, political speeches and literary works, what early twentieth-century

Americans meant by the common expressions "America First" and the "American dream". But the book is much more than a study of these catch-phrases, and she deftly relates them to wider social, political and cultural developments' Colin Kidd, *Guardian*

'Sharp, polemical ... Churchwell is determined to break through the received wisdom of the two sayings by studying primary sources ... Ideas of equality of opportunity, justice and democracy for all are retreating from what she calls the "rising tide of domestic fascism". If she is correct, her work as an arbiter of the public understanding of the humanities has never been more important. She is Boudicca rising up against the ascendancy of "America First" and the prostitution of the "American dream"' *Irish Examiner*

'Literary journalist and professor Sarah Churchwell digs a little deeper than most, providing a thoughtful long view on a highly topical subject' *BBC History Magazine*, Summer Reads

A NOTE ON THE AUTHOR

SARAH CHURCHWELL is Professor of American Literature and Chair of Public Understanding of the Humanities at the School of Advanced Study, University of London. She is the author of *Careless People: Murder, Mayhem and the Invention of* The Great Gatsby and *The Many Lives of Marilyn Monroe*. Her literary journalism has appeared widely in newspapers and she comments regularly on arts, culture and politics for television and radio, where appearances include *Question Time, Newsnight* and *The Review Show*. She has judged many literary prizes, including the 2017 Baillie Gifford Prize for Nonfiction and the 2014 Man Booker Prize, and she was a co-winner of the 2015 Eccles British Library Writer's Award.

BEHOLD, AMERICA

A History of America First and the American Dream

Sarah Churchwell

BLOOMSBURY PUBLISHING
LONDON · OXFORD · NEW YORK · NEW DELHI · SYDNEY

BLOOMSBURY PUBLISHING
Bloomsbury Publishing Plc
50 Bedford Square, London, WC1B 3DP, UK

BLOOMSBURY, BLOOMSBURY PUBLISHING and the Diana logo are trademarks of
Bloomsbury Publishing Plc

First published in Great Britain 2018
This edition published 2019

A catalogue record for this book is available from the British Library

ISBN: HB: 978-1-4088-9480-4; TPB: 978-1-5266-0113-1;
eBook: 978-1-4088-9479-8; PB: 978-1-4088-9477-4

2 4 6 8 10 9 7 5 3 1

Typeset by Newgen KnowledgeWorks Pvt. Ltd., Chennai, India
Printed and bound in Great Britain by CPI Group (UK) Ltd, Croydon CR0 4YY

To find out more about our authors and books visit www.bloomsbury.com
and sign up for our newsletters

MIX
Paper from
responsible sources
FSC® C020471

CONTENTS

x Coolidge CONTENTS

LIST OF ILLUSTRATIONS

Oh, critic and cynic, dreamer and doubter, behold America, as this day she stands before her history and her heroes. See her millions of people, her free institutions, her equal laws, her generous opportunities, her schoolhouses and her churches; you see misfortunes and defects, for not yet is fully realized the American dream; you surely see her mighty progress toward the fulfillment of her philosophy.

Oration in honour of President Ulysses S. Grant, 1895

It was an effort toward some commonweal, an effort difficult to estimate, so closely does it press against us all ...

F. Scott Fitzgerald, 1933

INTRODUCTION

There is great power in loaded phrases, as anyone willing to pull the trigger knows.

'Sadly, the American dream is dead,' Donald Trump proclaimed on 16 June 2015, announcing his candidacy for president of the United States. It seemed an astonishing thing for a candidate to say; people campaigning for president usually glorify the nation they hope to lead, flattering voters into choosing them. But this reversal was just a taste of what was to come, as Trump revealed an unnerving skill at twisting what would be negative for anyone else into a positive for himself.

By the time he won the election, Trump had flipped much of what many people thought they knew about America on its head. In his acceptance speech Trump again pronounced the American dream dead, but promised to revive it. We were told that the American dream of prosperity was under threat, so much so that a platform of 'economic nationalism' carried the presidency.

Reading last rites over the American dream was shocking enough. But throughout the campaign Trump also promised to put 'America first', a pledge renewed in his inaugural speech in January 2017. It was a disquieting phrase for a presidential candidate, and then president-elect, to keep using. Think pieces on the history of 'America first' began to sprout up in the national press and on social media, informing their audiences that the slogan 'America first' stretches back to the Second World War, and to the efforts of the America First Committee to keep the United States out of the European conflict. 'America first' had been invented by high-profile isolationists like Charles Lindbergh, they explained, whose sympathy with the Nazi project was often inextricable from an avowed anti-Semitism. 'America first', they said, was a code for neo-Nazism.

Meanwhile, other pundits were weighing in on the 'American dream', as writers asked if it was indeed dead.[1] Nearly all of these pieces began with a shared understanding of what the American dream was supposed to entail: namely, upward social mobility, a national promise of endless individual progress. But now, thanks to epidemic levels of inequality, that dream was widely viewed as under threat, a story that had been endlessly recycled across the international press for the decade since the financial crisis beginning in 2007. Trump had weaponised this inequality, they said, convincing his followers that only an outsider could redeem a corrupt system. (That he was in fact a plutocratic insider, a self-styled billionaire corporate tycoon, was hardly the last bit of cognitive dissonance his followers were prepared to disavow.)

But most did not question what the American dream meant; they only debated its relative health. A *Guardian* editorial from June 2017, for example, called 'Is the American Dream Really Dead?', summed up not only the questions everyone was asking, but the premises from which they began.

> The United States has a long-held reputation for exceptional tolerance of income inequality, explained by its high levels of social mobility. This combination underpins the American dream — initially conceived of by Thomas Jefferson as each citizen's right to the pursuit of life, liberty and the pursuit of happiness. This dream is not about guaranteed outcomes, of course, but the pursuit of opportunities … Yet the opportunity to live the American dream is much less widely shared today than it was several decades ago.[2]

Few would dispute any of this: the American dream is widely understood as a dream of personal opportunity, in which 'opportunity' is gauged primarily in economic terms, and those opportunities are shrinking. The idea that the American dream was 'initially conceived' by Jefferson is similarly axiomatic, despite the fact that happiness and opportunity are not, in fact, synonymous.

But what Jefferson conceived – at least in terms of life, liberty and the pursuit of happiness – was a dream of democratic equality. He doesn't mention economics, or opportunity, for good reason. In fact, Jefferson took John Locke's phrase, 'life, liberty and property', and changed property into happiness. While it is true that in the eighteenth century 'happiness' was often used to mean 'flourishing', which can clearly imply prosperity, Jefferson nonetheless removed specific economic guarantees from the nation's founding entitlements. Democratic equality and economic opportunity are not the same thing, but the American dream has, for decades, been used as if they are.

The *Guardian* piece ends by noting the self-defeating nature of the 'dream' as understood in these terms. 'Ironically, part of the problem may actually *be* the American dream ... Indeed, the dream, with its focus on individual initiative in a meritocracy, has resulted in far less public support than there is in other countries for safety nets, vocational training, and community support for those with disadvantage or bad luck.' The dream is of the individual capitalist striving in a free-market world, one that is inimical to the 'safety nets' of social democracy. Again, this understanding of the dream is entirely typical of how it is construed today – not just by Americans, but around the world.

But although this meaning of the dream is unquestionably the one Americans inherited, this book will show that it is exactly the reverse of the ideas the 'American dream' was coined to advance. Gradually in 2017 a few writers began to notice that the American dream had once included higher dreams of personal fulfilment, beyond the wish to live in an up-to-date department store (as an American historian put it back in 1933).[3] But its reduction to sheer materialism is, in fact, the least of the expression's changes in meaning.

The *Oxford English Dictionary* defines the American dream as 'the ideal that every citizen of the United States should have an equal opportunity to achieve success and prosperity through hard work, determination, and initiative'. Certainly Americans have always built individual aspiration into a mythology. But upward social mobility is not an idea associated with the expression 'the American dream' until much later than most people think – a fact that has profound implications for the cultural and political fight the US (and indeed much of the West) now finds itself in, for how America sees itself and its own promises.

The received wisdoms about 'America first' are similarly misunderstood or delimited – including those offered by eminent historians. Timothy Snyder gave a highly representative description of 'America first' in a 2017 interview, explaining – as nearly every pundit has – that 'America first' goes back to the Second World War. 'Trump and Bannon's idea of "America First" is technically from 1940,' Snyder stated, 'but it is meant as nostalgia for the period before America entered the world in WWII and before the welfare state. The "America First" movement included many populists and white supremacists.'[4] While it is true that 'America first' always included many populists and white supremacists, it is not true that it emerged in response to the welfare state that was created in the 1930s, or that it represented a nostalgia for the period before the 1930s. In fact, the phrase was popularised well before the 1930s, and the nostalgias it represented were considerably more complicated than this abbreviated, widely recycled, version of its origins suggests.

By 1940 'America first' had been entangled in America's political narrative for decades. Charles Lindbergh and the America First Committee of 1940 were not the beginning of the story of 'America first'. They were the end – until Donald Trump resuscitated the term.

And the American dream isn't dead, either – we just have no idea what it means any more.

Behold, America tells the history of these two loaded phrases, a tale that upends much of what we thought we knew about both, perhaps even about America itself.

It turns out that America first and the American dream were always connected, and contested, terms in a nation finding its way. A nation losing its way might do well to contest these terms once more.

* * *

History rarely starts when we think it did, and it never seems to end when we think it should. Nor does it tend to say what we think it will. The phrases 'American dream' and 'America first' were born almost exactly a century ago – and rapidly tangled over capitalism, democracy and race, the three fates always spinning America's destiny.

Received wisdoms can become self-fulfilling prophecies – loaded dice, rigging the conversation. When what's on the table are national values, and our language obscures from us important truths about those values, the stakes grow very high. Returning to original sources can overturn those common wisdoms, exposing the gaps between what we tell each other that history shows, and what it actually says.

Behold, America offers a genealogy of national debates around these two expressions, most of which have been forgotten. The evolution of these two sayings – both their myths and their truths – has shaped reality in ways not fully understood. We cannot understand the subtexts of our own slogans if we do not understand their contexts; we risk misreading our own moment if we don't know the historical meanings of expressions we resuscitate, or perpetuate. We cannot hear a dog whistle if we are not in its range.

Phrases can form chains of association, conceptual paths that the mind follows intuitively, even unconsciously, as one word, or idea, seems to lead naturally to another. Those chains of association help define political and social realities, and it's only by tracing the words, how people skip from one to the next without necessarily even being aware of it, that we understand how these ideas have evolved.

Take, for a different example, Ronald Reagan's often cited 'city on a hill', in which he suggested that America was a shining ideal held up to the world to emulate. That is a very Cold War idea, and it's basically the antithesis of what John Winthrop, who coined the phrase 'city upon a hill', said in 1630.

Winthrop used 'city upon a hill' not to suggest the nation would be a glorious beacon. Instead, it was a metaphor for a place everyone could see and judge: the singularity of the American experiment meant that the world would be watching.

> We must Consider that we shall be as a City upon a Hill, the eyes of all people are upon us; so that if we shall deal falsely with our god in this work we have undertaken and so cause him to withdraw his present help from us, we shall be made a story and a byword through the world, we shall open the mouths of enemies to speak evil of the ways of god and all professors for God's sake.

Our equivalent simile would be a goldfish bowl: Winthrop was urging Americans to strive for moral excellence, because the world would judge the outcome of the experiment. The message of Winthrop's 'city upon a hill' amounts to: 'We mustn't fail, because everyone is watching. If we fail, we'll become a laughing stock, and bring our ideas into global disrepute.' It's not self-congratulation; it's a warning.

We need to be able to tell the difference between alarm bells and victory peals. Compared to Winthrop, Reagan's speech was the goldfish preening himself on being watched as he bumps blindly into the glass. The degradation of ideas matters to our society: anyone who doubts that should look at the current state of our toxic civil discourse, about which there is almost nothing civil left at all. Reagan's 'city on a hill' became a shorthand that distorted ideas of American exceptionalism. America wasn't supposed to be an exceptional place because its citizens had dreams, or even because those dreams sometimes came true. That's true of everyone. It was supposed to be exceptional in being a place dedicated to the proposition of helping those dreams to be realised – but the nation's dreams were meant to be exceptional, too.

The American dream and America first have similarly been misunderstood, and misrepresented. The American dream – far from validating a simple desire for personal advancement – once gave voice to principled appeals for a more generous way of life. And America first was no mere temporary pushback against Roosevelt's creation of the welfare state. The nationalism embedded in the phrase had a long-standing and profound purchase on many Americans' understanding of their country, and its connection with anxieties about American fascism did not begin in 1940.

In 1941, an American journalist named Dorothy Thompson, who had been in Europe during the rise of fascism in the early 1930s, wrote about Charles Lindbergh, at the time (and now once more) the most famous embodiment of America first.

> Lindbergh's behavior is confusing only if one fails to remember that it can be a political tactic to confuse. If one assumes that Lindbergh confuses *consciously*, then his behavior fits a pattern. Lindbergh's behavior does fit a pattern – a thoroughly familiar pattern. It is the pattern of revolutionary politics designed by Adolf Hitler. Lindbergh's technique, his whole campaign, is singularly without inventiveness. It has all happened before. To anyone who has studied the rise of popular demagogues bent on making New Orders of Society, Lindbergh is old stuff.
>
> I am absolutely certain in my mind that Lindbergh is pro-Nazi; that Lindbergh hates the present democratic system; that Lindbergh intends to remake that system and emerge as America's savior and that Lindbergh intends to be President of the United States, with a new party along Nazi lines behind him.[5]

The similarities between what Thompson says in 1941 and our political situation today might seem like a coincidence. But what looks at first like historical coincidence may, instead, simply be a pattern we haven't discerned yet.

* * *

We're all asking urgent questions about the present, but there are far more surprising answers than many think to be found in the past. The backstory of these two charged expressions might help us understand how we found ourselves facing these problems today – and even, perhaps, how to resolve them.

After the end of the Cold War, the triumph of Western liberalism gradually became taken for granted, the 'end of history' even famously pronounced. Many were deeply shocked by the sudden rise of authoritarian nationalism around the world in the first years of the twenty-first century, particularly in the United States, which liked to proclaim that 'it can't happen here'. But of course it can – and it has. There has always been a tension, in America, too, between liberal democracy and authoritarianism.

And for a long time you could fairly say that in the United States that debate played out between ideas represented by the phrase 'American dream' and those represented by 'America first'. In the first half of the twentieth century there was a clear contest over the national value system, and the two expressions came to voice opposing views. One might be tempted to call it a battle for the nation's soul, if that weren't a cliché. So call it a battle over the moral economy, instead; or even a battle for the nation's future, a battle still being fought.

There is a clear and powerful strain of populist demagoguery in American history, from President Andrew Jackson to Louisiana Senator Huey Long, one that now extends to Donald Trump. Eruptions of American conservative populism are nothing new. A country in which the theocratic religious right has so often achieved political power, in which the Ku Klux Klan has periodically imposed sweeping regimes of terror, in which McCarthy and his witch hunts took hold, is far from immune to indigenous strains of authoritarianism.

As this story will show, reactionary populism in the United States has historically defined itself against the same enemies – urban elites, immigrants, liberals, progressives and organised labour; and for the same beliefs – evangelical Protestantism, traditional 'family values' and white supremacy. Trump has once again brought Americans face-to-face with a deeply rooted populist conservatism, one that defines itself in opposition to groups of people it constructs as 'alien' or 'un-American'. And that populism is consistently drawn to demagogues and authoritarians.

* * *

The protagonists of this book are thus not people, or historical events, but these two expressions – America first and the American dream – as they were used in regional and national newspapers, magazines, books and speeches that circulated around the country in the first half of the twentieth century.

The story begins as the last Gilded Age was drawing to a close, a hundred years ago. The end of the Civil War in 1865 had marked the coming of American modernity, the dominance of finance capitalism and the new industrial technologies that transformed the nation, both physically and psychologically. The power of modern America was built on the ruins of institutionalised slavery; the post-bellum generation they called 'Big Money' energised the country, galvanised its desires, and began to glorify the enduring mercenary strains in American life.

This is when most of the people whose words fill this book were born, as the Gilded Age yielded to the Progressive Era, at the moment when sheer, indiscriminate acquisitiveness was becoming America's secular religion.

There are only a handful of 'important' authors in what follows, including F. Scott Fitzgerald, John Steinbeck, Theodore Dreiser, Sinclair Lewis and William Faulkner, whose novels about the 'American dream' as it is now understood and transmitted are so central to our ideas about the phrase that it would distort the story to exclude them.[6]

Most of the voices speaking in this book are not famous authorities, however. They are anonymous, forgotten, the voices of ordinary citizens writing in their local newspapers. There are plenty of politicians, and newspaper editors, yes – and the occasional newspaper owner – along with the lesser influence of reporters and columnists, many of whom, though famous in their day, are all but forgotten now. But there are also ministers, professors, businessmen, headmasters, housewives, valedictorians, speakers at county fairs and society lunches, Americans from all walks of life, and from all over the country, who gave voice to these emerging ideas in ways their local papers saw fit to record and share with the community around them. They are liberal and conservative, white and black, Christian and Jew, male and female, foreign-born and nativist. And they show that these expressions meant things to significant portions of the country that are very different from what most Americans assume today they have always meant.

In an origin story about the ideas of a nation, words matter – especially because their rhetoric informs so much of our own political reality. Furthermore, many of these anonymous Americans were frankly more thoughtful, and more informed, than we may be about our own assumptions. They were often acutely aware of what was at stake in their debates; when they spoke of an American dream they tended to invoke one that is richer, more textured and more expansive than the one we refer to, and when they spoke of America first they were speaking of far more than an anti-Semitic pilot's tacit support for Hitler.

While the turbulent and complex history of American national politics forms a backdrop here, this book is thus almost exclusively drawn from primary sources, to try to resist received wisdoms. As we shall see again and again, nuance gets lost in transmission; returning to the originals lets us reconsider what we thought we knew.

Moreover, a traditional 'historical account' can't help but suggest that its conflicts and debates have been consigned to the past. But the battles being fought in this book are by no means over, and these forgotten opinions and comments may show us a different way to fight them. These are not the dead fights of a distant culture – these are traditions inherited and replayed, without being truly understood.

One of the benefits of this approach is that it reminds us of a central distinction between American political discourse in the first half of the twentieth century and in the first half of the twenty-first. A hundred years ago, Americans got their facts from the same collective sources: first newspapers and then radio broadcasts and newsreels. (This history ends before television begins.) They had their own opinions and judgements about those facts, of course; but the facts were not in dispute. This meant it was possible to have far more shared understandings of political reality than is now the case, thanks to our hyper-fragmented, hyper-partisan, hyper-marketised new medias. We have managed to produce a world in which facts and the news themselves are in constant dispute from voices at the very top of our government and media chains. That is, as most people recognise, a very big problem.

It's often remarked that the American dream is there to compensate for the nightmare of reality, American society as a lottery that everyone plays and no one wins. We know that dream – its assurances, its betrayals – so well that we think they're the only meanings available to us, that these ever-receding promises are all the American dream ever meant. And 'America first' is treated as a sudden aberration, the anomalous return of a fascist ghost that briefly stalked American history for a few months before the US joined the fight against Hitler. Turns out we were wrong on both counts.

The loss of cultural memory is a kind of death, for culture is sustained by memory. We do not have to accept others' narrow understanding of our meanings. Here is another version, told by the voices of the past.

First, America First

On Monday 30 May 1927, a cool day with showers forecast, New Yorkers were gathering for the annual Memorial Day parades around the city. It was only nine years since the end of the great European war, into which America had been so reluctantly drawn, and Europe had suddenly become closer than ever before. Precisely ten days earlier, Charles Lindbergh had completed the first solo flight across the Atlantic in the *Spirit of St. Louis*, and no one had yet stopped celebrating. Front pages around the country reported that Lucky Lindy had been mobbed in London, greeted by rapturous crowds of 150,000. Few Americans were talking about much else than the newest national hero, but in New York that day different kinds of mobs were about to gather.

Around 8 a.m., a group of Italian immigrants living in the Bronx set out for the elevated train on their way to Manhattan to join the parade. But they were not going to honour the American soldiers who had died in the service of their country. They were supporters of Mussolini, planning to join four hundred American Fascists who were marching in Manhattan's Memorial Day parade as part of the official Fascist movement in America. They had been invited by the parade's organisers, to the outrage of many anti-Fascists, including Italian nationalists and anarchists who threatened violence if the invitation wasn't rescinded. It wasn't.

Like all his fellow Fascists intending to march that day, Joseph Carisi was wearing the blackshirt uniform, sporting leather boots, jodhpurs, a black cap, and carrying a steel-tipped riding crop. When he stopped to buy a newspaper, Carisi was jumped by two men, stabbed in the neck and left to die on the sidewalk. Another Fascist, Nicholas Amoroso, who was running either to catch up with his group or away from the killers (reports vary), was shot four times, once right through the heart. One of the two murdered men had served in the American army during the Great War, the other with the Italian army, papers reported.[1]

The parade they had meant to join took place without them, a Fascist delegation of several hundred that was guarded by police 'to avert disorder'.[2] After the parade the American blackshirts returned to their headquarters, in the heart of Times Square. There another of the Fascists, standing outside, was set upon by three men. He defended himself with his riding crop, as his fellow blackshirts charged out brandishing clubs and whips, chasing the assailants through theatre crowds in Times Square, who fled as 'the black-shirted mob tore through traffic'.[3] A hundred Fascists, reported the *New York Times*, rushed the attackers; a 'melee' ensued that was quickly dispersed by the police.

There was also violence in Brooklyn, where a parade of Fascisti marched from the Angelo Rizza Fascista League at 274 Troutman Street, in Bushwick. The *LA Times* reported 'several hundred men' were parading, 'including forty or fifty in the black shirt uniform'. Fights broke out between supporters and protesters mingling on the sidewalks, and an anti-Fascist was found lying on the ground, stabbed in the back. He survived, and identified a Fascist as his assailant. Accompanied by thirty police reserves to forestall violence, the marchers made their way through Brooklyn, stopping at the Wilson Avenue station, where the Fascisti came to attention and gave the Fascist salute. They ended at a Roman Catholic church, where the priest blessed them under large American and Italian flags while the police remained on guard.

The biggest outbreak of violence that Memorial Day, however, occurred in Queens, where it centred around a different right-wing group: not Italian-Americans, but the self-proclaimed 'one hundred percent American' kind.

By 1927, the Ku Klux Klan had spread across the United States
since its rebirth in Georgia twelve years earlier. The first Klan was
formed in the immediate aftermath of the Civil War, as former
Confederate soldiers in Tennessee created a secret society to
promote white supremacism and terrorise the newly freed slaves
in the South during the Reconstruction Era. (The name is generally
believed to have originated from the Greek word for 'circle', *kuklos*,
while 'klan' pays homage to the mystified Celtic heritage supposedly
shared by white Southerners.) Within a decade or two, the first
Klan had been successfully suppressed by law enforcement, and
died out by the turn of the century. But in 1915, it was resuscitated
in Georgia, and by the early 1920s the Second Klan had achieved
a powerful political presence in the United States, not only in the
South, but across the country.

The Klan had an active presence in New York City and Long
Island by 1927, with favourite slogans, which they even attempted
to copyright at various points. That year the Klan was 'call[ing]
attention to the fact that it first announced the program of one
hundred per cent "Americanism" and of "America first"'.[4] They
were not, in fact, the first to adopt these mottos, as this book
will show: in 1927, both phrases had been around for a decade
or more.

But as far as the Klan – busily copyrighting hate – was concerned,
'America first' belonged to them, and on Memorial Day in Queens a
thousand or so of them had gathered to march, many in white robes
and hoods. They were accompanied by four hundred women from
the so-called 'Klavana' (the 'feminine branch' of the Klan). Some of
the reported 20,000 spectators in Queens that day objected to the
Klan's presence, as others defended their right to march; scuffles
broke out, and it turned into a riot. 'Women fought women and
spectators fought the policemen and the Klansmen, as their desire
dictated.' Klan banners were shredded, and 'five of their number'
were arrested, said initial reports, while a few others were caught
up in the confusion as well.[5]

Although the police in Queens had been ordered to keep the Klan in check, 'the Klan worsted detachments' of police 'on four separate occasions during its four-mile march and surged triumphantly past the reviewing stands, little the worse except for a number of tattered robes and dismantled hoods and five marchers in the custody of the police'.[6]

The police commissioner announced that neither American Fascists nor the Ku Klux Klan should have been allowed to parade in the first place. 'Ku Klux Klan members involved in the Memorial Day parade riot in Queens, "clearly were guilty of a breach of faith with the police",' said the commissioner. '"Neither the Klan nor the Fascisti have a proper place in a parade dedicated to the soldier dead of the United States."'[7] Within a week, New York had banned any public appearance by either 'the white-robed Ku Klux Klan' or 'the black-shirted Fascisti'.[8]

SCENE AS POLICE AND KLAN CLASH IN QUEENS PARADE

Scene in Queens blvd., where police tried to turn Klansmen out of Memorial Day parade. Officer at left is about to swing his nightstick over the head of white-sheeted knight, whose friends rushed to assist, causing a free-for-all with two auto loads of policemen.

After the riots, public support for the Klan was voiced in the New York area more than once. One Long Island citizen complained that 'the police were grossly to blame for this disgraceful affair', calling their 'interference' in the clashes 'a detestable outrage'. 'The Klan had a perfect right to march and thank God they exercised that right.'⁹ The tone of more than one local report suggested the Klan was the injured party: Klansmen and women 'ran the gauntlet of attacks', which 'the police were powerless to prevent', wrote one upstate New York editorial. 'Many Klansmen had their robes torn off and many of the men and women marchers were struck by flying missiles.'¹⁰

The Klan, meanwhile, blamed the police for being Catholic. In a circular headed 'Americans assaulted by the Roman Catholic Police of New York City', the Klan protested against 'Native born Protestant Americans' being 'clubbed and beaten when they exercise their rights in the country of their birth'. Casting themselves as the victims of police brutality, they added: 'We charge that the Roman Catholic police force did deliberately precipitate a riot,' beating 'defenseless Americans who conducted themselves as gentlemen under trying circumstances'. As far as the Second Klan was concerned, Catholics couldn't be loyal Americans because their higher allegiance was to the Pope.

In the days after the riot, the *New York Times* revealed the names of a total of seven men who had been arrested in Queens. Five of them were identified as 'avowed Klansmen' who'd been marching in the parade,¹¹ and were arrested for 'refusing to disperse when ordered'. A sixth was a mistake: he'd had his foot run over by a car and was immediately released. The seventh, a twenty-one-year-old German-American, was not identified in the press as a Klansman. The reports only stated that he was arrested, arraigned and discharged.¹² No one knows why he was there, but it appears that he wouldn't leave. His name was Fred Trump.

It meant nothing at the time.

America first = KKK

PART ONE

1900—1920

I

THE AMERICAN DREAM 1900–1916:
The Spirit of American Dreams

Beware resentful multimillionaires, for they will destroy the American dream.

That, in a nutshell, was the warning issued by an article in the *New York Post* in 1900, which cautioned readers that 'discontented multimillionaires' form the 'greatest risk' to 'every republic'. The problem was that multimillionaires 'are very rarely, if ever, content with a position of equality'. But if the rich were to be treated differently from other Americans, 'it would be the end of the American dream'.[1]

The article, reprinted in regional papers around the country, argued that multimillionaires insist on special privileges, their own rules, demanding to be treated as an elite class. All previous republics had been 'overthrown by rich men', it added, and America seemed to have plenty who were ready to wreak havoc on democracy without consequence, 'deriding the constitution, unrebuked by the executive or by public opinion'.[2]

As it happens, this forgotten editorial in the newspaper established by Alexander Hamilton appears to be one of the earliest uses of the phrase 'the American dream' in a context we would recognise. And instead of assuming that multimillionaires are the realisation of the American dream, it says their lack of belief in the equality upon which republics are founded will destroy it.

Most Americans today almost certainly believe the opposite: that a multimillionaire proves the success of the American dream. But in 1900 the *Post*'s editorial writer presumed that everyone would agree that the 'American dream' was of equality, and that wealth would kill it. And local newspapers around the country reprinted the item – from Wilmington, North Carolina, to Galena, Kansas, to Santa Cruz, California – suggesting they found currency in it.

Before about 1900, there is little discernible trace in American cultural conversations of the phrase 'American dream' being used to describe a collective, generalisable national ideal of any kind, let alone an economic one.

The phrase does not appear in any of the foundational documents in American history – it's nowhere in the complete writings of Thomas Jefferson, Alexander Hamilton or James Madison. It's not in Hector St. John Crèvecoeur or Alexis de Tocqueville, those two great French observers of early American life. It's not found in the works of any of America's major nineteenth-century novelists: Washington Irving, James Fenimore Cooper, Nathaniel Hawthorne, Herman Melville or Mark Twain. It's not in the supposedly more sentimental novels of Harriet Beecher Stowe, Louisa May Alcott, or even Horatio Alger, whose 'rags to riches' stories are so often held to exemplify it. Nor does it crop up visibly in political discourse, or newspapers, or anywhere noticeable in the public record.

There were references in newspaper articles or histories to specific, particular American dreams: the American dream of naval supremacy, or the American dream of continental expansion (a dream that 'proceeds from a sense of social and political superiority', a New York paper helpfully explained in 1877).[3] A New Orleans paper reported that a new interest in recreational sports marked a change in 'the spirit of American dreams'.[4] A story that Napoleon had been urged to flee to the United States was reprinted around the country in 1880 under the headline 'Napoleon's American Dream'.[5]

There was the American dream of rehabilitating China.[6] There was the (surprising) 'bastard American dream of Empire' in the

Philippines, as well as the 'pan-American dream' of hemispheric travel, or conquest.[7] By 1906, 'the American dream of a republic in Cuba appear[ed] to be over'.[8] 'Mexico in American hands is the American dream,' readers were told in 1916.[9] There was even the 'American dream of a railway project through Anatolia' as late as 1922.[10]

Most of these American dreams are noteworthy primarily for the fact that they have little or nothing to do with life in the United States, its values or meanings. Often the expression denoted dreams of empire – but it was always a distinct, individual dream of what activities America might get up to, not a collective sense of what it might be, or mean.

ash

In these earliest years of the phrase's appearance in print, there were only a handful of invocations of 'the' American dream, rather than 'an' American dream, because there were so many to choose from. And when 'the' American dream did appear, it was almost always in contexts that make it clear the phrase was not being used to denote anything about individual aspiration or economic opportunity at all. But those are the meanings that are universally ascribed to the phrase today, with no sense that it could ever have meant anything else.

Certainly the individual pursuit of prosperity, the self-made man, the success story were all familiar American ideals, as the immense popularity in the second half of the nineteenth century of Horatio Alger's books about impoverished boys rising to middle-class prosperity does attest. But the 'Alger ethic', as it's been called, of rags-to-riches meritocratic bootstrapping was not associated with anything named 'the American dream' until much later.[11]

Instead, there were references to the American dream of liberty under representative democracy, the American dream of self-government,[12] or the American dreams of the poets Southey and Coleridge, who imagined a utopia there. The earliest iterations of the phrase 'American dream' tended to use it to describe the political dreams of the framers, the dreams of liberty, justice and equality.

The problem for the United States has always been how to reconcile the three. Liberty is in tension against both justice and equality: one person's freedom to pursue property or power soon infringes upon principles of social justice and democratic equality. The friction has remained, but the 'American dream' would switch sides, as we shall see. Today the phrase is used all but exclusively to denote an individual's pursuit of property, whereas when it first crept into American political discourse, it did so to represent the social dream of justice and equality *against* individual dreams of aspiration and personal success.

From the early years of America's history the nation's political dreams have also been referred to as the 'American creed', the belief system that broadly fused liberal democracy, individual opportunity, equality, liberty and justice. The problem wasn't merely how to square these principles with each other, given how often they come into conflict. It was also how to balance a doctrine of explicitly stated values against the behaviours of individual Americans that implicitly betrayed those ideals on a daily basis.

As early as 1845 another *New York Post* editorial was widely circulated, objecting to the fact that a new political movement called nativism was contrary to Americanism and the American creed. 'The great principle of true *Americanism*, if we may use the word, is, that merit makes the man,' it observed. Because people should never be judged by 'purely accidental' distinctions, but only by personal characteristics, any form of nativism was 'contemptible' bigotry, based on 'low and ungenerous prejudices – prejudices of birth, which we as a people, profess to discard'.

What is the effort to confine the political functions incident to citizenship to native-born Americans, but the attempt to found an aristocracy of birth, even a political aristocracy, making the accident of birth the condition of political rights. Is this

Americanism? Shame on the degenerate American who pretends
it! He is false to his American creed, and has no American heart.[13]

As a concept, Americanism would not get appreciably better at
remembering its creed, or having a heart, but many individual
Americans, believing in an inclusive polity established (at least in
theory) by the framers, would continue to make principled appeals
for tolerance, justice and equality. At stake was the character of
modern America, whether it would be shaped by tribal loyalties or
constitutional principles.

* * *

The earliest use I have found of the 'American dream' to denote a
mutual value system – one akin to the older idea of the American
creed – is from 1895, when a celebration was held in Chicago
on what would have been the seventy-third birthday of Ulysses
S. Grant. The festivities included a (very long) commemorative
oration thanking Grant for protecting the Union, first as a general
in the Civil War and then as president. At one point, the orator
turned his expansive attention to the character of the nation Grant
was being lauded for having saved:

> Oh, critic and cynic, dreamer and doubter, behold America, as
> this day she stands before her history and her heroes. See her
> millions of people, her free institutions, her equal laws, her
> generous opportunities, her schoolhouses and her churches;
> you see misfortunes and defects, for not yet is fully realized the
> American dream; you surely see her mighty progress toward the
> fulfillment of her philosophy.[14]

The nature of that unrealised dream, that unfulfilled philosophy,
is unspecified, taken as a given – but a shared value was being
assumed. The national philosophy being summoned is obviously
not limited to economic success or upward social mobility: this

is a speech about the ideal of American democracy, of which 'generous opportunities' are just one aspect, alongside institutional freedom, religious freedom, equality under the law and universal education.

And when the 'American dream' was used in a context that referred to economic prosperity, the expression usually suggested that the accumulation of wealth was 'un-American', that the American dream was opposed to economic inequality and laissez-faire capitalism.

In 1899 the *Brooklyn Daily Eagle* published an item criticising a Vermont landowner's decision to build an estate of four thousand acres with sixty rooms, which would make it the largest individual property in America. 'Until a few years ago the thought of such an estate as that would have seemed a wild and utterly un-American dream to any Vermonter,' protested the reporter. Vermont had always been 'a state of almost ideally democratic equality, where everybody worked and nobody went hungry'.[5]

If the concentration of wealth was an 'un-American dream', then preserving the American dream would mean resisting individual success at the expense of others. This vision looks a lot more like social democracy than free-market capitalism – and it's a vision that continues through the earliest uses of the phrase.

A Kansas editorial asked in 1908 why a baseball pitcher earned twenty times more than a settlement worker, why the president of an insurance company made so much more than a headmaster. 'Why does the world offer fortunes to the man who shows us how to make money and starvation wages to the man who shows us how to make beautiful lives? Why do we accord highest place to money mongers and lowest place to teachers of ideals?' False standards were leading people astray; but 'thank goodness, a change is coming over the spirit of American dreams'. The country was beginning to concern itself with more than 'the material things'. Having 'solved the problems of the production of wealth', 'now we must stop!' The country had bigger problems than making money, contended that editorial from the American heartland. It was time to enable 'the equitable distribution of wealth'.[16]

Enough Americans had been dreaming of material wealth for an editorial to praise a change in their spirit; there is no question that American energies have always been focused on acquisition, but the idea of the 'American dream' was summoned as a corrective, not as an incentive. Individual Americans' dreams would need to improve to live up to national ideals of equality and justice, or toxic inequity would blight the American dream of democracy.

* * *

It was the heart of the so-called Progressive Era (roughly 1890 to 1920), which responded to the Gilded Age of unregulated capitalism with clashes between labour and industry, and a series of attempts (mostly frustrated) at economic reform. In the 1890s severe financial crashes and recessions led to soaring inequality; riots ensued. Droughts were ravaging the upper Midwest: the notorious Dust Bowl of the 1930s was presaged by the terrible droughts of the 1890s forty years earlier. Monopoly capitalism had taken such a stranglehold over the United States that in 1890 Congress passed the Sherman Anti-Trust Act, the first major federal law to regulate the power that giant corporations could exert over ordinary Americans – and over government itself. In 1893 a financial panic led the nation to debate the creation of federal aid programmes, which the United States had never enacted. That same year, President Grover Cleveland denounced governmental 'paternalism' in his second inaugural address, informing the nation that 'while the people should patriotically and cheerfully support their Government its functions do not include the support of the people'.[17]

Republican Theodore Roosevelt was elected in 1900 on a progressive platform promising, in the name of free markets, to 'bust the trusts' – the massive national corporations that were consolidating industrial power, making it impossible for small businesses to compete, and were seen as eroding the foundations of the middle classes. At the turn of the twentieth century in the United States, the rich were getting richer and the poor were getting poorer, despite the incremental growth of the middle class.

National conversations were highly attuned to the rampaging inequality created by industrial robber barons and monopoly capitalism. A few months before Theodore Roosevelt announced his candidacy, a widely reviewed book called *The City for the People* argued:

A hundred years ago wealth was quite evenly distributed here. Now one-half the people own practically nothing; one-eighth of the people own seven-eighths of the wealth; one per cent of the people own fifty per cent of the wealth and one-half of one per cent own twenty per cent of the wealth, or 4,000 times their fair share in the principles of partnership and brotherhood. A hundred years ago there were no millionaires in the country. Now there are more than 4,000 millionaires and multi-millionaires, one of them worth over two hundred millions, and the billionaire is only a question of a few years more.[18]

Monopolies were fundamentally opposed to social good, it said. 'Diffusion is the ideal of civilization, diffusion of wealth and power, intelligence, culture, and conscience.' But instead of diffusion, America had created 'private monopoly of wealth, private monopoly of government, private monopoly of education, private monopoly even of morality, and the conditions of its production.'[19] The *Labor World* in Duluth, Minnesota, protested 'the spectacle of one per cent of our families owning more wealth than all of the remaining 99 per cent!'[20]

The symbol of the 'one per cent' that so dominates discussions of economic inequality today comes, like the American dream it accompanies, from a century ago. The difference is that a hundred years ago many people considered billionaires un-American.

That's where the story of the 'American dream' as a saying begins — in the Progressive Era, protesting inequality. After a few decades of scattered references to particular American dreams of sovereignty or conquest, the phrase began to coalesce, used in an increasingly consistent way by people around the country to remind Americans of a shared ideal about equality of opportunity — which may sound like our American dream of individual success. But for them the American dream of equal opportunity could only be protected by *curbing* unbridled capitalism, and protecting collective equality.

When they invoked the American dream it was a sign of moral disquiet, not triumphalism, reflecting the fear that America was losing its way. The phrase was a warning siren, reminding Americans to look at the ground upon which they stood — not towards nebulous dreams of individual future advancement, but back towards the nation's shared founding values.

That American attitudes were changing in response to the growth of monopoly capitalism was clear to all; wealth was no longer an easy virtue to pursue. It had become a test for American society.

Soon even the *Manchester Guardian* was noting that although a 'loose individualism' balanced by Hamiltonian federalism had long been the 'chief substance of Americanism', shifting circumstances 'caused a change to pass over the spirit of this American dream'. Opportunities for 'the ordinary man' were becoming more restricted, while 'economic, social, and political potentates have arisen in the shape of trusts, bosses, railroads, labour unions', meaning that 'a wide gulf has opened up between wealth-ownership and the condition of the workers'.[21]

Again there was a sense that 'the spirit of the American dream' was undergoing a dangerous alteration, and that change involved the concentration of wealth in the hands of the few; again the 'American dream' described not the accumulation of riches, but the risk posed to ideals of justice and equality by such accumulation.

As the American dream began to develop into a popular way to articulate a collective national ideal, the phrase was used to talk about stopping the rich and powerful from destroying democratic equality, and with it economic opportunity for all.

The American dream is usually imagined today as a nostalgic return to some golden past of national prosperity and harmony, in which happy small capitalists ran an agrarian, softly mercantile society and professionals earned the same as farmers, and everyone was content. But if you examine the actual history of the phrase, you find a society always grappling with inequality, uneasily recognising that individual success would not redeem collective failure.

* * *

A writer named David Graham Phillips was murdered in 1911 outside the Princeton Club of New York by a (Harvard) man impressively named Fitzhugh Goldsborough, who thought Phillips had slandered Goldsborough's sister in his most recent book. At the time of his death, Phillips was working on a novel called *Susan Lenox: Her Fall and Rise*, which was published posthumously six years later, and is primarily remembered now as the source novel for a 1931 Greta Garbo film. But it also provides a comparatively well-known early use of 'American dream', thanks to the *Oxford English Dictionary*'s decision to include a passing quotation in its definition of the American dream as an ideal of self-determination: 'The fashion and home magazines ... have prepared thousands of Americans ... for the possible rise of fortune that is the universal American dream and hope.'

At the beginning of the twentieth century, thanks to the explosion of advertising, the rise of celebrity culture, the use of photographs in newspapers and the imminent dominance of Hollywood in the American imagination, consumer capitalism – which included the 'fashion and home magazines' – was becoming aspirational: 'the universal American dream and hope'. Ordinary Americans could scrutinise the lives of the rich and powerful, in all their glamorous and luxurious detail. They could see what their houses looked like, and not just tiny glimpses of exteriors through hedgerows or over stone walls. Readers could now look at their furniture, their fashions, their cars, their yachts. Conspicuous consumption had arrived with a vengeance, and it taught people as never before in full sensory detail what having money might *feel* like. Unsurprisingly, most people concluded that it would feel pretty good.

Such is the experience Phillips ascribes to his tiresome heroine, Susan Lenox:

> And the reading she had done – the novels, the memoirs, the books of travel, the fashion and home magazines – had made deep and distinct impressions upon her, had prepared her – as they have prepared thousands of Americans in secluded towns and rural regions where luxury and even comfort are very crude indeed – for the possible rise of fortune that is the universal American dream and hope.[22]

But the entire force of Phillips's mammoth novel – it clocks in at well over nine hundred pages – is to undercut the idea that meritocracy or self-determination has anything to do with the realisation of such dreams and hopes. Susan Lenox grows up illegitimate in a small Indiana town, where local bigotry forces her into the prostitution everyone assumes is her birthright. After many (many, many) misfortunes, which endlessly lead her back into prostitution, she falls in love with a wealthy playwright. Unfortunately, her former pimp murders the playwright; fortunately, the playwright has left her his estate. The 'exultant' look on her face when she learns this shocks the playwright's valet, 'for to his shallow, conventional nature Susan's expression could only mean delight in wealth, in the opportunity that now offered to idle and to luxuriate in the dead man's money'. Not so! cries Phillips. Such assumptions are merely 'the crude dreamings of … lesser minds'.[23] For Susan, wealth simply means freedom, from poverty and sexual exploitation.

This does indeed appear to be one of the earliest uses of the 'American dream' to suggest upward social mobility – but only to rebuke the idea as a 'crude' dream for 'lesser minds'. In *Susan Lenox*, a rise of fortune may be the universal American dream and hope, but it means everyone in the country is wishing for the wrong thing. Moreover, whether it comes to you is an accident of fate, not a measure of character or merit. Phillips's stern rejection of luxuriating in wealth notwithstanding, inheriting a fortune because your pimp murders your rich lover is hardly a ringing endorsement of the Puritan work ethic. It certainly doesn't suggest the ideal of 'achieving success and prosperity through hard work, determination, and initiative', which is the definition the *OED* wants that passage from *Susan Lenox* to exemplify.

And at any rate the 'American dream' continued to be used far more frequently to discuss democratic equality than individual aspiration. In 1912 the *Chicago Tribune* was writing of 'the American dream of justice, equality, and the noblest liberty', an American dream by no means synonymous with the one David Graham Phillips had suggested a year earlier.[24] At the very least, the meanings of the phrase remained unsettled, and plural.

Two years later saw the first appearance of 'American dream' in an important book by an influential writer, one that used the phrase to discuss democratic individualism in practice, and has occasionally been identified as the earliest known use of the phrase.[25] It isn't really: it's neither the earliest, as we've seen, nor does it begin to articulate an American dream that anyone today would identify with the expression. But it is a significant early use all the same.

In 1914, a young writer named Walter Lippmann set out to write a book that would diagnose the problems of the Progressive Era and propose a solution. Just twenty-five years old, Lippmann was a recent philosophy graduate from Harvard, where he had studied with the great philosopher George Santayana (who ranked Lippmann with T. S. Eliot as one of the two most brilliant students he ever had). Lippmann's ambitious book, *Drift and Mastery*, was a huge success, establishing him as a pre-eminent public intellectual, as well as an important spokesman for the progressive movement.

As part of his diagnosis of what ailed American society, Lippmann referred to something he called 'the American dream' – but it is neither the economic dream of individual success with which the world today is so familiar, nor the political dream of democratic and economic equality that we have been looking at.

Lippmann argued that recent social and cultural revolutions in America – transformations in old models of manufacturing, distribution and access to jobs and profit – meant that traditional institutions and theories no longer applied to modern society. The new industrial world was bewildering: changes had been so rapid that everyone was uprooted from former certainties and paradigms.

Lippmann chose a striking metaphor to describe how it feels to be confronting massive technological disruption: 'We are all of us immigrants in an industrial world,' he wrote, 'and we have no authority to lean upon. We are an uprooted people, newly arrived, and *nouveau riche* ... The modern man is not yet settled in his world.'[26] It was a new world, but Americans were still trying to organise their political system around the old one.

In particular, Lippmann worried that a free-market economy of unchecked capitalism, trusting in the abilities of markets to self-regulate and of people to exercise rational self-interest, would lead only to what he called 'drift' – the inadvertent and unpredictable, created by atomised liberty. Perverse outcomes would abound. Lippmann thought society needed a strategy, which he called (somewhat problematically) 'mastery'. He envisioned a kind of planned economy, although not the kind of planned economy that would be espoused in the near future by Maoists and Stalinists.

Lippmann's social plan sought to balance capitalism and socialism using the scientific method: it would be evidence-based, rational, forward-looking and progressive, broadly socialised in its belief in sharing benefit and abilities, while controlling individual access to wealth. In effect, Lippmann was arguing in *Drift and Mastery* for social democracy, for government regulation of big business in order to protect both small-business owners and workers, rather than merely busting monopolies and assuming the market would then regulate itself. Government did not necessarily mean federal government, of course: local government could also regulate and police the workings of business. But the goal was the democratisation of the economy.

Like most American progressives of his time, Lippmann was far from opposed to market forces, but he thought the nation needed a moral economy, in every sense. The problem was not capitalism; it was unrestrained capitalism. The government had to ensure that a moral system – otherwise known as justice – was operant in the nation's economic systems. Without it, men could be guaranteed to 'drift' right back into the law of the jungle – precisely what humans created government to prevent. ('If men were angels,' as James Madison famously wrote, 'no government would be necessary.')[27]

For Lippmann, the 'American dream' was bound up in the illusions that were crippling democracy, and allowing capitalists to run roughshod over the common man. But Lippmann did not merely blame the capitalists; he blamed the common man, too – and this is where the 'American dream' comes in. Pure democracy was a chimera, Lippmann held, because it led to a dangerous populist nationalism, to mob rule and the rise of dictators.

The problem was that Americans kept being led astray by an illusion. 'The American temperament leans generally to a kind of mystical anarchism, in which the "natural" humanity in each man is adored as the savior of society,' he warned.[28] 'Mystical anarchism' – or, as it would later be known, libertarianism – depends on total faith in the wisdom and justice of the common man, his ability to redeem a country debilitated by intellectuals and false experts.

That misplaced faith, for Lippmann, was the 'American dream'.

'If only you let men alone, they'll be good,' a typical American reformer said to me the other day. He believed, as most Americans do, in the unsophisticated man, in his basic kindliness and his instinctive practical sense. A critical outlook seemed to the reformer an inhuman one; he distrusted ... the appearance of the expert; he believed that whatever faults the common man might show were due to some kind of Machiavellian corruption. He had the American dream, which may be summed up, I think, in the statement that the undisciplined man is the salt of the earth.[29]

The American dream here suggests the dangers of democracy, its illusions and mythologies. Lippmann is attacking America's blind faith in individualism, in the undisciplined, unpolished, unschooled, natural person as the source of all wisdom. This American dream is not an aspirational fantasy, but a deluded and dangerous illusion: believing that the country could flourish without experts, that every citizen can be sufficiently discerning about everything, especially in an age of proliferating information and propaganda, to be what Lippmann would later call 'omnicompetent'.

Lippmann feared that the American dream of some golden past when unsophisticated people ran the country just fine would tempt voters into following a populist demagogue who told them they could return to the Jeffersonian fantasy of a village of happy yeoman farmers, despite living in an industrial age. Lippmann called *this* the American dream: all-knowing ordinary folk, like Benjamin Franklin's 'Poor Richard', the farmer-sage who could advise the nation. Lippmann deplored what he called America's 'fear economy' of unchecked capitalism, suggesting that the nation's 'dream of endless progress' would need to be restrained, because it was fundamentally illusory, another kind of American dream. This dream of endless progress is just as foolish, Lippmann maintained, as 'those who dream of a glorious past'.

Disputing America's image of itself as a 'nation of Villagers', Lippmann criticised the nostalgic ideal of the agrarian idyll championed by Jefferson. Why would rural life necessarily create better, or wiser, people? The nation needed to accept change, and to adapt to it. 'Those who cling to the village view of life may deflect the drift, may batter the trusts around a bit, but they will never dominate business, never humanize its machinery, and they will continue to be playthings of industrial change.'[30]

The American dream, Lippmann thought, was a naive faith that democracy would always work in its purest form without education or regulation to support it. Trusting democracy to work on its own would paradoxically destroy it. Equality wouldn't just happen naturally; it had to be protected, planned for, educated into people. Society had to create defences against the plutocrat and the swindler, the fake man of the people who affected a folksy style and encouraged his listeners to take pride in ignorance.

For the next twenty years, the 'American dream' would be associated with a recognition that dreams of endless progress could be as socially destabilising as unregulated competition or vast economic inequality.

* * *

Dreams of individual progress were by no means lacking, of course, and they were not easy to disentangle from the relationship between property and self-determination. America had always represented a fantasy of easy wealth, one that was often in conflict with the political experiment of democratic government. But the problem was not simply a matter of condemning greed (although that's doubtless worth doing). For better or worse, the associations among property, liberty and happiness are inescapably knotted into the rhetorical fabric of America's founding ideas.

When Jefferson enshrined 'life, liberty and the pursuit of happiness' as inalienable rights, there is little doubt that he changed the course of the human events he was charting. The phrase, as is widely recognised, was adapting the philosopher John Locke's declaration that 'life, liberty and property' were fundamental human rights – but in fact, Jefferson was not really rewriting Locke. Rather he was fusing two of Locke's phrases from different essays. In his *Essay Concerning Human Understanding*, Locke declared 'the necessity of pursuing true happiness the foundation of liberty'. Man's 'intellectual nature' could only be perfected by distinguishing 'true and solid happiness' from any desires we mistake for real happiness. 'So the care of ourselves, that we mistake not imaginary for real happiness, is the necessary foundation of our liberty.'[31]

Locke was arguing in essence that pursuing imaginary forms of happiness is a kind of enslavement; higher freedom comes from knowledge of ourselves, from self-realisation. Jefferson then embedded that idea in the American imaginary – but progress kept getting tangled back up in property. Both were allied with individualism, with autonomy, with equality. Similarly, Ralph Waldo Emerson's widely hailed nineteenth-century ideal of self-reliance presupposed a certain level of common prosperity. Widespread poverty was no one's democratic fantasy, but the question was where individual prosperity ended and national inequality began, because that would also crush the democratic dream.

Democracy would have to find equilibrium among everyone's right to pursue property and/or happiness, and that has proven a difficult – indeed so far an impossible – balance to strike. That this would be so is clear enough from the fact that Jefferson's lofty belief in liberty as the foundation of human happiness was belied by his willingness to turn other people into property to fund his own happy freedoms. This point is often made, but it bears repeating.

Put another way, one of the luxuries the wealthy acquire is the luxury of discovering that money isn't everything. This was the lesson offered by a 1916 novel called *Windy McPherson's Son*, by Sherwood Anderson, which is the mostly unremarkable tale of a young man who leaves small-town Iowa to make his fortune, and having done so, learns how little it means.

When Sam McPherson realises that chasing the gods of success has led him astray, he decides to throw away everything he has and start over again. 'I will leave the money hunger behind me,' he declares, 'and come up to Truth through work.'[32] It's the Puritan work ethic in its purest form: work for work's sake, because work is a positive good that leads to personal wisdom. He will seek spiritual, not financial, enrichment.

But his new resolve also strikes Sam McPherson as ironic. 'He, an American multimillionaire, a man in the midst of his money-making, one who had realized the American dream, to have sickened at the feast and to have wandered out of a fashionable club with a bag in his hand and a roll of bills in his pocket and to have come on this strange quest – to seek Truth, to seek God.'[33] Here is the 'American dream' describing the self-made businessman, the small-town man who becomes a multimillionaire through hard work and determination. But instead of an ideal to be celebrated, it is an illusion to be rejected.

This should still be surprising; never in Horatio Alger's hundred-odd novels do any of his heroes wonder if wealth was worth it in the end. But it's also worth remembering that most of Alger's stories end with their heroes rising from poverty to middle-class respectability, not to vast plutocratic fortunes.

The middle class was growing at the same time that the 'American dream' was gathering momentum: the *Oxford English Dictionary* finds its earliest use of the phrase 'white collar' in Indiana, in 1910: 'He follows the lure of the white collar to the city and gets a job in which he can wear a white collar all the week.' The lure of the white collar was real, and increasingly attainable for more and more Americans, as universal education and transformations in industry and business created more office jobs.

Just as the 'American dream' began to converge with the rise of the American white collar success story, however, it was interrupted by the explosion of conflict in Western Europe. And despite its growing economic implications, the 'American dream' as a shorthand for democratic liberty was by no means defunct. Nor was the phrase yet fixed as 'the' American dream, which is hardly surprising given the different ways in which it was still being used.

In 1914 a Virginia paper was writing of 'An American Dream', in this case, the hope that America might help end 'the terrible struggle now drenching Europe in blood'.

> **An American Dream**
>
> ONE dream fills the heart of many Americans at this time, when all but us of the big and many of the little powers of the world are in the throes of the horrid nightmare of war. It is a big dream, and one

Such an ambition might 'seem a wild dream' in the midst of war, but it filled the 'imaginations of true American patriots'. 'Cynics and pessimists do not have it, because of its seeming wildness. Jingoes do not have it, for their dreams are always lurid and never beautiful. But President Wilson has it,' the author averred, as did 'the people, as a whole'. Everyone would share in the glory of peace, if it came; but whether it did or not, all would 'be better for the dreaming'.[34] The prospect of tyranny has always had a way of stimulating dreams of liberty.

But despite the Virginia editorial's fond hopes, it was not the case that everyone in the United States thought the nation should join the European conflict. Many believed that America should remain neutral, a campaign for non-intervention that rapidly acquired the motto 'America first'.

America was never of one mind on the subject of liberty – or indeed on much of anything else.

2

AMERICA FIRST 1900–1916:
Pure Americanism Against the Universe

Unlike the 'American dream', 'America first' was always a political slogan. What both expressions shared were their attempts to identify a national value system, and they emerged at the same moment in America's history – as it came into its own as a world power at the beginning of the twentieth century, and began debating in earnest the role it would play in the world. By no coincidence, the two moments of crisis in defining these terms arose when the United States faced the urgent question of how to respond to each of the century's world wars.

'America first' was also like the 'American dream' in not suddenly being invented by an individual, although it was popularised by one. The phrase appears as a slogan in the American political conversation at least as early as 1884, when an Oakland, California, paper ran 'America First and Always' as the headline of an article about fighting trade wars with the British.

America First and Always.

A Wisconsin congressman gave an 1889 speech declaring that while there was no danger of war between America and Germany, there was also 'no doubt of the loyalty of German-Americans to the land of their adoption ... We will fight for America whenever necessary; America first, last and all the time; America against Germany; America against the world; America, right or wrong; always America.'[1]

The *New York Times* shared among its 'Political Notes' in 1891 the observation made by 'a wild Western turnip-fed editor out in the State of Washington' that 'the idea that the Republican Party has always believed in' was 'America first; the rest of the world afterward'.[2] The Republican Party agreed, adopting the entire phrase as a campaign slogan by 1894. The *Morning News* in Wilmington, Delaware, described a Republican 'monster parade' of victory, in which jubilant Republican voters wore 'America First' badges in honour of 'the redemption of the state from Democratic misrule': 'nearly every man seen on the street wore a badge bearing the words "America First, the World After"'.[3]

That same year a politician responded to the toast of 'Government by the People' by saying he 'believed in America first', that 'patriotism is loyalty to America first'.[4] By 1899, there were a few scattered references in regional papers to an 'America First Committee', its official purpose unclear.[5]

'See America First' had become the ubiquitous slogan of the newly burgeoning American tourist industry by 1906, one that adapted easily into a political promise, as was recognised by an Ohio newspaper owner named Warren G. Harding, who successfully campaigned for senator in 1914 using the slogan 'Prosper America First'; he would return to the motto before long.[6]

The expression did not become a national catchphrase, however, until April 1915, when President Woodrow Wilson gave a speech declaring: 'Our whole duty for the present, at any rate, is summed up in the motto: America First.' At that point, it took off.

Western Europe was a full year into the Great War, while the United States remained neutral. Although public sentiment veered strongly towards protecting fellow neutral nations like Belgium from German occupation, many Americans viewed the conflict as an imperialist quarrel between two equally unsympathetic foes. Despite a strong animus against what was widely perceived as a baldly nationalist venture by Kaiser Wilhelm, there was plenty of anti-British sentiment to balance that out. The sun had not yet set on the British Empire, and it was not at all clear to many Americans why they should support the nation they had fought so hard (and within the memory of living people's grandparents) to overthrow. Irish-Americans in particular were outraged at the idea of an allegiance with Britain, as most of them had emigrated to America to escape conditions created by British rule, an offence that only deepened after the British government's brutal response to the 1916 Easter Rising. Neutrality also meant that US citizens could contribute relief to victims in war zones, and the nation gave generously.

American neutrality was by no means always motivated by pure isolationism, in other words; it mingled pacifism, nationalism, anti-imperialism, anti-colonialism and exceptionalism – and it was widespread. Wilson gave many citizens the tuning note they sought in declaring America 'too proud to fight'.

A Democrat who campaigned on progressive lines, Wilson had been president for three years when he gave his 'America first' speech with an eye on re-election a year later. This line has often been quoted, although almost never in association with its resuscitation a century later, and usually taken out of context from Wilson's speech. Detail tends to be the first casualty of reproduction.

'I am not speaking in a selfish spirit,' Wilson began, 'when I say that our whole duty, for the present, at any rate, is summed up in this motto, "America First." Let us think of America before we think of Europe, in order that America may be fit to be Europe's friend when the day of tested friendship comes.' Wilson argued that America could demonstrate its friendship best not by shows of 'sympathy' for either side, but by preparing 'to help both sides when the struggle is over'.

Neutrality didn't mean indifference or self-interest, he insisted. 'The basis of neutrality is sympathy for mankind. It is fairness, it is good will at bottom. It is impartiality of spirit and of judgment. I wish that all of our fellow citizens could realize that.'[7]

All of his fellow citizens evidently could not realise that, for the phrase was rapidly taken up without any of Wilson's subtlety – or mendacity, depending on your perspective. Certainly the decision to maintain neutrality in the face of evil can be immoral, as history would demonstrate all too savagely within twenty years. Walter Lippmann, for one, now co-editing the *New Republic*, argued strenuously for America's intervention in the war on the basis that bystanders could not affect the justice of the outcome, or protect democracy.

But Wilson had something else noteworthy to add in his 1915 'America first' speech – a warning about being taken in by 'fake news'.

Fake News Condemned.

Wilson told the country there was a growing problem with news that 'turn[s] out to be falsehood', or that is false in 'what it is said to signify', which, if the nation were 'to believe it true, might disturb our equilibrium and our self-possession'. The country could not afford 'to let the rumors of irresponsible persons and origins get into the United States. We are trustees for what I venture to say is the greatest heritage that any nation ever had, the love of justice and righteousness and human liberty', and so it was vital that Americans defend that heritage of justice and freedom.

There were 'groups of selfish men in the United States' working to undermine that legacy, creating 'coteries where sinister things are purposed'. But 'the heart of America' would stay true, Wilson was confident, and it should put America first by staying out of the conflict.[8]

Wilson explicitly differentiated 'America first' from self-interest and indifference, and it can't reasonably be said that this speech enjoins isolationism per se. Nonetheless, he was campaigning on the basis of keeping America out of the war, and 'America first' was taken up in the name of isolationism almost instantly.

Some of his critics objected to the flexibility in Wilson's use of the term 'America first'. In November 1915, the president of 'Friends of Peace and Justice' challenged Wilson on what it meant in real terms to put 'America first', demanding: 'What would "America First" mean if we had a President who was not a mere trickster in phrases?' It would mean having a president who cared for 'that mass of Americans who are living today in poverty or in fear of want, because of the robberies which are being perpetrated upon them by the highwaymen of modern finances'.

'America first' was a mere ploy, he added, to distract the people with flag-waving from the brazen corruption of 'subservient politicians' who served only the nation's 'mighty financial interests', not its ordinary citizens.[9] This unholy alliance between the 'highwaymen of modern finances' and the politicians who truckled to them was 'the most extraordinary conspiracy' to consolidate power in 'the entire history of our Republic'.

Meanwhile the US Bureau of Education was creating an 'America First' campaign, with an explicitly assimilationist agenda. Its stated purpose was to encourage immigrants and new American citizens to put loyalty to the United States above allegiance to the nations they had left; but it also explicitly stated that no one expected, or desired, immigrants to reject their own culture, language or histories in order to embrace America's. Arguments over whether English should be a compulsory national language flared; what it meant to be an 'American' in a country absorbing waves of immigration became an urgent question, the answer to which, for many, was to impose an American ethno-nationalism, one that upheld old prerogatives of white, Protestant, male establishment power.

By no coincidence, the American 'melting pot' as a metaphor for assimilation emerged during roughly the same period, comparing the mixing of immigrant communities together to the practice of melting different metals together in order to mint new coins – no less valuable, but in a different form. The phrase was in use by 1889. 'For present uses coagulation and not separation of the race elements in our National melting pot is the thing to be desired,' wrote the *Chicago Tribune* that year. 'The common word "American" is good enough for any of us.'[10]

The United States was a country, added the *New York Times* a few months later, 'in whose mysterious melting-pot all nationalities and races lose their homogeneity and are quickly reduced to the condition of American citizenship'.[11] It was six years after Emma Lazarus composed her poem 'The New Colossus', which would be mounted on the Statue of Liberty in 1903, inviting the world to send America its tired and poor, its huddled masses and wretched refuse. Within another ten years, the 'melting pot' had become a cliché, increasingly used in a pejorative sense: 'Dregs of Europe ... America the Melting Pot into which Races are Poured', read a typical 1912 headline.[12]

Over the next twenty years, assimilation and immigration would become incendiary issues, and during the Great War they joined forces with political isolationism under the banner 'America first'.

*   *   *

As the war inflamed tensions, even in an ostensibly neutral country, immigrant communities, especially German-Americans, Italian-Americans and Irish-Americans, were being attacked as 'hyphenates', whose allegiance to the United States could not be trusted because their divided identities implied divided loyalties. Irish and Italian immigrants were suspected of choosing the Pope over the president, while Jews had long been said to be a 'nation within a nation', 'mercenary minded – money mad', 'unmergeable', 'alien and unassimilable'.[13] The Chinese Exclusion Act of 1882 had sought to ban Chinese immigrants altogether, and before long other Asian immigrant communities would also be directly targeted.

During the First World War, however, it was German-Americans who bore the brunt of xenophobic reaction against 'hyphenates'. People of German descent were harassed and victimised (in response many anglicised their names, as did the British royal family); the German language became verboten in schools. Even sauerkraut was renamed 'liberty cabbage'.

Across the United States, this growing animus against 'hyphenates' was frequently identified with 'America first'. The *New York Times*, for example, argued in 1915 for the virtue of 'Hazing the Hyphenates' – which amounted to harassing German-American citizens out of any supposed sympathies they might have felt for Germany in the European conflict. ('Hazing' had meant initiation rites that involved tormenting younger students at schools and universities since the nineteenth century.) The *Times* article began with a recent speech President Wilson had given to the Daughters of the American Revolution, in which he remarked upon a general impression 'that very large numbers of our fellow-citizens born in other lands have not entertained with sufficient intensity and affection the American ideal'.[14]

In response to this impression, the president called upon every American 'to declare himself, where he stands. Is it America first or is it not?'

The *Times* editorial heartily approved of the president's demand. No one 'worthy of his American citizenship' could possibly object, it pronounced, before endorsing what it called the president's 'humorous' suggestion that hazing was an appropriate cure for any 'un-American habits' thus detected. German-Americans may not have seen the humour in a suggestion by the president of the United States that they should be terrorised by their fellow citizens if they failed arbitrary loyalty tests.

'Probably they will take heed,' the editorial ended. 'There is no alternative if they are to continue to live among us, to do business in the United States, to retain their citizenship. Life is hardly worth living under continual "hazing".'[15] Its necessity may have been regrettable, the national paper of record implied, but harassment in the name of 'America first' was perfectly justified.

Regional papers also praised Wilson's remarks. His appeal to 'pure Americanism' in this '"America first" speech' went 'to the mark like a cannon shot', reported a Kansas paper. 'One might as well try to obstruct the ocean's tide as to stand in the way of "America first." Every new immigrant instinctively knows this.'[16]

'Ostracize the hyphen,' urged a columnist ten days later. 'Citizens of German birth or parentage are guilty more than any others for this divided allegiance, this half-hearted loyalty, this hindering of the development of simon-pure Americanism.' ('Simon-pure', from the name of a character in a popular play, meant 'ultra-pure', the genuine article.) All 'foreign-born citizens', he insisted, 'should take occasion to put themselves on record as cherishing no loyalty to the country of their origin', and affirm that 'with them, absolutely and unqualifiedly, it is "America first"'.[17]

Hyphenate hysteria would not abate any time soon, and it continued to affiliate itself with 'America first'. In a 1916 editorial called 'No Room for the Hyphen', the *New York Times* was pleased to report that both presidential nominees that year – Woodrow Wilson and his opponent, Republican Supreme Court Justice Charles Evans Hughes – had given speeches in which they'd 'put the hyphen and the hyphenate out of the campaign'. Wilson had again castigated American citizens who had insufficiently absorbed the spirit of America, at least according to their compatriots.

'We ought to let it be known that nobody who does not put America first can consort with us,' stated Wilson. Hughes had said something virtually indistinguishable, the *Times* added: 'his attitude is one of "undiluted Americanism"', as purity became the measure of patriotism. Hyphenates were impure, alloyed, defiling true Americanism with their suspicious foreign ways.

'Anybody who supports me,' Hughes promised, 'is supporting an out-and-out American, and an out-and-out American policy.' The *Times* out-and-out applauded. The entire East Coast, they warned, would be lost to any party that tried 'catering to the hyphen vote'. The candidates had both 'put the hyphen out of American politics. Keep it out.'[18]

'Shall we give aid and comfort to the disloyal hyphenate,' demanded a reader a few months later, 'to the Germans and their associates?' President Wilson, wrote the author, 'stands for America first, but also equally and bravely and nobly for all mankind'.[19] All mankind excepting, of course, the disloyal hyphenate, the Germans, and their associates.

In fact, 'America first' had become so popular, and so powerful, a political statement in America by 1916 that both presidential candidates adopted it as a campaign slogan. Hughes's slogan was 'America First and America Efficient', while Wilson went simply for 'America First'.

'The Administration's efforts to keep the United States out of war and at the same time maintain the national honor' was the domestic platform of the Democratic National Convention in the summer of 1916, while its 'foreign affairs plank will align the party behind the President placing "America first" with reference to all questions, both international and domestic'.[20]

The promise to put 'America first' had several implicit meanings. It meant that they would keep America out of the European conflict, and in the case of Hughes, it meant he would support protectionist trade policies. 'We commend to every voter,' wrote the *Scranton Republican* on election day, 'the slogan of Charles Evans Hughes, "America First, America Efficient."' There was one word, they added, that embodied this slogan more than any other. 'It is Protection. The protection of American labor and enterprise is imperative to conserve the markets of the United States.'[21]

A department store in Pennsylvania advertised an 'All American Sale', selling goods that were made in America. 'Be Neutral,' it urged. 'America First.'[22]

'America first' also strongly connoted, however, promises to protect 'real' Americans from the threat of treachery by 'hyphenate' Americans with supposedly divided allegiances. One senator gave a speech in which 'he deplored the hyphenated American, saying that people in this country could not afford to have two flags'. He criticised any public figures who took the side 'of aliens when they should be for America first, last and all the time'.[23]

The *North American Review* endorsed Hughes's candidacy in October 1916, stating that Hughes's 'entire career confirms' that he stands 'for *America* first', whereas, 'disappointingly', 'Mr. Wilson stands for *Wilson* first'.[24] '"America First, Last and Always And No 'Hyphens,'" Says Hughes,' read the headlines in October 1916, after

Hughes gave a speech repudiating the vote of anyone who had 'any interest superior to that of the United States'.[25]

In his speech, Hughes announced: 'I am an American, free and clear of all foreign entanglements,' a deeply coded statement – what today we would call a dog whistle.

Saying that as an individual he had no 'foreign entanglements', Hughes was invoking a ubiquitous justification for isolationism, which held that in George Washington's farewell address of 1796 he had warned America against 'all foreign entanglements'. It was a frequent and long-standing misquotation; indeed, the phrase is still attributed to Washington, but in fact, those words are not quite what Washington said – and what he really said matters to this history.

Why, by interweaving our destiny with that of any part of Europe, *entangle* our peace and prosperity in the toils of European ambition, rivalship, interest, humor or caprice?

It is our true policy to steer clear of permanent alliances with any portion of the foreign world; so far, I mean, as we are now at liberty to do it; for let me not be understood as capable of patronizing infidelity to existing engagements. I hold the maxim no less applicable to public than to private affairs, that honesty is always the best policy. I repeat it, therefore, let those engagements be observed in their genuine sense. But, in my opinion, it is unnecessary and would be unwise to extend them.

Taking care always to keep ourselves by suitable establishments on a respectable defensive posture, we may safely trust to temporary alliances for extraordinary emergencies. [emphasis added]

Washington never said 'avoid all foreign entanglements', nor does the passage really urge that. The final sentence makes it clear: Washington was not saying that the United States should never enter any alliances at all, but was only warning against *permanent* alliances in Europe. And he explicitly allowed for 'temporary alliances for extraordinary emergencies'. The First World War could reasonably have been described as an extraordinary emergency, quite apart from the question of whether one statement from 1796 should dictate all of American foreign policy in perpetuity.

But in denying that he *himself* had any foreign entanglements, Hughes was not raising the possibility that a Supreme Court Justice had colluded with a foreign power. He was, rather, covertly reassuring his audience that he was not a 'hyphenate', which meant 'one hundred per cent American', which meant a native-born white Protestant.

The idea of 'one hundred per cent Americanism', as it was frequently called, itself began as a code for debates about 'hyphenate' Americans versus 'pure' Americans, before rapidly evolving into ways to suggest – without specifying – other kinds of 'un-American' people or behaviour. One suggested slogan for the 1916 Republican campaign, according to the *Los Angeles Times*, was 'pure Americanism against the universe', which is certainly comprehensive.[26]

'Pure Americanism' and 'one hundred per cent Americanism' in turn became surreptitious ways to suggest racial and ethnic purity in a society that had long been dominated by the 'one-drop rule', which said that one drop of 'Negro blood' made a person legally black in the United States. 'Wherever there was a drop of negro blood in a man he was a negro,' noted a North Carolina paper in 1903. 'It took one hundred per cent of Anglo-Saxon blood to make a white man, but one per cent of negro blood makes a black man.'[27]

The 'one-drop rule' was the foundation of slavery and miscegenation laws in many states, literally used to determine the legal status of individuals, whether they would be enslaved or free. Its logic extended from the notorious three-fifths compromise in the Constitution, which computed slaves as three-fifths of a person for purposes of counting the population when apportioning representation to government. Slaves could not, of course, vote; but white slave owners wanted them to count as part of the population so that their states could send more representatives to government,

surely one of the more outrageous instances of having it both ways in human history. America was a nation long accustomed to quantifying people in terms of ethnic and racial composition, as words like mulatto and half-caste, quadroon and octoroon, make clear.

Declaring someone 'one hundred per cent American' was no mere metaphor in a country that measured people in percentages and fractions, in order to deny some of them full humanity.

The associative chains ran along the eugenicist idea of racial purity, and all these phrases began to suggest each other. It was all too easy to conflate 'pure American', 'one hundred per cent American' and 'one hundred per cent Anglo-Saxon', and many Americans in the first decades of the twentieth century were eager to do so.

'Our great American melting pot,' stated a 1917 Arizona editorial, 'contains a mixture that boils, fumes, bubbles, steams. In the semi-solution are held all sorts of elements. Some observers are pessimistic concerning the possibilities of a perfect blend,' it added, while others believed 'that the crisis [of war] had proved a magic element to precipitate the foaming mixture into clear, hard, shining crystals of pure Americanism'. Sadly, even the catalyst of war was insufficiently magical to create a crystalline Americanism. 'We still have in our midst men who love Germany more than they love American liberty.'[28]

Charles Evans Hughes was congratulated for demanding 'an Americanism that is "100 per cent pure",' one that 'leaves no room for any hyphenated constituent element. Only "an undivided, unwavering loyalty to our country," only "a whole-hearted, patriotic devotion, overriding all racial differences" will be tolerated.'[29] Pure Americanism rejected hyphenate elements, but patriotic devotion was meant to override racial differences: the logic became self-cancelling, but that didn't stop anyone from deploying it.

Anyone who was less than one hundred per cent American could thus, by the long-standing logic of the one-drop rule, be rejected as non-white, non-American, or both. Nativism – combining racism, xenophobia and inherited position – created a syllogism, in which 'one hundred per cent' denoted both pure white and pure 'American', which became rhetorically interchangeable.

Within six months of Wilson's 'America first' speech, the association was clear enough that a self-styled 'Southern Democrat' in Kansas was announcing that the 'next big national issue will be America for pure Americans'. The 'main issue', he stated, 'has already been defined by President Wilson in two words, "America First"', which meant that the United States must determine 'whether in its national aspirations, ideals and sympathies it is to be all American or half alien'.[30]

Soon it became impossible to disentangle the codes – which is one of the points of deploying them. Codes create plausible deniability, and not merely in public. They can also give people who use them a way to evade their own cognitive dissonances. The codes are there to muddy the waters, to keep people from seeing their own faces in the pool.

Perhaps the most prominent advocate of 'America first' isolationism was the newspaper magnate William Randolph Hearst, who supported Hughes's candidacy. Hearst's editorials were reprinted throughout the country, urging America to put 'America first' and steer clear of 'entangling alliances', another popular mangling of Washington's words.

The Hearst syndicate's 'great anxiety for "America first"' was frequently remarked. 'In big black type, Hearst has said repeatedly "America first."'[31] '"America first!" was the text of his campaign', a constant refrain in the American papers to keep the country out of the war.[32] Tiny local papers like the *Hardin County Ledger* in Iowa reprinted Hearst's editorials in their entirety, in which he argued for months: 'We should inflexibly resolve to keep out of entangling alliances, to fight our own war in our own way; to use American money and American men only for the defense of America.'[33]

Being free of 'foreign entanglements' was thus another way of conflating 'anti-hyphenate' xenophobia and nativism with isolationism and 'America first'. They were all knotted up – because it's not as easy to steer clear of all entanglements as some would like to believe.

Woodrow Wilson always tried to differentiate his use of 'America first' from isolationism, insisting the slogan was actually internationalist, meaning America should take the lead. 'AMERICA FIRST is a slogan which does not belong to any one political party,' he later said. For the Democrats, as opposed to the isolationist Republicans, it meant, he insisted, that 'in every organization for the benefit of mankind America must lead the world by imparting to other peoples her own ideals of Justice and Peace'.[34]

It was a neat ploy, worthy of the wily old diplomat; but Wilson's other 1916 slogan for re-election was balder: 'He Kept Us Out of the War.'

* * *

As an expression 'one hundred per cent American' is often attributed to a 1918 speech Theodore Roosevelt gave called 'Speed up the War', in which he declared: 'There can be no fifty-fifty

Americanism in this country. There is room here for only 100 per cent. Americanism, only for those who are Americans and nothing else. We must have loyalty to only one flag, the American flag.'[35]

But the phrase was in circulation by at least 1915, when a rabbi urged his synagogue to follow 'Ten Commandments of True Americanism', instructing them: 'True Americanism means 100 per cent. Americanism.'[36] And in a 1916 letter that was reprinted in the *New York Times* and then around the country, Charles Evans Hughes thanked Roosevelt for endorsing his candidacy. 'No one is more sensible than I of the lasting indebtedness of the nation to you for the quickening of the national spirit, for the demand of an out-and-out – 100 per cent – Americanism.'[37]

During his post-presidency in fact Theodore Roosevelt gave many speeches about '100 per cent Americanism' and 'hyphenates', including 'America for Americans' in 1916, in which he also tended consistently to add that the question was strictly one of loyalty to the United States, not of a person's ethnic origins. He routinely mentioned his own Dutch heritage, while promising he would personally vote for president 'any American of German, Irish, Scandinavian or other parentage, of whatever creed'. It was 'a violation of every principle of true Americanism to discriminate' against anyone because of their heritage.[38] But these qualifications were rapidly lost in translation (and it's worth noting that he only named Northern Europeans).[39]

Before long, America first, one hundred per cent American, pure American and patriotism were being used more or less interchangeably. A nationally syndicated *Baltimore Star* editorial in 1918 described a local man as 'a one-hundred per cent patriot, [and] not only one-hundred per cent American – for there are, it is to be regretted, many one-hundred per cent Americans who are not even fifty per cent patriots'.[40]

What is being measured in thus sifting Americanism? Not patriotism, for if it were, there would not be a distinction between fifty per cent patriots and one hundred per cent Americans. It had to connote 'real American', which almost certainly translated into white and native-born. 'All willing to pledge full one hundred per cent allegiance to our government, and then give it, should alone be entitled to the honored name of "American citizen",' stated a South Dakota editorial in July 1918.[41] Similarly, in a widely circulated article titled 'Confessions of a Hyphenate', a recent immigrant explained that nothing he did was sufficient to earn him the label 'One Hundred Per Cent American'. 'Three years ago I believed that I was a full-fledged American, as indistinguishably merged in the stream of American life as one drop of clear water merges with another. I should have known better,' he wrote in *The Century*. 'The immigrant can no more turn himself into a one hundred per cent American than the rabbit can grow a mane. Whether he be a Pole in Germany, a Chinaman in Japan, an Italian in the Argentine, or a German in America,' he concluded bitterly, 'the immigrant must always remain a citizen of the second class.'[42]

When Congressman Julius Kahn of California ('perhaps the leading Jew in American public life')[43] announced, 'I am an American, for America first, last and all the time; no other country appeals to me,' the *San Francisco Chronicle* put this declaration under the subheading '100 Per Cent American', although Kahn never used that phrase. The expressions had become synonymous enough for an editor to treat them as interchangeable.[44]

It is therefore also likely the case that when the *Chronicle* declared above its masthead from 1918 to 1920, 'This Newspaper is One Hundred Per Cent American', it was sending a dog whistle to all its readers that it was for 'America first', and for 'pure Americans', as well as signalling political isolationism.

In fact, the more you pull on the threads that knot 'America first' and 'one hundred per cent American' together, the more you find other strands pulling the knot tighter.

Julius Kahn was himself a German-born immigrant — a 'hyphenate' — who was elected to Congress in 1899. Soon he had co-authored the Kahn–Mitchell Chinese Exclusion Act of 1902, a law making the Chinese Exclusion Act permanent. (In other words, a German Jew could, with hard work, good fortune and a willingness to exclude other minorities, be accepted into the one hundred per cent club. The Chinese, however, were out of luck.)

Another immigrant congressman was proclaimed one hundred per cent American not long after Senator Kahn was — and this case is equally instructive. When Senator Knute Nelson died, he was hailed in obituaries across the land as 'one hundred per cent American' — despite having been born in Norway.

Nelson got a free pass to pure Americanness because (as his obituary helpfully spelled out) he was descended from 'the true Nordic line', 'from the race which set up strong gods and bred strong men'. Like the list of hyphenates Teddy Roosevelt was prepared to accept as true Americans, Nelson came from the right part of Europe, the northern part. His years of public service could thus demonstrate 'the value to America of men born over the seas who become Americans in the fullest meaning of that phrase which distinguishes the best among us: "He was a one-hundred-per-cent American."'[45]

The reason why being Nordic made Nelson one hundred per cent American (which might seem oxymoronic) was that 'Nordic' and 'one hundred per cent American' were *also* intertwined. As if all of this weren't confused enough, 'Nordic' was yet another code, used in the first decades of the twentieth century in the same ways that the Nazis would use 'Aryan'.

'Nordicism' held that people of Northern Europe were biologically superior to those of Southern Europe, a theory espoused by white supremacists like Madison Grant, whose 1916 *The Passing of the Great Race: or The Racial Basis of European History* became one of the most influential works of eugenicist scientific racism. 'The Nordics,' Grant wrote, are, all over the world, a race of soldiers, sailors, adventurers, and explorers, but above all, of rulers, organizers, and aristocrats in sharp contrast to the essentially peasant character of the Alpines. Chivalry and knighthood, and their still surviving but greatly impaired counterparts, are peculiarly Nordic traits, and feudalism, class distinctions, and race pride among Europeans are traceable for the most part to the north.[46]

Grant warned of the imminent 'great danger' in America of 'replacement of a higher type by a lower type', unless the 'native American' (i.e. nativist, white descendants of early European settlers) 'uses his superior intelligence to protect himself and his children from competition with intrusive peoples drained from the lowest races of eastern Europe and western Asia'.[47] Grant's proposed solutions to this impending crisis including the building of ghettos and the sterilisation of 'inferior' humans.

But in practice, 'Nordic' was used to describe anyone who was blonde, or white, or 'Caucasian', or 'Anglo-Saxon', or Northern European, as well as anyone who was actually from Norway. (This could lead to entertaining mix-ups, when racists got confused about who they hated, as we shall see.)

None of it was pretty, and none of it was lost on contemporary observers – nor was it intended to be, as a North Carolina woman made clear in a letter to her local paper in 1920. 'I do not relish all this "One hundred per cent. American," "America first" propaganda to the exclusion of other nations, not because I am not a loyal American, but because I am.'[48]

But many Americans embraced it. A Colorado rancher whose son had been killed in action told an audience in the Midwest: 'You folks do not seem to take this war seriously enough. With us out west it is a matter of life and death. We have our One Hundred Per Cent American societies, and I want to tell you that any disloyal utterances or actions will result in a necktie party with a rope, a tree and a Hun the principal factors.'[49]

Patriotism, citizenship, ethnic purity and racial purity were all being conflated: it was a short rhetorical step from 'One Hundred Per Cent American societies' to lynching, because of the associative chains that had been created. Loaded phrases slamming into each other with sufficient force could detonate into real violence; slogans are not mere words when they create political realities.

That this was no idle threat was made all too brutally clear a month after the Colorado rancher threatened to lynch any German he deemed insufficiently loyal – when a Midwestern mob did just that. 'Mob May Have Made a Fearful Mistake,' admitted a Florida headline in 1918, reporting the story of a 'socialist lynched' in Illinois for 'disloyal utterances'. The victim prayed in German before being 'strung up'; his killers subsequently found in the dead man's pockets a statement of loyalty to the United States.[50]

Threats of lynching were directed with some frequency against hyphenates. And although the term 'hyphenate' was most often applied to immigrants, it would have also implicitly conjured for many listeners the hyphenate term 'African-American', a phrase used by abolitionist newspapers as early as 1835.[51] By 1855, an abolitionist was distinguishing 'African Americans' from 'Saxon Americans'.[52] 'The two greatest questions which, in the progression of the age, cannot be escaped, were the Anglo-American and the African-American,' said another in 1859.[53]

Fifty years later, avowed hostility towards 'hyphenate' identities did not have to explicitly name African-Americans to implicitly differentiate them from 'Anglo-Americans' or 'Saxon Americans'. Nor should this be a surprise: race and immigration have been intertwined in America since at least the antebellum days of Know Nothing nativism in the 1850s, when the 'Native American Party' formed from the remnants of the Whigs to oppose the influx of European immigrants fleeing revolution and famine, but equally to oppose the abolitionist policies of the nascent Republicans, whom Lincoln would soon lead.

By the early years of the twentieth century, as with 'America first', so the animus against all 'hyphenates' had become something that many Republicans and Democrats could agree on.

* * *

Although seven presidents lobbied against lynching, Woodrow Wilson was not one of them; under pressure, he gave just one speech denouncing it. Nor would he likely have been made uneasy by the increasing associations of his campaign slogan with eugenicist ideas of racial purity. Wilson's speeches against hyphenates were no mere campaign tactic. Although an internationalist whose administration passed progressive legislation including the Federal Reserve Act, Wilson was reactionary in matters of race. In fact, Wilson was one of the many white supremacists who have inhabited the White House, going right back to the ones who had slaves build it for them.

A native Virginian born nine years before the Civil War began, Wilson came of age with the national romance known as the Lost Cause. In the aftermath of the South's crushing defeat in the Civil War, Southerners began trying to reclaim what they had lost – namely, an old social order of unquestioned racial and economic hegemony. They told stories idealising the nobility of their cause against the so-called 'War of Northern Aggression', in which Northerners invaded the peaceful South out of a combination of greed, arrogance, ignorance and spite. Gentle Southerners heroically rallied to protect their way of life, with loyal slaves cheering them all the way. This Edenic myth of a lost agrarian paradise, in which virtuous aristocrats and hard-working farmers coexisted peacefully with devoted slaves, predated the war: merging with Jeffersonian ideals of the yeoman farmer, it formed the earliest propagandistic defence of slavery.

Since the Civil War, the Democrats were the party of the South, opposed to Lincoln's Republicans, the party of the North and Union, over the question of slavery and civil rights (itself a phrase associated with the rights of African-Americans as far back as antebellum abolition arguments). After the war the party of

Lincoln gradually evolved into the party of urban industrialism, while the Democrats were firmly aligned until the 1940s with Southern agrarianism. And because of this ideological allegiance to Southern agrarianism, the Democrats were also the party of states' rights, Jim Crow segregation and white supremacism.

Although Woodrow Wilson was not a typical 'Southern Democrat' – he had been governor of New Jersey, and was elected in 1912 as a progressive – his views were not always distinct from theirs. As president, Wilson instituted segregation in the federal government, including separate toilets in the US Treasury and Interior Department. His Treasury Secretary, who then became his son-in-law, William G. McAdoo (born in Georgia in 1863, in the midst of the Civil War), defended the decision by arguing that it was 'difficult to disregard certain feelings and sentiments of white people in a matter of this sort'. Luckily for them, it was easy to disregard the feelings and sentiments of black people.

A delegation from the National Independence Equal Rights League came to the White House in 1914 to express their dismay at federalising segregation. Wilson insisted that it was 'enforced for the comfort and the best interests of both races in order to overcome friction'. Told that his support for segregation would likely result in the united opposition of African-American voters in the 1916 election, Wilson took umbrage, 'saying that if the colored people had made a mistake in voting for him they ought to correct it, but that he would insist that politics should not be brought into the question because it was not a political problem', but 'a human problem'. The delegation left, informing reporters that Wilson's 'statement that segregation was intended to prevent racial friction is not supported by the facts'.[54]

In 1915 Wilson became the first president to show a movie in the White House: *The Birth of a Nation*, directed by D. W. Griffith, who was himself the son of a Confederate colonel. The now notoriously racist film was based on an even more racist novel called *The Clansman*, by Thomas W. Dixon – with whom Woodrow Wilson had become acquainted at Johns Hopkins University. Dixon was himself a staunch upholder of the one-drop rule, as he had explained to a local reporter in North Carolina. 'There is no reconciling the essential difference between the negro and the Anglo-Saxon,' Dixon announced, because 'one drop of negro blood makes a negro'.[55] Dixon wrote a series of books mythologising the rise of the Ku Klux Klan, part of the 'moonlight and magnolia' school of plantation fiction, of which another member was the writer Thomas Nelson Page – whom Woodrow Wilson appointed his ambassador to Italy.

Page's novels, such as *In Ole Virginia* (1887) and *Red Rock* (1898), helped establish the formula: devoted former slaves recount (in dialect) their memories of a halcyon plantation culture wantonly destroyed by militant Northern abolitionists and power-crazed federalists. A small band of honourable soldiers fought bravely on the battlefield and lost; the vindictive North installed incompetent or corrupt black people to subjugate the innocent whites; Southern scalawags and Northern carpetbaggers descended to exploit the battle-ravaged towns. Pushed to the limits of forbearance, the Confederate army rose again to defend honour and decency – in the noble form of the Ku Klux Klan. It was a pernicious fiction turning the armed defence of institutional slavery into a *beau geste*.

The Birth of a Nation outlines this myth in fulsome, false detail, telling a story in which 'the former enemies of North and South are united again in common defense of their Aryan birthright', as an intertitle declared. Dixon reportedly said that his purpose 'was to revolutionize Northern audiences', writing a story 'that would transform every man into a Southern partisan for life', while Griffith said that one of his hopes for the film was that it would 'create a feeling of abhorrence in white people, especially white women, against colored men'.[56]

It worked. *The Birth of a Nation* was a national phenomenon. Northern white audiences cheered; black audiences were horrified. The film prompted riots and racist vigilante mobs in cities across America, as well as at least one homicide, when a white man killed a black teenager – in Indiana, not in the Deep South.

The Birth of a Nation was single-handedly responsible for rekindling interest in the Ku Klux Klan, resuscitated by 'Colonel' William Joseph Simmons after viewing *The Birth of a Nation* and its depiction of Klansmen as heroes. Before long, slogans like Wilson's 'America First' and Roosevelt's '100 per cent Americanism' would give the resurgent Klan its own codes.

For all the Klan's divisiveness, its extension across the country also worked perversely to reconcile North and South just as *The Birth of a Nation* imagined, as 'Anglo-Saxons' united against perceived threats from groups they sought to subordinate; the election of the Southern segregationist Wilson functioned in the same way, helping to reunite the nation in the wake of Reconstruction.

And in the meantime, even without the help of the Klan, white people had continued to brutalise black people across the country. Between 1889 and 1922, according to the National Association for the Advancement of Colored People (NAACP), 3,436 people were lynched in America – and that's just the official records.[57] No one knows how many more victims went unidentified, and unaccounted for. Although the vast majority of victims were African-American, Catholics and Jews were also lynched, as were women. The Mexican government sued the United States for failing to prosecute those responsible for the lynching of Mexican nationals; Italian nationals were lynched as well, including eleven suspected of a murder in 1891.

Lynching was not always, or even primarily, a furtive outbreak of violence in the dead of night. By the turn of the century, in many parts of America lynching had turned into entertainment, a blood sport. Public lynchings took place in the cold light of day, with plenty of advance warning, so people could travel from outlying areas for the fun. There were flyers and notices letting spectators know when and where the lynching would take place; local newspapers ran headlines announcing impending plans; reporters were sent to cover it; families brought children, and had picnics. Victims were frequently tortured and mutilated first; pregnant women were burned to death in front of a peanut-crunching crowd.

A Jewish man named Leo Frank was lynched in Georgia in October 1915, scapegoated for the death of thirteen-year-old Mary

Phagan. Two months later, 'Colonel' Simmons lit his vicious fire on Stone Mountain, Georgia, and proclaimed the Ku Klux Klan reborn. In Texas in May 1916, a black farm worker named Jesse Washington, accused of murdering the white woman he worked for, was lynched in front of the Waco city hall. Washington was not hanged. First he was castrated, then his fingers were cut off, then he was raised and lowered over a bonfire for two hours, until he finally died. His charred body was then dismembered, the torso dragged through the streets, and other parts of his body sold as souvenirs.

It happened in broad daylight, in the middle of the day, as some 10,000 spectators watched, including local officials, police officers and children on their school lunch break. Photographs were taken of Washington's carbonised body hanging above grinning white people and turned into postcards.

That's the reality of what being 'one hundred per cent American' and for 'America first' meant to a great many citizens of the United States in the first decades of the twentieth century.

3

THE AMERICAN DREAM 1917–1920:
What Do You Call That But Socialism?

When the United States entered the First World War in 1917, it did so after a speech in which President Wilson famously insisted that 'the world must be made safe for democracy'. It would not have been surprising, however, if he had said the world must be made safe for the American dream, for during the war years the phrase was used almost exclusively to describe what America was, or should, be fighting for in Europe, as any economic senses dropped almost entirely from the expression. 'Sound a trumpet call to every loyal American to remember what America stands for,' read an Oregon advertisement. 'Make the American dream come true of a world set free for Democracy.'[1]

While the US continued to debate whether it should join the conflict, the 'American dream' could still denote peace. 'We are at the parting of the ways as regards realization of the American dream of promoting universal peace.'[2] But increasingly it was used to justify America's involvement in the war, as when the *Chicago Tribune* argued that America could only uphold liberty by fighting for the American dream in Europe.

If the American idea, the American hope, the American dream, and the structures which Americans have erected are not worth fighting for to maintain and protect, they were not worth fighting for to establish. And America has won its place in the world by fighting. If it had not fought for political and personal liberty the equality of man would today be abstract theories rather than established facts.[3]

Although the *OED* uses an excerpt from this very *Tribune* quotation as an early example of its familiar definition of the 'American dream' (namely, 'the ideal that every citizen of the United States should have an equal opportunity to achieve success and prosperity through hard work, determination, and initiative'), there is nothing in the *Tribune*'s original passage about success or prosperity, or hard work, or initiative. The editorial explicitly refers to America's democratic structures, its ideals of political and personal liberty, and of defending equality.

As far as the *Tribune*'s editorial writers in 1916 were concerned, that was the American dream, not success. But once again the *OED* assumes that the meaning of the 'American dream' is so synonymous with prosperity and self-determination that quotations which do not support that meaning are used as if they do.

Nor was the *Tribune* alone in seeing the American dream as a promise of liberty that responded to the threat of tyranny. In February 1917, Mrs Mary E. T. Chapin (whose talks at Manhattan's Biltmore Hotel were 'the fad of the hour among the members of fashionable society who do not attend church but who feel nevertheless a need for spiritual ministration')[4] gave a speech reprinted around the country, urging the United States into the war. Mrs Chapin's words were almost certainly intended as a rebuke to the isolationists who endlessly misquoted George Washington to justify their arguments against 'foreign entanglements'.

Washington dreamed of greater freedom for mankind than the world had ever known ... and he made it a reality for this Nation. I believe that dream of Washington will be extended to Europe by the great war – that the United States will be called upon to settle the war in such a way that the American dream of liberty will spread through Europe and ultimately will encircle the world.[5]

The phrase was also used, less peacefully, but no less politically, to describe America's military might and rising power, criticising the country for timidity in its refusal to enter the war, as in a martial *Chicago Tribune* editorial in January 1917: 'George Dewey smashing the Spanish fleet was the perfect realisation of the American dream of triumphant power.'[6] There were articles discussing the 'American dream of dominating politics from the Equator to the Canadian line', while the *Washington Post* wrote of 'the American dream of a great merchant marine'.[7]

America joined the war, reluctantly, in April 1917. Six months later, Iowa papers were reprinting a Des Moines editorial declaring the war a contest between the 'Prussian dream' of empire and the 'American dream' of democracy.[8] In the face of tyranny, early uses of the 'American dream' would consistently pivot towards the protection of liberty as the defining principle that upholds democracy.

But meanwhile the American dream continued to take various political shapes, from economic equality to a vague idea of national progress. The *Chicago Tribune* was particularly fond of using it; one editorial, widely reprinted, chastised the country for its lack of foresight in planning the railroads. 'We must learn to look ahead in another spirit than the breezy optimism of the American dream. The war, with its giant pressure, is forcing us swiftly out of our complacency.'[9] The 'American dream' was beginning to float free of qualifying descriptors – no longer the American dream 'of' this or that, but rather the expression of a loose, collective optimism.

In April 1918 the *Chicago Tribune* again invoked the American dream of liberty, reflecting on a year in the war with some pride: 'it was evidence of the reality of the American dream of ordered liberty, an unforgettable pledge of American nationality, worthy of the noble men who in the war for independence and the war for union gave the last full measure of devotion'.[10] 'Are you interested in the preservation of the land of liberty in which you live?' demanded a Kansas editorial in April 1918. 'Does the American dream of everlasting peace appeal to you? Remember, we can't have peace without fighting for it. America didn't want war, but this is war to end war.'[11]

When the war did come to an end in November 1918, the American dream still suggested 'ordered liberty', but also democratic order. It was cited more than once to describe the proposed League of Nations, which would result, a Nebraska editorial maintained, in 'a substantial realization of the American dream' – in Europe. The peace plan created 'a constitution for confederate states of the world, laying down principles of government as between nations and peoples', in the same way that the US Constitution regulated relations between American states.[12] The American dream of democratic government could be replicated in Europe, the League's defenders insisted, to extend the American creed of equality, liberty, self-determination and justice.

European peace would not prove so easy to engineer, however. Wilson was 'Releasing American dream' at the Versailles conference, according to a 1919 California headline reporting that the chairman of the Democratic National Committee in 1919 had accused Republicans of deliberately attempting to derail the effort. 'President Wilson has endeavored to release for humanity the dearest dream that has come to the mind of man since the dawn of civilization.' That democratic dream was the American dream, as far as the editors of the *San Bernardino County Sun* were concerned.[13] But Republican leaders had no intention of supporting this particular American dream.

* * *

As America returned to questions about what kind of democracy it would have at home, the Russian Revolution was giving rise to the 'Red Scare', the fear that Soviet Communism would constitute a threat to American democratic institutions, and that the nation would be infiltrated by Bolsheviks. Inequality was still rising, and the May Day riots in 1919 indicated more than labour unrest. The Red Scare, along with associated acts of terrorism, including anarchist bombings, had combined with the jingoistic fervour of the war effort, and rising fears of 'foreign agents', socialists, anarchists and other 'un-American' social forces, to create a state of heightened nationalist tension. That year the traditionally peaceful May Day parades in Boston, New York and Cleveland led to violent clashes between demonstrators and police.

They also resulted in another outpouring of calls for 'one hundred per cent Americanism', and against the 'Sovietization' of the United States by anarchists and Bolsheviks, with endless animadversions against 'un-American' activities that would be revived forty years later during the Cold War. The May Day labour riots were followed swiftly by race riots that took place across the summer and autumn of 1919 in almost forty cities, including in Chicago and Washington DC, where black citizens fought back against white assailants.

That November, Republicans in Reading, Pennsylvania, took out an ad in their local paper declaring they were 'sound one hundred per cent Americans, with the will and the courage to resist all attempts to sovietize Reading, or to graft upon its government un-American ideas or practices'.[14] Two months later, a local Nebraska correspondent furiously argued the opposite case. 'The policy of attempting to control political ideas is un-American. The policy of deportation is czaristic. It certainly is un-American. Some one hundred per centers are right now considering the advisability of turning the Philippine islands into an American Siberia.

'The muzzling of speech and press is a boomerang,' the writer warned. 'Will the authorities never learn that you can't curb ideas by imprisonment or deportation of their expounders?'[15]

Assimilation was one response to xenophobia, and the American dream was beginning to be conjured as a corrective to white nationalism. The earliest instance I have found of the 'American dream' describing the immigrant experience and dreams of individual success comes from 1918. A review of an immigrant memoir called *An American in the Making* ends:

> We find how horrible seems New York ... to a young European fresh from village life. How dreadful seems the noise and filth of the Ghetto! How rough the manners of the motley crew he meets! What a terrible disappointment, heart-breaking, at first, is America! But this Max fights his way to success and at last begins to dream the American dream himself, for he confesses that, at last, it was his old friends and relatives in the Ghetto who seemed strange and backward to him.

It's an assimilationist dream, but also one of upward social mobility: in dreaming the American dream, Max leaves the other 'strange and backward' immigrants behind, embracing American dreams of success.[16]

But other influential voices continued to express suspicion and even alarm towards the idea of upward social mobility as a national aspiration. In 1919, Theodore Dreiser – not yet a famous novelist, but already a committed socialist – published *Twelve Men*, portraits of men who had influenced him. One, a now-forgotten short-story writer, was distinguished for Dreiser by the fact that he 'had not the least interest in American politics or society – a wonderful sign. The American dream of "getting ahead" financially and socially was not part of him – another mark royal.'[17]

The American dream of upward social mobility was evidently on the make – but it was by no means universally touted as a collective ideal, or as the 'American dream' to which the nation should aspire. This mutability does far more than show the obvious fact that ideas can change over time. As ideas of the American creed – liberty, democratic equality, social justice, economic opportunity, individual advancement – began to magnetically cohere around the phrase

'American dream', it also began taking on a more distinct shape. But that shape could shift, as current political or social pressures could tilt the balance of the phrase towards one point of the creed or another.

A popular writer of romantic fantasy adventures named George Barr McCutcheon published a novel in 1920 called *West Wind Drift*. A castaway tale set during the Great War, it is the deeply implausible chronicle of a random group of Americans who meet aboard a great ocean liner while travelling home from South America in 1917 to join the US war effort. Under the captain's watch are 'a Scotch-American', an 'Irish-American' and 'a plain unhyphenated American from Baltimore'. The plain – and plainly meant to be read as 'real' – American is, naturally, the novel's hero.

After the ocean liner is blown up by saboteurs in a plot obviously modelled on the 1915 sinking of the *Lusitania*, the survivors are cast ashore on an uncharted island, where they proceed to build an island paradise. Because the only thing that matters in a survivalist economy is labour, McCutcheon explains, the castaways devise a new currency for their society: time. Time spent working is the only value, and so that is what is traded.

They institute a weekly 'camp tax', as everyone pays in a set amount of time, out of which 'the school, the church, the "hospital" and "the government" were to be supported'. Everyone receives the same number of hours for their work. 'Greed was lacking, for there was no chance to hoard.' Instead resources 'travelled in a circle', from the people to the government, and the government to the people.[18] This results – quite miraculously – in a utopia.

The thin plot revolves around a few seditious elements, all foreigners, who must be eliminated from utopia to maintain its impeccability. An American bank president at first also bears all the hallmarks of a villainous bad capitalist (the scheming, arrogant, top-hatted and monocled monopolist is a Gilded Age stock character in American populist demonology). But even the banker is redeemed in the end, because at heart he's a decent American who respects democracy and justice, and comes to learn the value of equality.

In a striking passage, one American describes their society as

> the most exquisite state of socialism. This comes pretty close to being the essence of that historic American dream, 'of the people, by the people, for the people.' Up to date, that has been the rarest socialistic doctrine ever promulgated, but we are going it a long sight better. 'From the people, by the people, to the people.' What do you call that but socialism?[19]

Whatever most Americans call the American dream today, it seems safe to say that socialism isn't part of it. Taking Lincoln's 'government of the people, by the people, for the people' from the Gettysburg Address and fusing it with the familiar socialist slogan 'from each according to his ability, to each according to his needs', already a cliché by 1920, results in the realisation of the 'historic American dream'.

But the hero – the 'plain unhyphenated American' – is quick to point out that what they've created isn't really socialism: 'socialism is a game in which you are supposed to take something out of your pocket and put it into the other fellow's whether he wants it or not. This scheme of ours is quite another thing. We're not planning to split even on what we've got in our pockets so much as we're planning to divide what we've got in our hands.'[20]

Their system, in fact, is social democracy: the Puritan work ethic incentivising individual endeavour, with a taxation system for the support of collective services and mutual benefits. This 'American dream' incorporates social justice and equality of access to goods and services; it repudiates ideas of personal advancement. It is not advocating the redistribution of wealth, but it is opposed to the stockpiling of wealth.

West Wind Drift was syndicated from post to post, literally – from the *Washington Post* to the *Pittsburgh Daily Post* to the *St. Louis Post-Dispatch* – suggesting that no one in 1920 was overly troubled by this subversive image of a quasi-socialist American dream.

The fact is that in the first twenty years of the existence of the phrase 'American dream', it was usually employed to describe a political ideal, not an economic one; and when it was used to describe an economic aspiration, it was with the pejorative meaning of 'dream' as illusion, not ideal. Never in its earliest years that I have found was the 'American dream' cited to celebrate the freedom of free markets. It was a way to debate ideas about protecting individuals from corrupt forces of power and self-interest.

The American dream was about how to stop bad multimillionaires, not how to become one.

early 1900

freedom not

economic prosperity

4

AMERICA FIRST 1917–1920:
We Have Emerged from Dreamland

Like the 'American dream', 'America first' rapidly narrowed its meanings when the United States entered the First World War. Wartime patriotism made the phrase incompatible with isolationism; for the next two years it became more or less pure jingoism, with frequent comparisons to other nationalist slogans such as 'Vive la France!' and 'Rule Britannia' – while loudly deriding 'Deutschland über Alles' as repugnantly militaristic.

The hypocrisy in this position was frequently pointed out. 'The very people who are most insistent that "Deutschland ueber alles" is the device on the devil's banner are the people who are yowling most tremendously in favor of everybody's slogan of "America First",' observed a North Carolina editorial. But there was nothing to choose between militarist slogans in their implicit belligerence and nationalism. If 'America first' became the country's guiding principle, the editorial warned, it would inevitably lead the nation towards further conflict. 'We have faith to believe that this country is not, and never has been, for "America first",' it concluded. 'We hope and believe that it is for Justice first.'[1]

But such hopes were increasingly belied by the degree to which American xenophobia was now militarised and fully legitimated, with its own campaign slogan. It inspired some truly dreadful poetry:

America first! her traditions and laws,
Her ideals high to cherish our cause;
The soil on which only her freemen hath trod,

We will sacredly keep to her and her God;
All, all to the colors, we rally once more,
America first! from shore unto shore.[2]

And a great deal of equally silly fiction. In September 1917 *Hearst's Magazine* ran a story called 'The Pawn's Count', featuring a German-American, 'a Japanese', 'the villain, Mohammedan Hassan', and the heroine, 'Cammella Van Peyl', who despite her exotic name is 'the American girl "for America first, only, always".'

'You cannot frighten me, Hassan,' America-first Cammella announced in an illustrated advertisement that helpfully glossed her words ('Yankee girl hard to frighten'), amidst its casual anti-Muslim stereotyping.[3]

"You Cannot Frighten Me, Hassan."

SPIES—WAR

This illustrates E. Phillips Oppenheim's great story, "The Pawn's Count," in HEARST'S MAGAZINE for September.

A German-American, an Englishman, a Japanese and Cammella Van Peyl, the American girl "for America first, only, always," is the heroine.

This is a first-class Oppenheim story. Fair warning, if you read as far as Cammella's interview with the villain, Mohammedan Hassan, you will be a confirmed Oppenheim reader for the rest of your days.

Yankee Girl Hard to Frighten.

The wartime patriotism that swept America in 1917 and 1918 was not restricted to invocations of the American dream or America first, of course. The 'American creed' also made a comeback, courtesy of a descendant of President John Tyler named William Tyler Page, who won $1,000 in a 'national citizen's creed contest'. Page's American creed begins:

I believe in the United States of America as a government of the people, by the people, for the people, whose just powers are derived from the consent of the governed; a democracy in a republic and a sovereign nation of many sovereign States;

a perfect Union, one and inseparable; established upon those principles of freedom, equality, justice and humanity for which American patriots sacrificed their lives and fortunes.[4]

Page's creed was recited in schools and town halls across America for the next several decades, inculcated into tens of thousands of American citizens. Like the pledge of allegiance, which was composed in 1892 and popularly recited for decades before it was made official in 1945, so would Page's American creed return in the fight against totalitarianism.

* * *

When the First World War ended, 'America first' quickly shifted its meaning back from wartime jingoism to pure isolationism. No contradiction registered, for its nationalism remained consistent.

Wilsonian attempts at characterising 'America first' as a slogan for American world leadership were overpowered by a wave of popular resistance to any further entangling alliances. The country's sentiment had not broadly changed; a majority of the population still felt that Europe's problems were its own, and that the US government should focus its energy domestically. They had made an exception for the Great War; that exception was over and it was time to return to the isolationist norm.

In particular, Wilson's position on the Treaty of Versailles and his advocacy of the League of Nations was not popular at home. Progressives objected to its harsh reparations and the huge debt burden it imposed on Germany, as well as to its arbitrary disposition of territories, viewing these as a betrayal of the principles of justice for which they had fought. Conservatives despised Wilson's attempts to establish the League of Nations, seeing it as a nightmare of permanent entangling alliances – and this time Washington's farewell address was more accurately cited.

Congress was baulking especially at Article X, which allowed for collective action to maintain peace, enjoining all member nations to 'respect and preserve … against external aggression the territorial integrity and existing independence of all Members of the League'. This was anathema to non-interventionists certain it cloaked imperialist tendencies and was a pretext for enforcing the will of the imperial League. Its opponents argued that Article X bound the United States to a permanent, global commitment to send troops to any place, at any time, if the League detected 'external aggression'.

America first had backfired against Wilson: now it was leading his opponents to call his desire to join the League of Nations 'indefensible'.

One of the problems with Article X was the widespread view, shared by progressives like Walter Lippmann, that the post-war settlement of territories was unjust, and it would force America to defend that injustice. Lippmann predicted it would lead to 'endless trouble for Europe', warning, all too accurately, that the Versailles Treaty would surely prove 'a prelude to quarrels in a deeply divided and hideously embittered Europe'.[5]

But others were opposed to the League of Nations for the way it seemed to transfer democratic agency away from individual citizens, and towards cabbalistic foreign powers and international financiers. Many white male owners of small farms and businesses, in particular, saw in the League of Nations yet another encroachment on their political hegemony, yet another incremental degree of influence transferred away from them and towards 'alien' groups, diluting the concentration of their power.

As American politicians and press called for protectionist tariffs, they began debating the question of what they called 'economic nationalism', another phrase that would be revived a century later. Bankers argued that the US must 'meet and compete with the economic nationalism of other peoples'.[6] A widely reprinted *New Republic* leader countered that the establishment's opposition to German democratic autonomy was clearly a pretext for creating what would later be called the military-industrial complex, 'a future structure of armament, militarism, economic nationalism, and power politics' in America.[7]

'America first' was soon taken up as a rallying cry for protectionist tariffs and against the League of Nations. Citizens wrote in to the papers explaining why Republicans were the most patriotic party. 'The Republican party may rightly be called the American party,' claimed a letter to the *New York Tribune*. 'Let our motto be America First.'[8]

William Randolph Hearst was the nation's most relentless opponent of Article X. For Hearst, the League of Nations and Article X would inevitably entangle America in foreign conflicts in Europe, and he led the domestic campaign against Wilson's efforts to persuade Congress to sign the Treaty, reiterating that the League of Nations and the World Court were 'loathsome' organisations, whose sole purpose was to enmesh the United States in foreign conflicts that could destroy it.

In editorials and letters to the press, Hearst openly threatened politicians who supported the Treaty. Surely any patriotic statesman, Hearst ruminated in one, would want American citizens 'to know how he voted and to REMEMBER how he voted'. Hearst was prepared to use his publications – 'read now by twenty-five million Americans and increasing daily in the number of their clientele' – to 'keep those statesmen and their votes for as many years as may be necessary before the American people'.

If, in the end, the Treaty was accepted by Congress, Hearst vowed to 'consecrate' his publications 'to the formation of a new party ... whose dominating idea will be "America First," and whose sole devotion will be to the Liberty, Democracy and INDEPENDENCE which have made America first of all nations of the world'.[9]

The *Scranton Republican* warned readers that internationalism, with 'its subtle illusions', 'its glittering generalities and its appeal to universal sentiment', was deluding American citizens. 'The people of this country must not lose sight of the fact that a principle to which they must tenaciously adhere is "America first."'[10]

Fears of international propaganda infiltrating America were not assuaged by reports like the one revealing a 'Fake News Bureau in Europe', a plan 'whereby news without foundation, or entirely distorted, is given out for transmission to America for purely speculative purposes'.[11] Propaganda was itself a new and worrying idea, exposing for the first time how easy it was to use false or distorted information to manipulate opinion.

Concerns about propaganda had emerged during the war; the threats that systematic propaganda posed to democracy were instantly apparent, as the fragility of any system depending on the wisdom of crowds became all too clear. Modern ideas about advertising showed that political slogans could help create a campaign brand, persuading voters to choose not only a candidate but a political position. Where in the nineteenth century name recognition was often sufficient (think 'Tippecanoe and Tyler, too'), in the twentieth century, candidates increasingly aligned themselves with ideologies – like 'America first'.

'America first' and associated ideas of Americanisation, including calls for English as a national language, were touted as antidotes to foreign propaganda and alien ideas. 'America first must be stamped upon every heart. There should be but one language in the public grade schools – the language of the Declaration of Independence, of Abraham Lincoln, of Theodore Roosevelt,' pronounced General Leonard Wood, who had commanded Roosevelt's rough riders and was seeking the Republican nomination in 1920. 'Avoid loose-fibred internationalism as you would death, for it means national death.'[12]

Despite these efforts to claim 'America first' as an improving ideal, many leading educators publicly despised it. Charles W. Eliot, former president of Harvard, wrote to the *New York Times* in withering terms:

America first: this is the lowest estimate of the intelligence and good sense of the American people that has ever been made by native or foreigner. That such an estimate should be made by public men who had the means of watching the way the minds and hearts of the common and uncommon people in the United

States worked in 1917 and 1918 would seem incredible, but is a humiliating fact.[13]

More representatively, Republican Senator Walter Edge of New Jersey announced that there was 'a distinct difference between an "America first" citizen', and those seeking a dream of 'world power' that would 'engulf' the United States 'in the maelstrom of Europe without qualification'.[14] Editorials around the country agreed, criticising Wilson's 'tenacious adherence' to an ideal of international brotherhood for which 'the world is not yet prepared'.[15] 'In brief, Americans want to safeguard America first.'[16]

Before long, 'America First, Last and All the Time' had been resuscitated around the country. Local papers from Wilmington, Delaware, to Green Bay, Wisconsin, adopted it as their motto, printing it on the editorial page of every issue.

AMERICA FIRST, LAST,
AND ALL THE TIME.

By early 1920, Hearst's *New York American* — declaring that its 'inspiration is "America First"' — was offering a $500 prize, and one hundred '"America First" Silver Medals', for the best student essay written in celebration of George Washington, who 'was for AMERICA FIRST, LAST AND ALL THE TIME'.[17] Off and on for the next two decades, Hearst would add 'America First' to the mastheads of his newspapers from coast to coast.

The Washington Herald
AMERICA FIRST

On 19 March 1920, the Senate refused for a second time to ratify the Treaty of Versailles, sending it back to President Wilson (about whose stroke six months earlier rumours were finally beginning to circulate). The next day, the *New York Times* shared outraged letters from American citizens insisting that the country should take a leading role in the peace process, trying to reclaim the old Wilsonian internationalist meaning of 'America first' as first to do right in the world.

'With indignation and shame we behold America fallen from her position of leadership among the nations,' one attested. '"America First" ought to mean America first (not last, as now), to redeem her pledge; America first, not last, to pay her debt of honor; America first, not last, to make a willing sacrifice.'[18]

In the summer of 1920, Republicans nominated Warren G. Harding, who had successfully campaigned for the Senate back in 1914 on a platform of 'Prosper America First'. Now Harding adopted it as his presidential campaign slogan. 'Call it the selfishness of nationality if you will, I think it an inspiration to patriotic devotion – To safeguard America first, to stabilize America first, to prosper America first, to think of America first, to exalt America first, to live for and revere America first.'[19]

Many Americans did indeed call it the selfishness of nationality. A North Carolina paper reported that Harding was being denounced as 'an exponent of "the reactionary, mediaeval creed of selfish, egotistic, jingoistic nationalism"'.[20] Jingoism, the *Indianapolis Journal* had told its readers back in 1895, was a British term for those who seek power 'by browbeating and crowding other nations with threat of war'. Jingoism was patriotism for bullies; it picked on weaker nations, and never spoke of principle, only of glory; never of justice, only of self-interest.[21]

That summer, Senator Henry Cabot Lodge delivered a keynote speech at the Republican National Convention, denouncing the League of Nations in the name of 'America first'. The American people would never accept the Treaty of Versailles, Lodge warned, declaring that 'no man who thinks of America first need fear the answer' to Wilson's 'imperious demand'.[22]

By 30 June Harding had recorded 'America first' on a new device called a phonograph as part of the campaign; a month later he cited it in accepting his nomination, promising to use 'America first' to oppose 'the supreme blunder' of Wilsonian internationalism and the League of Nations. Others noted the irony. 'Candidate Harding is making a great to do about "America first." The trouble with that slogan in Republican mouths is that it is borrowed from the Wilson Administration.'[23] So, on the face of it, was Harding's campaign poster, which was markedly similar to Wilson's of four years earlier.

The *American Economist* endorsed Harding's candidacy in a leader reprinted around the country, promising that Harding ('a clean man of upstanding character') would usher in 'an era of nationalism, instead of internationalism, that we shall have as the Head of the Nation a man who thinks for "America First"'.[24]

Not everyone was convinced. A North Carolina editorial objected: 'Senator Harding prates about "America first." Who wants to put America second? Had it not been for the Republican Senators in Washington, among whom Senator Harding is one, America would today really be first, sitting at the head of the table in the great concert of powers for the preservation of the peace and liberty of the world.'[25]

But for many Americans, the motto quickly came to seem axiomatically patriotic. An ad was taken out in Texas for Independence Day: 'Tomorrow – July 4th – the American people will again renew their allegiance to the greatest of all flags, and will again avow their faith in the great principles embodied in the Declaration of Independence. America First has become the slogan of all loyal Americans.'[26]

This paean to civic virtue was slightly undermined by the fact that it was selling a laundry service ('Long Live your Linen – Long Live Your Clothes') in which Uncle Sam was pictured pensively mulling 'America First'.

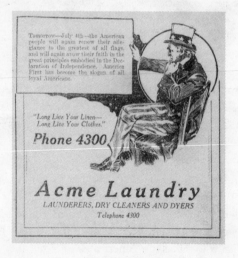

Whatever the ad's unintentional comedy, the point is that 'America first' had become so fully absorbed into the national conversation that by 1920 it seemed to many Americans as iconic as the Fourth of July, the Declaration of Independence and Uncle Sam.

* * *

But it also remained divisive. Americans all over the country wrote to their local papers and to the *New York Times*, repudiating the expression and its sentiments, seeing in them, as others had done, an ugly ultra-nationalism. 'When [Harding] closed his first home-coming speech with "America first" six times reiterated, one felt that surely he would have something like "Deutschland über Alles" to say,' one correspondent observed.[27]

Another announced more baldly: '"America first" seems to me a mighty mean slogan.'[28]

The *Pittsburgh Post* censured Harding in July for implying that those who disagreed with him were not putting 'America first'. Americanism, the editorial argued, should not be judged only by love of country during war, but 'also by loyalty to its principles in peace. If there is one principle that stands out more than another in the American creed for all times it is tolerance of opinion. It follows that an intolerant man is far from being an ideal American.'[29]

But Harding was routinely impugning the integrity of those who disagreed with him, including progressives in his own party who dared to challenge the Republican old guard. Now, the leader added, he was attacking his political opponents by despicably claiming 'that Democrats are not for America first'. The sooner Harding realised it was beneath contempt to accuse his opponents of being traitors just because they disagreed with him, the better it would be for everyone.[30]

The *New York Times* did the *Post* one better. It dismissed 'America first' as itself beneath contempt, roundly mocking the 'banality' of the phrase, 'the greatest volume of commonplace ever uttered. "America first!" "Aye, my countrymen, let us all love our native land." Thrilling cries like these have been dinned into all ears from every Republican stump.' The best thing about Harding's speeches, the editorial concluded, was that they furnished 'such complete intellectual relief' for anyone with a brain.[31]

The motto continued to play well to crowds, however, and specifically to the xenophobic fears that politicians were busily stoking. That autumn, in what became known as his 'Address to the Foreign Born', Harding offered 'America first' as an antidote to the dangers of 'hyphenate Americans'. Declaring himself 'unalterably against any present or future hyphenated Americanism', Harding warned that the League of Nations would only 'drive into groups' Americans 'whose hearts are led away from "America First!" to "Hyphen First!"'

America must guard against an 'organized hyphenated vote', Harding maintained, so as to avoid having control over the nation 'transferred to a foreign capital abroad'.[32] All of these euphemisms – internationalism would drive voters into groups, the nation must block an organised hyphen vote, there were foreign cabals waiting to grab American wealth – amounted in real terms to the demonisation of any immigrant communities voting as a bloc, internationalism deliberately conflated with xenophobia.

Criticising the Democrats for failing to make a positive case for their own values, Harding pronounced: 'We do not know what our opponents stand for. I stand for a united America, a humane America, an efficient America, America first.'[33]

The subtexts of these coded phrases were not lost on Harding's audience. 'The slogans "America first" and "I am in favor of staying out" bring a chill,' wrote one angry citizen just before the election, on 31 October 1920. 'America may "stay out" of the League, but she will not "stay out" of history.'[34]

In October, Will Hays, chairman of the National Republican Committee, had proclaimed that he could see 'Republicans "Marching to Victory" Under "America First" Banner'.[35] On 3 November, they did just that, sweeping the White House and Congress against a Democratic ticket that included a vice-presidential nominee named Franklin Delano Roosevelt.

After Harding's victory, he stated that the Great War had been fought not to secure democracy, but to secure American rights abroad: internationalism would only be in the service of nationalism. European politicians, worried about America withdrawing from the world stage, assured each other that 'while Senator Harding's success is momentarily a victory of the ideas represented by the slogan "America First"', it did not mean that the United States would hold that line for long.[36] Surely it was just a campaign tactic, and America would return to a position of world leadership.

Once Harding won, for many Americans the phrase seemed legitimised; soon it was viewed as an administrative policy, rather than merely a slogan. A letter to the *New York Times* just after the 1920 election defended the idea: '"America first," as every well-informed person understands, simply means the protection and defense of our own domestic affairs at home against the invasion or interference of any unfavorable outside influences,' including 'the discussion or practice of nihilism, radical socialism or alien propaganda'. A defence against these 'disintegrating influences' was all that was intended by 'America first', a slogan 'approved in the late election' that was now government policy. 'Every one within the United States should fall in step.'[37]

The threats of nihilism, radical socialism and alien propaganda that 'America first' was meant to combat were, by no coincidence, all corrupting influences associated with European intellectuals, many of whom were also Jewish. These radical intellectuals, with their alien ideas, were construed as threats to 'ordinary' supporters of 'America first', which – through another chain of associations – thus became a defiantly anti-intellectual position, as well. Rural populations felt that smug cosmopolitan elites – like the writer H. L. Mencken, who became famous for insulting the 'rubes' and 'yokels' of the Middle American 'booboisie' – were sneering at their morality and religion.

The result was that 'America first' was by no means only taken up by Republicans. Just after the election, Democrat Senator

James Reed of Missouri told an 'America First Thanksgiving' celebration in Madison Square Garden: 'We have emerged from dreamland.' Reed was one of a bipartisan group of congressmen known as the 'Irreconcilables', who unilaterally rejected the Versailles Treaty in any form. 'The American people have refused to haul down the American flag. We have emerged from dreamland. The people can always be trusted. Our Anglo-Saxon fathers realized that,' Reed added, throwing in a little racial fillip for his listeners. 'They knew, as Jefferson knew, that the common sense of the people was greater than all the knowledge of a few intellectuals.'[38]

This calculus unites Anglo-Saxons, the Founding Fathers, and the common people against foreign intellectuals who inhabit an unreal dreamland. (We should pause here and enjoy for a moment the idea that the erudite Jefferson, America's first ambassador to France, was opposed to foreign intellectuals.) The charge that urban, intellectual, cosmopolitan citizens are less American, or less 'real', than rural, plain-spoken, provincial Americans is nothing new; it has underwritten the nation's periodic eruptions of anti-elite populism for most of its history. And by 1920, it was associated with 'America first'.

Reed's 'real America', emerging from 'dreamland', was embracing what Walter Lippmann had deemed an illusion, the dream of the unvarnished wisdom of the common man, the power of anti-intellectualism writ large. By no coincidence, Lippmann himself was a first-generation German-Jewish immigrant from New York – exactly the kind of 'alien' public intellectual Senator Reed was encouraging his constituents to dismiss in the name of their 'Anglo-Saxon' fathers. Each group routinely accused the other of embracing delusions, of inhabiting a bubble of unreality.

Earlier in 1920, a former senator named Albert J. Beveridge addressed a 'monster crowd' in Indiana in similar terms, measuring the reality of his fellow Americans against their homogeneity.

Beveridge was not merely for America first, he affirmed: he was for America only.

> I am a nationalist; I am opposed to the League of Nations. I am a nationalist by birth, by conviction, by thought and for prudential reasons. Why, when this country was established it was a homogeneous nation. We are not such a nation now, but a conglomerate of racial groups with none outweighing any other. We are not a people as the French are a people, as the Italians are a racial entity. And until we are a people and racial lines are wiped out and we have become homogeneous in blood as well as in name and purpose, we cannot be the greatest nation possible, a distinctive race in the world. Not America first and Italy second, not America first and France second, not America first and Germany second, but America only should be our slogan.

The monster audience responded to these appeals for a purified 'American race', and its appeals to an entirely mythical racially homogenous past, with thunderous applause.[39]

* * *

All of this should make it come as little surprise that the Ku Klux Klan had also adopted 'America first' as a motto by 1920. In 1919 a Texas Klan leader gave a Fourth of July speech declaring, 'I am for America, first, last and all the time, and I don't want any foreign element telling us what to do.'[40] The fantasy of an America once populated solely by the racially pure Nordic 'common man' was the Klan's genesis myth as well, the prelapsarian past to which they hoped to force America to return – by violence if necessary.

Lynching posed enough of a national crisis that during the 1920 presidential campaign, Republicans were urged to add a plank to their platform that would make it a federal crime. That summer, the

New York Tribune printed a letter from a reader advising the Republican Party to do so. On the same page, another correspondent argued that there had been 'far too much appeal to racial elements. The country must be purged of all alienism.' Americanism, he insisted, stands not for "America First" – that implies doubt, as if there were secondary choices – but for "America Only."' Alienism and foreign elements were leading the country astray; 'as Americans we can solve our own problems, so that every class, every race, every sect may be satisfied'.[41] The author did not seem to see any contradiction in following his objection to too much pandering to racial elements, and a call for purging of all alienism, with an assurance that 'every race may be satisfied'. The Republicans did not adopt an anti-lynching policy in their platform that year, making it unlikely that every race in America was satisfied.

Instead, states' rights continued to be invoked as the pretext for allowing local governments to decide how, or whether, to prosecute lynching. Mostly they didn't, and in the four years between 1918 and 1921, at least twenty-eight people were publicly burned at the stake in the United States.

Most American newspapers at least publicly denounced lynching by 1920. But the cognitive contortions required to rationalise racial violence have always created astonishing blind spots. For example, in July 1920, a North Carolina paper ran an editorial suggesting that the 'America first' slogans of Wilson and Harding were 'just a little selfish': 'A year ago America led the world; today we are completely isolated.'

Right next to that leader condemning selfishness, the paper (ironically named the *Washington Progress*) ran an editorial threatening black Americans with lynching. 'Another horrible outrage has been committed on a white woman by a brute of a negro and as a result another white man has been killed and several others wounded,' it began, before descending into hysterical incoherence: 'This is the second occurrence recently and the former negro was lynched and an attempt to lynch the last one [*sic*].'

Having paid brief lip service to morality and the law – 'lynching is deplorable and cannot be approved' – the editorial quickly got on with the business of blaming the victim:

> But conditions are growing worse and will not be tolerated. The negroes might as well realize this fact once for all. If the best element of the colored people will [choose to,] they can aid in stamping this crime out and retain the good feeling that now exists between the races. No matter how much lynching may be deplored if this thing continues the crime of lynching will multiply.[42]

Summary violence would continue as long as black Americans did not improve their ways – by accepting the fractional citizenship allotted to them by white people.

Historians would later demonstrate beyond any reasonable dispute that violence against African-Americans was a backlash against the political and economic gains they made in this period, and that policing sexual boundaries was usually a pretext. The fact that 'economic competition' led to lynching was acknowledged by local American papers as early as 1903.[43] The more minorities achieved economic autonomy and integrated themselves into the nation's social fabric, the more retaliatory violence they provoked. (The idea of being 'uppity' – failing to know your place – is also the logic that allows oppressors to convince themselves that their victims had it coming, that provoking violence is the same as deserving it.)

That violence against black people was overwhelmingly eco-nomically motivated was occasionally impossible to ignore, even at the time. A local Nebraska paper reported in 1920 that 'thousands of negroes' had been forced by 'white capped' 'night riders' to work in the cotton fields of South Carolina. The headline described this enforced labour in slightly different terms, however: 'Cotton Crop Saved by Action of Night Riders Wearing the Garb of the Kuklux Klan'.[44] It seems that congratulations were in order for the Klan's heroic decision to save a cotton crop by trying to temporarily resuscitate slavery.

Meanwhile, lynching was spreading out of the South. In 1920 the *Dallas Express* ('The South's Oldest and Largest Negro Newspaper') noted that five years earlier a lynching in the North was so rare that it would dominate the news reports when it happened, whereas in the South it garnered much less attention.[45] But in 1919, out of eighty-two reported lynchings in the United States, two were in Colorado, one in Washington state, one in Nebraska and one in Kansas.

In June 1920, three black men, circus workers named Elias Clayton, Elmer Jackson and Isaac McGhie, were lynched in Duluth, Minnesota, accused of raping a white girl. The alleged victim was later examined by a doctor who found no evidence of physical assault. No one was ever prosecuted for the murders.

Two months later, a mob of over a thousand people stormed a Texas jail and lynched Lige Daniels, accused of murdering a white woman; photographs of his dangling body were turned into souvenir postcards. As ever, there were smirking white crowds below, including children.

Later that year, there was another triple lynching in Santa Rosa, California, in front of spectators, one of whom offered a 'vivid' eyewitness account of the 'sickening' event to the press.[46]

It was observed even at the time that the excuses offered for lynching had grown ever thinner, as if mobs could no longer be bothered to rationalise torture and murder. Once the only 'adequate provocation' acknowledged by public opinion was 'the ravishment of a white woman by a Negro', noted the same *Dallas Express* article. But now 'public opinion has become more indulgent'.[47] Among the 'reasons' offered for the summary execution of black Americans in the early years of the twentieth century were 'wild talk', 'gambling dispute', 'wage dispute', 'debt dispute' and 'circulating literature'.

For the Klan, 'America first' offered a fig leaf: a xenophobia that was socially and politically acceptable was covering for a vigilante racism that was (at least officially) not, as they protested that they were purging 'alien elements', and that they had nothing against black people. But the fact is that the Klan only rarely attacked foreigners, whether recent immigrants or visitors from other countries. Instead the 'alien element' was a nativist euphemism for the wrong kind of American: the hyphenate kind, the kind with alien ideas, an alien name, an alien religion, or of an alien race.

* * *

But because the one-drop rule was impossible to prove (all drops of blood in fact look the same, after all), racial purity was much harder to police than groups like the Klan cared to admit. The possibility that people might be hiding their real origins, 'passing' as white, or even as American, is the kind of possibility that might make a nativist very anxious indeed. Anxious enough to develop conspiracy theories about the origins of people in power.

Which is why, in 1920, just before Harding was elected, he was accused of being black.

In October 1920 the press revealed a whispered underground conspiracy theory against the presidential candidate, designed by his opponents to keep his party out of the White House. It was, shouted the *New York Herald* headline, an instance of 'Political Depravity and Moral Degeneracy to Shock the World'. They had uncovered 'a dastardly conspiracy' to 'steal the election from the Republican party through an insidious assertion that Warren G. Harding, Republican candidate for President of the United States, is of Negro ancestry'.[48]

The accusation depended on widespread agreement that to be part 'Negro' was not only to be dishonoured, but to be disqualified from the presidency by virtue of not being 'one hundred per cent American' – which could be construed as being black, or foreign, or treasonous, or all three.

An outraged Republican chairman assured voters that Harding was 'pure Anglo-Saxon', while objecting that the unfounded charges being generally circulated, and widely believed, constituted 'the most contemptible and scurrilous attack ever made by anyone on a candidate for this high honor'.[49] It came as a shock to many that even in modern times the honour of the presidency was insufficient to shield a candidate from scurrilous rumours about his origins.

In an editorial reprinted around the country, a newspaper from Harding's home state of Ohio angrily denounced the 'whispering lies' attacking the presidential candidate's legitimacy. America was supposed to be moving on from ad hominem personal smears. 'The presidential campaigns of the present century have been fought out chiefly in the open with arguments about principles and the characters and intentions of candidates.'[50]

But now Democrats were attempting to revive an ugly 'underhanded partisanship' in circulating the rumour that Harding had a black grandmother. No Democrat had endorsed this 'sneaking propaganda' officially, but they had all passed the pamphlets around behind closed doors.[51]

Defences of Harding sprang up, sharing his ancestry and family tree, carefully explaining exactly where his family came from

(Lanarkshire, Scotland) and when (seventeenth century), while promising 'to prove that there was not one drop of negro blood in any one of them'.[52]

'As a rule Americans object to lies,' the letter finished, 'and particularly to that type of lie which flourishes only in the dark. Unless the character of our people has changed they will show on election day exactly what they think of the subterraneous campaign' to discredit a president's legitimacy on racial grounds with a whispering campaign. 'A political campaign that cannot be run in the open free press of America is not to the credit of any party or candidate,' they were certain.

The *St. Louis Post-Dispatch* reported that three Ohio papers had 'denounced' the rumour, declaring that 'Warren G. Harding, pure in heart, pure in his Americanism, splendid in his fine patriotism, has in his veins only the pure blood of the white man, given him by a long line of culture ancestry, men and women of whom he may well be proud – proud in achievement, proud in their fine home life and ideals and proud in their pure race integrity'.[53]

All of these 'purities' were presented as, if not equivalent, then correlated: pure heart, pure Americanism, splendid patriotism, pure white blood, admirable culture, high achievement, fine ideals, pure race integrity – each becomes inextricable from the other.

From the 'pure Americanism' of 'America first' to 'the pure blood of the white man' in a few easy rhetorical steps. Nor would it be the last time in American history that the idea of too much 'black blood' was used to imply that a president was less than 'one hundred per cent American' and thus unqualified for office, although no one appears to have asked for Harding's birth certificate.

That December, William Allen White, the nationally beloved journalist known as the Sage of Kansas, wrote a letter. 'What a God-damned world this is!' he said. 'If anyone had told me ten years ago that our country would be what it is today … I should have questioned his reason.'[54]

america is racist

America was still a nation of isolationism. But world war two led to aggression (xenophobia).

After wars the anti. 74, (not letting blacks into office (lording)). The american dream came into conflict with America first when they wanted to kick them out

PART TWO

1920—1930

5

THE AMERICAN DREAM 1921–1923:
Salesmen of Prosperity

As the Harding presidency focused America's attention on 'America first', the 'American dream' continued, gradually, to emerge as a way to burnish the prestige of key national values – perhaps even of idealism itself in an increasingly worldly society. It also contributed to a growing sense of national self-regard.

In January 1921, Walter Lippmann wrote an essay that was never published, but was saved among his papers, in which he argued that American Jews should assimilate, rather than support Zionism: 'It is a splendid thing to build Zion in Palestine, but it is no less splendid to fulfill the American dream.'[1]

Quite apart from its potentially controversial political stance (which is why Lippmann's biographer mentioned it), this previously unpublished quotation in fact represents one of the earliest extant uses of the phrase 'American dream' in a context that we would recognise, to describe aspiration, assimilation and the immigrant experience. The idea was clearly on Lippmann's mind, for he would return to the phrase in another important essay within two years.

But it was only slowly gathering cultural momentum. A year later, the *Pittsburgh Press* recounted a story about three enterprising playwrights who rented a home on Long Island 'for a hide-away where they expected to fashion the great American dream', a very early mention of the American dream as a combination of professional ambition and get-rich-quick scheme: the attitudes of the 1920s were increasingly infiltrating the Progressive Era ideal.[2]

By the beginning of 1922, it was still possible for the *Akron Beacon Journal* to write of 'the American dream of world peace', but uses of the phrase in economic contexts were on the rise, at least partly because so was the economy.[3] In the 1920s, the dream that every American might be able to become rich – not just prosperous, but downright wealthy – began to spread, as the stock market promised that everyone could win the lottery by gambling a few dollars, just as Broadway and Hollywood suddenly seemed to suggest that everyone could become a star, or write a hit show.

As the national preoccupation with dreams of prosperity became a fixation, several writers responded in the 1920s with novels that are now regarded as classic treatises on the 'American dream', even though none of the novels in question uses the phrase.

The bestselling American novel of 1922 was *Babbitt*, by Sinclair Lewis, a ferocious popular satire of American conformity, crude materialism and the national cult of business. In the novel's opening pages, George Babbitt gazes upon a bank tower with supreme satisfaction, beholding 'the tower as a temple-spire of the religion of business, a faith passionate, exalted, surpassing common men'.[4] Babbitt is a man of his tribe, unthinkingly following the rules; his reflexive Republican Presbyterianism, Lewis writes, 'confirmed business men in the faith'.[5] That faith is philistinism, although Babbitt is for the most part a fairly innocent philistine, even almost lovable in a hapless kind of way. Babbitt would be shocked by the ugliness of the 'Americanism' understood by some of his real-world counterparts; he is foolish and selfish, but not vicious.

Lewis has quite a lot of fun lampooning 'America first' Republicans and the '100 percenters'. Babbitt is a member of the Good Citizens' League, to which, Lewis explains, 'belonged most of the prosperous citizens of Zenith', which included 'Regular Guys' like George Babbitt, the 'salesmen of prosperity', but also the local bourgeois aristocrats, 'that is, the men who were richer or had been rich for more generations: the presidents of banks and of factories, the land-owners, the corporation lawyers, the fashionable doctors'.[6]

The Good Citizens' League share a belief 'that the working-classes must be kept in their place; and all of them perceived that American Democracy did not imply any equality of wealth, but did demand a wholesome sameness of thought, dress, painting, morals, and vocabulary'.[7] Skewering 'America first' conformity, Lewis was satirically reminding his readers of an American dream that did indeed imply 'equality of wealth', that dream of which Americans had been speaking and writing for the previous twenty years, but one increasingly repudiated by a Republican Party proselytising the benefits – for them – of unchecked capitalism.

Babbitt's Good Citizens' League also supports 'an Americanization Movement, with evening classes in English and history and economics, and daily articles in the newspapers, so that newly arrived foreigners might learn that the true-blue and one hundred per cent. American way of settling labor-troubles was for workmen to trust and love their employers'.[8]

The notion that capitalism's response to 'the labor question' is to teach workers that patriotism means loving your boss is no mere joke (although it is funny). Most of the spleen in *Babbitt* is directed against the idea that business is the religion of America, that money is what the nation worships. During America's rapid age of expansion in the nineteenth century, business had been elevated to the point of a patriotic virtue. As historian James Truslow Adams would argue in 1931, business ceased to be an occupation that was as subject to the moral code as all other endeavours, and began to transcend morality. 'Money-making having become a virtue, it was no longer controlled by the virtues but ranked *with* them.'[9] This logic would lead a century later to the frequently espoused belief that millionaires must be good people or they wouldn't be so successful, an extension of the vulgarised Calvinist idea that wealth is a sign of God's grace.

As early as 1913, on a trip to New York City, the British poet Rupert Brooke had commented on his astonished realisation that Americans truly worshipped business. 'It all confirms the impression that grows on the visitor to America that Business has developed insensibly into a Religion, in more than the light, metaphorical sense of the words.'[10]

Babbitt's popularity sparked debates and conversations around the country, making 'a Babbitt' a recognisable character type, while also making Lewis internationally famous. The UK edition was published with a glossary translating such incomprehensible American slang as Gee ('puritanical euphemism for God') and liberal ('label of would-be broadminded American'), a notable early instance of what a later generation would call throwing shade.

That autumn the *New York Times*, remarking that Midwesterners had taken umbrage at Lewis's parody, cautioned New Yorkers against enjoying the joke at the expense of philistine denizens of the heartland too much, for New Yorkers 'are themselves the frequent victims of a like error. By far too many dwellers in other parts of the country they and their city are called "un-American".' (In fact, the article went on to argue, 'New York is the most American of American cities', for the simple reason that it had inhabitants from 'practically every village, town and city in the United States' living in it.)[11]

Babbitt was the stereotypical Middle American: ignorant, complacent, gullible, accepting without question all the nostrums of his day. But for all Babbitt's apparent self-regard, he is troubled by a perennial, niggling dissatisfaction, dimly sensing the spiritual sterility and hypocrisy in his world, without knowing how to identify or remedy it. His story is now routinely discussed as one of the pre-eminent novels critiquing the hollowness of 'the American dream'. But Lewis never mentions the American dream; such analyses begin with the assumption that the American dream means materialism, and thus will be found hollow.

Even as Lewis was writing there were other American dreams available, but now they have disappeared from view.

* * *

Not until 1922 have I found any record of the immigrant 'American dream' explicitly linked with the old idea of America as a land of opportunity, although in Lippmann's unpublished 1921 essay that meaning is certainly implicit. And once again, as in most of the earliest references to the American dream as personal aspiration, it is presented not as a hope, but as a failure. 'American Dream Blasted', shouted an Oregon report of a German immigrant family in 1922 who 'dreamed of America as a land of opportunity' only to encounter 'virtual bondage and near starvation' in a contract that amounted to indentured servitude.[12]

This also seems to be one of the first uses of 'American dream' in a headline, suggesting its growing intelligibility as a shorthand; from Walter Lippmann writing about Jewish nationalism on the East Coast, to an editor in the Pacific Northwest reporting on local German immigrants, the 'American dream' was becoming recognisable across the country.

As it became more familiar, it slowly became less specific. Not an American dream of this or that particular thing – just *the* American dream, a usage that assumes everyone shares the same dream, and knows what it is without being told.

But even as people gradually began to use the expression as if its meaning were fixed, they did so in contexts that make clear that its meanings in fact continued to shift. In the Progressive Era the American dream had been identified with corrective dreams of controlling inequality and protecting democracy. In the 1920s it began to appear far more often in tandem with glorifications of wealth – and also with anxious stories about the incursions of new wealth into old strongholds of power – while debates about immigration continued to rage across the country.

As a phrase the 'American dream' could bring all these conflicting ideas together in an uneasy mix. In 1923 the *Chicago Tribune* ran an editorial urging the United States to 'Keep the Gates Closed', arguing that lifting restrictions on immigration would be 'shortsighted self-interest disguised as humanitarianism'. Maintaining that the economic case was against increased immigration, it added: 'If we are to be a harmonious and homogeneous people we must be free to do this work of assimilation without a perpetual flux of new elements.' In other words, immigration could be reconciled with the idea of racial homogeneity through the work of assimilation – but only if the country squeezed heterogeneity out of the 'elements' that were already in the country. No new elements would fit in the melting pot.

The article concluded that even if the economic argument that immigration would provide cheap labour were correct, 'we should still be opposed to opening the gates. For the future of our American dream depends upon the character of American citizenship, not upon the cash in our pockets.'[13] Here is the Progressive Era 'American dream', recognisably persisting in the idea that America should be judged by its values, not by its wealth. But the progressive ideal was being used to justify a racialised xenophobia that assumed the country must be 'homogeneous', and that these 'new elements' entering the country could not, by definition, have good character. Even if they brought in money, these 'elements' would be degrading the ideal of the 'American dream'. Old immigrants were in; new immigrants were out.

'America first' xenophobia was creeping into ideas about the 'American dream' – exactly what the 1845 *Post* editorial had warned would constitute a degradation of the American creed, the self-serving nativism of someone with 'no American heart'.

* * *

The question of how to judge the 'worth' of immigrant communities and ethnic minorities continued to gain urgency, and for many in the early 1920s, scientific racism provided the obvious answer. One of the most effective, and tenacious, attempts to institutionalise eugenicist assumptions about biologically determined merit was the development of the Stanford-Binet intelligence tests, first published in 1916.

By the early 1920s IQ tests were being used to justify any number of group classifications, and thus stratifications. In 1922 Walter Lippmann sat down to write a groundbreaking series of essays for the *New Republic* attacking their use in the military. These in turn paved the way for his argument a year later that IQ tests would undermine the American dream, a usage sometimes (erroneously) identified as the first appearance in print of the phrase 'the American dream'.[14]

Lippmann began by sharply warning that intelligence tests were an 'instrument for classifying a group of people, rather than "a measure of intelligence." People are classified within a group according to their success in solving problems which may or may not be tests of intelligence.'[15] Lippmann was scathing about the faulty premises of such efforts: 'we cannot measure intelligence when we have never defined it'. Moreover he could see clearly the eugenicist underpinnings of the claims about 'inherent' intelligence, which, as he pointed out, 'had no scientific foundation': 'we cannot speak of its hereditary basis after it has been indistinguishably fused with a thousand educational and environmental influences from the time of conception'.[16]

By July 1923 Lippmann viewed the biological determinism of intelligence tests as a direct threat to the American dream of equality of opportunity for individual self-realisation. Considering that within half a century, and for decades to come, access to education would be widely held as a foundation to achieving the American dream of upward social mobility, Lippmann's position is all the more striking – for he argued precisely the opposite.

In 'Education and the White Collar Class', an essay syndicated around the country, Lippmann predicted that supply for professional-managerial jobs would outstrip demand within a generation, because of widening access to higher education. Lippmann had been asked to advise high-school students interested in pursuing journalism careers, as they selected among 'the various vocations that are open to them'. Just how many white-collar jobs awaited graduates?

Lippmann estimated that roughly 10 million professional-managerial positions existed, but the country was annually producing half a million graduates. The competition was already fierce for existing jobs; either experienced people had to be fired to make room for a younger generation with modern skills, or younger people would be excluded from the opportunities for which they'd been educated. What should a nation facing a surplus of graduates qualified for jobs that were not materialising, thanks to rapidly changing industrial conditions, do?

What America had begun surreptitiously doing, Lippmann argued, was to try to limit enrolment in competitive high schools and universities by using standardised tests, which were being employed in some quarters to justify denying 'inferior' groups, including Jews and African-Americans, access to elite educations. These tests were 'a heap of nonsense', Lippmann insisted, as they purported to show 'that only a percentage of the population is by *nature* fitted for secondary and higher education'. This would artificially limit the pool of graduates applying for a diminishing number of white-collar jobs.

The real problem, Lippmann maintained, was 'not the scarcity of intelligence, but the scarcity of jobs'. And this problem would only grow worse if America continued to insist that higher education had to result in office jobs, instead of believing that educated people could work in 'skilled manual trades'. 'The real remedy', Lippmann believed, would require erasing 'the snobbish association' between professional-managerial roles and social superiority.

Education needed to be regarded 'as the key to the treasure house of life', not as 'a step ladder to a few special vocations'.

The alternative, to keep 'higher education confined to a small and selected class', would 'mark the end in failure of the American dream'.

As in his 1921 essay about Jewish assimilation, Lippmann here seems to be invoking an American dream we would recognise, but he is explicitly arguing for personal development over upward social mobility: for Lippmann preserving the American dream meant *rejecting* upward social mobility. The American dream entailed helping all citizens realise their own intellectual and spiritual potential; focusing on mere financial advancement or status would mean the American dream had failed.

Without widespread access to higher education America would be left with 'a literate and uneducated democracy, which is what we now have', Lippmann added for good measure. The distinction between literacy and education was crucial: what would happen to a nation in which voters could read, but weren't well informed?

Lippmann predicted that such a democracy would 'be governed increasingly by Hylans and Thompsons and Mussolinis'.

John F. Hylan, mayor of New York City from 1918 to 1925, was widely mocked for his ignorance, and in particular for his inane, often garbled speeches. Four months into Hylan's term, the *New York World* wondered if the city could survive four years of him. 'Those four months have been enough to reveal his incapacity,' although Hylan's 'unfitness for the office was revealed during the campaign'. Hylan's campaign speeches 'were a complete revelation of his ignorance, his demagogy and his unfitness for an office that is second only to the presidency in administrative difficulties'. As a candidate, Hylan had exposed 'everything about himself that an intelligent voter needed to know, and what he told was a prophecy that has been fulfilled'. It was astonishing, but 'the voters saw him, heard him and chose him'.[17]

William Hale 'Big Bill' Thompson was the mayor of Chicago from 1915 to 1923, and is still ranked as one of the most corrupt mayors in American history, not least because of his open association with

Al Capone, although that would come later. (In 1927, he would successfully run for mayor again, this time on a platform of 'America first', as we shall see.) And in 1922 Benito Mussolini had just come to power in Italy.

An uneducated but literate democracy would, Lippmann warned, elect the incompetent, the corrupt and the fascistic.

Today the American dream is widely identified as dependent on education for access to upward social mobility. But for Lippmann it was the other way round: education was a public and personal good in and of itself, not an instrumental means to the creation of wealth or status. It's the earliest use I've found of the American dream associated with education – but only to distinguish education from social or material ambition, not to unite the two.

* * *

When 'Education and the White Collar Class' appeared in *Vanity Fair* in July 1923, it was almost certainly read by F. Scott Fitzgerald, who that month had begun drafting what he intended to be the 'great American novel', a story about the attenuation of the American dream of human fulfilment into mere desire for wealth and power.

A few months earlier, Fitzgerald had published his least known work, a play called *The Vegetable: Or, From President to Postman*, a satire of the Harding presidency. One review offered a pithy summary of *The Vegetable*'s message, namely 'that a man may be an egregious misfit as the president of the country and cause incalculable damage, but that he may have in him the makings of the best postman in the world'.[18]

The play begins on the night in 1920 when Warren G. Harding was selected by the Republican Party as its nominee for president. The play's brainless protagonist, Jerry, awaiting the results, gets drunk and in the second act dreams that he's been elected president. He installs his family in the cabinet, declares war on the world, presides over rampant corruption, and is impeached at the end of his delirium.

The Vegetable is an acidic satire of the American dream of success, lampooning the promise of American opportunity as symbolised by the idea that anybody *can* be president, in order to suggest that not everybody *should* be president. Although it never uses the phrase 'American dream', the play is founded on the metaphor that American promises of power and prosperity to all citizens are not merely a dream but a delirium.

Fitzgerald was far from the only one to have noticed that 'a serious alteration in what we may call the American spirit has been taking place in recent years', as a *Chicago Tribune* editorial put it that summer – but different people identified different causes for that alteration. Fitzgerald thought America's spiritual impoverishment was caused by its mercenary ambitions. The *Tribune*, by contrast, thought it was caused by too much regulation. With an increase of 'envy and suspicion' among American citizens, it protested, 'has come the disposition to regulate the individual ... to disrespect the private conscience and to enlarge the dominance of government over individuals or minorities'. Such domination 'is contrary to the American ideal, a defeat of the American dream. Americanism meant freedom from all tyrannies and unconquerable faith in the individual. But of late years we have developed more and more the ancient fallacy of the state and given up more and more the inspiring and vitalizing belief in the individual and his liberty.'[19]

Increasingly, the American dream of liberty, which by definition is unregulated, was coming into conflict with American dreams of equality and justice, which by definition (or at least by human nature) require regulation to be realised. Some were beginning to see in the American government an authoritarian engine suppressing liberty, rather than a regulatory system that secured it for all. In this version of the national imaginary, the 'real American' populating rural areas was also a revolutionary upholder of freedom. And the regulations that might infringe upon the prerogatives of that freedom – including those that were instituted to protect the freedoms of other American citizens – were figured as un-American, imperilling the stalwart, sovereign individual.

That intractable problem of how to balance the needs of the individual against the needs of all the other individuals – the problem faced by every society in human history – continued to arise in international questions as well, where it took the form of debates over nationalism and isolationism. And for Americans seeking to articulate the need for mutual, collaborative values – Americans who were by no means only political liberals – the American dream continued to be a way to suggest that pursuing selfishness as a means to collective success was a delusion, just as the Progressive Era had insisted. Three weeks after the *Chicago Tribune* argued that the American dream of liberty was opposed to regulation, a Pennsylvania paper mentioned the American dream as an illusion to denounce isolationism. 'Isolation is only an American dream. "We're part of the world we're in and we might as well play our part."'[20]

That was not the view of 'America first'.

6

AMERICA FIRST 1920—1923:
The Simplicity of Government

During his 1920 'America first' campaign, Harding notoriously announced that 'government is a very simple thing'. If elected, he would just get things done. It would be very easy to be presidential, he promised.

'Good government has almost been allowed to die on our hands, because it has not utilized the first sound principles of American business,' he stated.[1] Harding would put an end to that, promising to run the American government like a business, a promise that was welcome to many Americans, who thought becoming a business was just the remedy the country needed. He would put 'less government in business and more business in government', Harding pledged.[2]

'The reactionaries are always talking about a businessman for president,' wearily noted a Salt Lake paper; the *Washington Herald* observed that Democrats were also responding to the 'widespread demand for a "businessman president"'.[3]

Assuring America he would liberate the nation from 'war's involvements', Harding committed to sweeping reforms of the executive, to make it more efficient and effective. When he took office in March 1921, Harding had complete control not only of the White House but of both branches of government. The Republicans would remain in power, virtually unchecked by any real opposition, throughout the decade, as the Democrats became so unelectable that the two-party system all but broke down.

As he was preparing to enter office, Harding declared: 'I believe most cordially in prospering America first.'[4] While still enjoying the heady days of self-confidence, he published a collection of addresses soon after his inauguration called *Our Common Country: Mutual Good Will in America*. In it, he mentioned 'America first' thirteen times, associating the motto with the principles of good business. 'All true Americans will say, as I say, "America First"! Let us all pray that America shall never become divided into classes and shall never feel the menace of hyphenated citizenship!'[5] In a book that called for the 'utter abolition of class' division, Harding did so by conflating class with ethnic background; suddenly, the dream of democratic and economic equality looked a lot like one hundred per cent Americanism.[6]

In fact, under Harding's presidency inequality would steeply rise. His definition of America first prosperity decidedly did not include social safety nets, enjoining an economic policy that 'yields opportunity to every man not to have that which he has not earned, whether he be the capitalist or the humblest laborer, but to have a share in prosperity based upon his own merit, capacity and worth – under the eternal spirit of "America First"'.[7]

'American business,' he continued, 'has suffered from staggering blows because of too much ineffective meddling by government.'[8] Harding kept his promise to stop ineffective meddling by ceasing to do much of any meddling at all. Although his administration is often described as 'laissez-faire', theirs was less a policy of let go than one of anything goes.

Within his first year in office, Harding had discovered that governing was considerably harder than he thought. A blistering 1921 North Carolina editorial called 'The Simplicity of Government' heaped scorn upon his administration. 'Mr. Harding remarked during his campaign that "government is a very simple thing after all",' it began. So it had proved, thanks to 'the simple proposition of much promise and little performance'. Republicans were 'loud-mouthed in the campaign', when 'almost anything was promised that looked like it might be a bait for the votes, but after the votes were procured, the party memory has suffered a lapse'.[9]

One of Harding's promises was the reduction of taxes, a promise that was very appealing to 'the fellows who had been making their barrels of profits' and disliked paying taxes on them. They had voted trusting in 'the time-honored republican custom of especially protecting those who protect the party', knowing they would be able to 'keep all their resources for their own use'.[10]

By 1922, many were mocking the self-exploding downward spiral of the GOP since their great 1920 victory.

Although we tend to describe the 1920s as a decade of economic boom, during which time the United States did experience eight

consecutive years of growth, the bull market didn't really take off until
1924, and lasted only until 1929. Harding inherited an economy in
which war spending had far outstripped tax collection in an era before
universal income tax. In an effort to balance the budget, the government
slashed spending, resulting in a sharp recession for the first two years of
the decade. Business failures between 1919 and 1922 trebled. Farmers
were particularly affected by the recession, having taken out loans during
the war at the government's urging, and then been forced to default on
them. Many never recovered; the foreclosure of small farms began not
during the Depression of the 1930s, but during the recessions of the
1920s. And even in the midst of the boom, banks were failing: nearly six
thousand banks were suspended during the 1920s at a rate of over five
hundred a year, mostly in the Midwest and South.

Moreover, the bubble was short-lived. Not only was the stock market
based on bogus values and commodities, including a vast number of
Ponzi schemes, bucket shops and other shady or frankly crooked
operations, but the stock market also had little to no effect on the real
economy. Inequality only sharpened, as money was siphoned to the top.

Americans were tired of the years of chaos and uncertainty, the
labour strikes and race riots, the bomb threats and progressive
agitators, the muckrakers and constant wars, from the Mexican
War to the Spanish-American War and then the Great War, which
they had been assured would end all wars. They wanted stability and
security, and Harding promised to deliver a 'return to normalcy' by
putting America first, and particularly by restricting immigration,
which had continued to explode in the wake of the war.

Between 1920 and 1921, 800,000 immigrants passed through
Ellis Island, so that anxiety about America's ability to absorb so
many 'foreign elements' merely increased. Many argued that an
influx of immigrants would only lead to further unemployment,
while the Red Scare continued to fan racially inflected fears of
domestic terrorism at the hands of anarchists. In early January
1920, at least three thousand people were captured and arrested as
part of the Palmer Raids, during which five hundred people accused

of being radicals and anarchists were abruptly deported, raids widely justified in terms of 'one hundred per cent Americanism', and supported by the Espionage and Sedition Acts of 1917 and 1918, passed by the Wilson administration, which had largely left its earlier progressivism behind.[11]

Although much reactionary violence was directed against blacks, Catholics and Jews in particular, a great deal of vigilantism was also targeted at radicals and socialists. In 1919, three former soldiers were shot and killed in Centralia, Washington, by snipers who were assumed to be members of the International Workers of the World. Locals 'made a dash to raid the I.W.W. hall and round up all suspicious characters', who were peremptorily 'thrown in jail'. The man believed to be their leader was seized by a lynch mob; 'they placed a rope around his neck, threw it over the cross-arm of a telephone pole and started to haul him up'. He was saved only when the police chief talked the crowd out of it, and was returned to jail, 'almost dead'.[12]

In 1920 Upton Sinclair published a novel called *100%: The Story of a Patriot*, partly inspired by the case of a radical named Tom Mooney, who was arrested and sentenced to hang for a 1916 San Francisco bombing on charges that were widely viewed as trumped up, and had been amplified by Hearst's red-baiting local press. Sinclair's novel is told from the perspective of Peter Gudge, 'a patriot of patriots, a super-patriot; Peter was a red-blooded American and no mollycoddle; Peter was a "he-American," a 100% American ... Peter was so much of an American that the very sight of a foreigner filled him with a fighting impulse'.[13]

Peter fully believes that

100% Americanism would find a way to preserve itself from the sophistries of European Bolshevism; 100% Americanism had worked out its formula: 'If they don't like this country, let them go back where they come from.' But of course, knowing in their hearts that America was the best country in the world, they didn't want to go back, and it was necessary to make them go.[14]

For men like Peter 'these were busy times just now. In spite of the whippings and the lynchings and the jailings – or perhaps because of these very things – the radical movement was seething.'[15] All over the country, people asserting their rights were blamed for the violence their assertions called forth.

The idea that all radicals were foreign agitators – and that all foreigners were radicals – had become axiomatic to many Americans by the early 1920s, and more of the political climate than is often now recognised was driven by, or intrinsically related to, anti-immigrant sentiment. Even Prohibition, which came into law in January 1920, was in large part a way to criminalise the customs of immigrant groups. Old Puritan Yankee communities were mostly temperate, especially after the evangelical fervour of the Second Great Awakening in the first half of the nineteenth century had inspired an animus against the 'demon liquor'.

Although the nineteenth-century temperance movement began, at least in part, as a broadly proto-feminist campaign (in an era when they were still legally and politically subject to their husbands, women sought prevention for alcohol abuse and domestic violence where there was no cure), temperance rapidly became entangled with anti-immigrant sentiments, as the Irish were associated with whiskey, Italians with wine. Just as religion offered a pretext for targeting 'foreign elements', so did alcohol offer a way to reject immigrant customs as inimical to a supposedly indigenous Americanism. It was also another way to demonise the elite, decadent pleasures of the city, to insist on the hearty purity of 'real' sober rural values over the delusive fantasies of urban sophistication.

Drinking was the vice of immigrants and aristocrats, the lower and the higher orders; those who repudiated it felt they represented 'real' Americans. Opposing alcohol was, as Walter Lippmann put it, 'inspired by the feeling that the clamorous life of the city should not be acknowledged as the American ideal'.[16] Thus a 1921 letter writer to the *Tampa Bay Times* complained that Mayor Hylan was not 'one hundred per cent American': 'New York is not an American city by any means. It has a mayor who is far from being a one hundred per cent American ... The real American favors the law and does not get together several thousands of foreigners, drunkards, gamblers, anarchists, white slavers, and such like, to enter a protest against the constitution of the government which is protecting them. If that crowd of un-Americans do not like the laws of this country the quicker they leave these shores the better for us.'[17]

For this correspondent, there was nothing to choose between drunkards, foreigners, anarchists and white slavers. They were all lumped together ('and such like'), equally unreal, equally criminal and equally un-American. And anyone who supported them was less than 'one hundred per cent American', too.

That went for any foreigners. When the American Ambassador to Great Britain made a speech in which he dared to mention 'the common interests of the United States and Great Britain', he was excoriated by Democrat Senator Reed. The speech would be 'treasonable if it were not idiotic', Reed announced, demanding the ambassador's recall. 'We ought to put in his place a 100 per cent American who believes in America first and all the time.'[18]

* * *

Over the first months of his administration, Harding and his advisers cited 'America first' constantly as they urged renewed isolationism. Harding 'stresses the America-first doctrine', noted an Ohio paper, 'and the menace of entangling foreign alliances'.[19] As early as January 1921, papers were reporting that '"America First" will be policy', that American 'sovereignty will not be surrendered'.[20] It was clear that '"America first" is the keynote of the platform of the new administration'.[21] By the summer of 1921 there were 'America First Societies' across the nation, advocating, among other platforms, the boycotting of British and European goods.

By the end of 1921, a year after election, the Harding administration was trying to pass a permanent protectionist tariff in the name of 'America first'.[22]

But for all its triumphalism, it was an expression that clearly continued to instil unease in many listeners. A few months earlier, a Pennsylvania editorial had written approvingly that Charles Evans Hughes should represent the Harding administration abroad, because he was '100 per cent. American. He stands for America first, but not for isolation.'[23]

Not everyone was convinced that America first could be so easily distinguished from isolationism. 'We all are anxious to be known as 100 per cent American,' a minister observed a few months after Harding's inauguration. But 'Americanism is not to think of America only', he insisted. 'If America first means America selfish, or America unmindful of world wrongs, we can hardly call it Americanism.'[24] Others similarly noted a strong social pressure towards a patriotism expressed always in the same terms: 'we must be 100 per cent American, we must be patriotic, we must stand by America first'.[25]

Just as Harding was inaugurated, the progressive *Capital Times* of Wisconsin demanded: '"America First?" For Whom? Is it America First for the financial rulers, or America First to make the world better? ... Just what is this new concept of "America First" that has been set up by the Harding administration? Is it "America First" or is it "America Uber Alles?"'

'America first', the leader charged, was a pretext for tightening the grip of 'the industrial octopus that is slowly fastening its tentacles on American life'. The protective tariff would 'make it "America First"' for 'the imperialists and financial rulers of this country to *get* what they can get out of the world'. What the nation needed was 'an "America First" that will seek to *give* to the world'.

Frequently breaking into outraged capital letters, the editorial urged that America should be 'FIRST in the world movement against war, against armament, against imperialism, against national and racial hatreds, against tariffs that isolate us'. Most of all, America should stand first 'against those sacred creeds of the economic rulers of the world that PROPERTY rights are above HUMAN rights ... The American citizen will be first when he has the courage to say: "I love my fellow man wherever he may be found. I AM A CITIZEN OF THE WORLD."'[26]

THE SIMPLICITY OF GOVERNMENT

The Harding administration was less certain about that. In February 1921, Harding's vice president Calvin Coolidge wrote an essay for *Good Housekeeping* called 'Whose Country Is This?' in which he declared: 'Our country must cease to be regarded as a dumping ground' and should only accept 'the right kind of immigration'.

Clarifying what kind of immigration he had in mind, Coolidge endorsed eugenics and Nordicism to the American people. 'Biological laws tell us that certain divergent people will not mix or blend. The Nordics propagate themselves successfully. With other races, the outcome shows deterioration on both sides. Quality of mind and body suggests that observance of ethnic law is as great a necessity to a nation as immigration law.'[27]

Not everyone agreed that keeping America 'pure' was possible, or even desirable. By the beginning of 1922, the Democratic candidate who had lost in 1920, James M. Cox, offered a biting assessment. 'The echoing cry of "America First" is a mockery of human intelligence, as unhappy experience tells us that we are a part of the whole world.'[28]

* * *

As the American government's association with 'America first' deepened, so did the Klan's. By February 1921, newspapers all over the country, from Indiana and Oregon to Colorado and New York, from Baltimore and Montana to Texas, were reporting the adoption of 'America first' by the KKK. 'The motto of the 1921 Ku Klux Klan is in its substance "America First",' wrote an Indiana paper in a feature reprinted throughout the state, noting that the Second Klan was a 'revival of the famous organization of the reconstruction period in the south'.[29]

The Klan had made its association with 'America first' official by 1921, issuing a proclamation of its 'ABCs', in a circular picked up by papers around the country: 'The ABC of the Klan is America First, benevolence, clannishness.'[30]

Some of the charter members of the Second Klan included 'a few survivors of the old Klan', the *New York Tribune* explained; it was now sharing its 'creed'. The Klan's creed included the promise: 'We shall be ever devoted to the sublime principles of a pure Americanism and valiant in the defense of its ideals and institutions. We avow the distinction between the races of mankind as same has been decreed by the Creator, and shall ever be true in the maintenance of white supremacy.'

At the same time, the Klan held a public meeting in Birmingham, Alabama, at which the 'Imperial Wizard' W. J. Simmons declared that the organisation stood for:

1. One hundred per cent Americanism and reconsecration to bedrock principles.
2. White supremacy.
3. To protect woman's honor and the sanctity of the home.[31]

Klan leaders circulated pamphlets around the country, repeating their 'creed' of 'America first, benevolence, clannishness'. They protested that the Klan did not support 'any propaganda of religious intolerance or racial prejudice'; the group was simply 'an association of real men' who believed 'in doing things worth while and who are 100 per cent American in all things'.[32]

The *Evening World* ran a front-page exposé of the Klan in September 1921. 'Secrets of the Klan Exposed', read the first headline.

In five years, the *World* noted, the Klan had grown from thirty-four members to almost 500,000 nationwide, spreading through the north and west more than twice as rapidly as it spread in the south, thanks to a 'highly organized sales force'. Millions of dollars were going to salesmen in commissions; the Klan was, to paraphrase later historians, America's most successful racist pyramid scheme.

Schoolteachers and local politicians who happened to be Catholic were being forced out of their positions; ministers who were Klansmen 'preach hatred of the Jew even in church pulpits'. Mobs of Klansmen had stripped and 'maltreated' white women, whipped, tarred and feathered white men for 'private conduct' of which they disapproved, and had 'warned' newspapers to be careful how they reported on the Klan.[33]

Over the next three weeks, the *World* published daily front-page reports of the Klan's secretive activities, and introduced Americans to such arcane rituals and codes as 'kleagles', 'klaverns' and the *Kloran*. The last item is a particularly ironic appropriation in light of reactionary American politics in the early twenty-first century, but the silliness of the Klan's occult nationalism was not lost on contemporary observers, who noted its willingness to embrace anything that sounded vaguely mystical or esoteric.

As an American historian would observe in 1931, reflecting on the Klan of the 1920s:

> the preposterous vocabulary of its ritual could be made the vehicle for all that infantile love of hocus-pocus and mummery, that lust for secret adventure, which survives in the adult whose lot is cast in drab places. Here was a chance to dress up the village bigot and let him be a Knight of the Invisible Empire.[34]

The *World* concluded its 1921 reports by denouncing the Klan as supporters of 'terrorism', who 'kidnap, beat, tar and feather victims, then turn them loose on other communities'. It listed four recent murder victims, as well as over forty floggings and twenty-seven 'tar and feather parties'.[35]

The revelations were reprinted around the country, reaching more than two million Americans a day. The *World*'s expressed opinion was that the exposure would destroy the secret organisation, but their optimism was misplaced. In fact, some historians have argued that the effort backfired, bringing much needed publicity to the Second Klan; recruitment surged, and the Klan established over two hundred new chapters in the four months after the *World*'s disclosures.[36]

It was perfectly clear to all at the time that the Klan was a terrorist organisation, and intended as one. (Indeed its rituals referred to Klan officers as 'Terrors'.[37]) The governor of Kansas stated outright: 'I am opposed to the Klan because it suggests terrorism.'[38] A 1921 cartoon reprinted around the country shows a leg wearing Uncle Sam trousers and labelled 'True Americanism' giving the boot to a figure in the robes of the Klan, who holds a sign reading 'Terrorism'.[39]

The Answer.

Philadelphia Public Ledger

No one in the 1920s was in any doubt about whether white men could be terrorists.

On 1 January 1922, many readers across America greeted the new year with a front-page report from the Tuskegee Institute that sixty-four people had been lynched in America during 1921; fifty-nine were black, five were white, and two were women.[40] Four had been burned alive.

Those were just the lynchings that were reported. Seventy-two were stopped; it is impossible to know how many others might have taken place around the country that were never discovered. Mississippi had the most in the country that year, at fourteen; there were seven in Texas.

A few weeks later a Klan parade in Alexandria, Louisiana, bore two flaming red crosses and banners with slogans including 'America First', 'One Hundred Per Cent American' and 'White Supremacy'. They also carried signs reading 'Race Purity', 'Good Negroes Are Safe, Bad Ones Beware, Whites Ditto' and 'Abortionists, Beware!'[41]

That summer the Klan took out an ad in a Texas newspaper, equating 'America first' with 'one hundred per cent Americans'.[42]

> The Ku Klux Klan is the one and only organization composed absolutely and exclusively of ONE HUNDRED PER CENT AMERICANS who place AMERICA FIRST.

A report in November 1922 that the Klan was attempting to establish an outpost in the heart of Times Square, at the Hotel Hermitage on Seventh Ave and 42nd Street, led Mayor Hylan (who clearly had his virtues) to announce that there was a 'Klan drive' on in New York City, and instruct the police to 'rout them out'.[43] They responded that they 'refused to be intimidated'; intimidation was a right the Klan reserved for themselves. The Hotel Hermitage, meanwhile, said they would not 'harbor a man who endeavored to foment bigotry'[44] and kicked the Klansman out.

Three weeks earlier, a young black man seen kissing a white woman had barely been rescued from a lynch mob on West 45th Street, about six blocks away.[45]

By February 1923, the *New York Times* was reporting that three flaming crosses had appeared 'to frighten Negroes in Long Island towns', while that summer 25,000 new Klansmen were said to have joined the organisation in an initiation ceremony near East Islip.[46]

Groups with names like the 100% Americans began recording songs glorifying the Klan:

> Lived there in the mystic city of the empire that's unseen
> A grand and noble wizard who once had a wondrous dream.
> In this dream he saw Old Glory and the cause of liberty
> Being supplanted by a people who had come across the sea,
> Bringing with them flags and customs belonging to primeval lands
> To affix and plant them firmly in this, our native land.
>
> *Chorus*
> Klansmen, Klansmen, of the Ku Klux Klan,
> Protestant, gentile, native-born man,
> Hooded, knighted, robed and true,
> Royal sons of the Red, White, and Blue,
> Owing no allegiance we are born free,
> To God and Old Glory we bend our knee,
> Sublime lineage written in history sands,
> Weird, mysterious Ku Klux Klan.

The Klan established an 'official' women's branch in November 1922, which published a pamphlet, 'Women of America! The Past! The Present! The Future!', outlining their beliefs and formally adopting the Klan's ABCs of America first, benevolence and clannishness.

> The Paramount Principles of the Women
> of the Ku Klux Klan:
> AMERICA FIRST: First above all
> other Nations on earth, first in thought
> and first in our love and affection. The
> Flag of our Glorious Country, the Star
> Spangled Banner, first and foremost
> before all other Nations or Principali-
> ties.

* * *

The earliest mention of 'fascism' in the American press seems to have been in early 1921, when an Italian correspondent in Rome wired a special to the *Brooklyn Daily Eagle* and the Philadelphia *Public Ledger*, in which he explained that 'no doubt Fascism is a transitory phenomenon', a reassuring message that was picked up by papers around the country.[47] But throughout 1922, as Mussolini's corporate state consolidated power in Italy, many American observers concluded that fascism looked all too familiar.

The *New York World* offered a homespun analogy to explain the 'Fascisti' to its readers within weeks of Mussolini's seizure of government: 'in our own picturesque phrase they might be known as the Ku Klux Klan'.[48] The *Tampa Times* agreed: 'The klan, in fact, is the Fascisti of America and unless it is forced into the open it may very easily attain similar power.'[49]

It no more requires hindsight to view the Second Klan as a fascist organisation than it does to view it as a terrorist one: once again their contemporaries could instantly see the likeness – and the danger – all too clearly. In fact, the comparison was widespread. 'Encouraged by the signal success of the Fascisti or Italian Ku Klux Klan,' wrote the St Paul *Appeal*, the American Klan was similarly seeking 'political power in the United States'.[50]

The Minneapolis *Star Tribune* had reported in the summer of 1921 that 'The Fascisti is a secret order having some of the Ku-Klux Klan method'.[51] In Philadelphia a year later they were described as 'Those obstreperous reactionaries who under the name of the "Fascisti" are playing a part in the public affairs of Italy closely analogous to that which in some sections of the United States has been assumed by members of the Ku Klux Klan'.[52] 'The Fascisti assumed some of the characteristics of the Ku-Klux-Klan,' agreed the *New York Tribune*, 'and their methods could hardly be justified in anything like a law-abiding democracy.'[53]

By November 1922 a Montana paper had noted that in Italy, fascism meant 'Italy for the Italians. The fascisti in this country call it "America first." There are plenty of the fascisti in the United States, it seems, but they have always gone under the proud boast of "100 per cent Americans."' 'The democrats may say it was the American fascisti that won the election in 1920,' the article surprisingly concluded, a Montana newspaper explicitly calling Harding's Republicans fascists.[54]

Three weeks after papers around the country reported that Mussolini's Blackshirts had seized power in Rome, with 'Italy Firmly in Grip' of the Fascists, the first mention of a rising German fringe politician also appeared in the pages of the *New York Times*. His name was Adolf Hitler.

Hitler's anti-Semitism seemed disturbingly violent, the *Times* reported in its first account of him, before quoting a senior German statesman who advised everyone not to worry. 'Sophisticated politicians' in Germany believed Hitler's anti-Semitism was merely a campaign tactic, a ploy to manipulate the ignorant masses. Because the general population can never be expected to appreciate the 'finer real aims' of statesmen, the politician explained, 'you must feed the masses with cruder morsels and ideas like anti-Semitism' rather than the higher 'truth about where you are really leading them'.[55] After the campaign, they were all certain that Hitler would shift to the centre, and become perfectly reasonable.

The *Times* correspondent clearly disagreed, warning, 'There is nothing socialist about the National Socialism' being preached in Bavaria, while Hitler 'probably does not know himself just what he wants to accomplish'. However 'the keynote of his propaganda is violent anti-Semitism', the correspondent repeated, adding that some Jews were already leaving Germany.[56]

That year, a young American journalist named Dorothy Thompson was living in Vienna, where she had just been made a foreign correspondent for the *Philadelphia Public Ledger* and *Brooklyn Daily Eagle*. Within a few months, Thompson was reporting on the rise of anti-Semitism in Vienna, and on 'what Fascistic Italy really thinks' from Rome.[57] By November 1923, Thompson was in Munich trying to get an interview with Hitler following his abortive Beer Hall Putsch; having failed, she filed articles describing 'Hitler's little Boy Scout show', including the many other factions in Bavaria plotting to destroy the German republic, and the way Hitler had updated 'Bismarck's dream' thanks to 'suggestions from Mussolini'.[58]

'The "fatherlandish" organisations', wrote the *Des Moines Register* that summer, are 'Germany's Ku-Klux Klan'.[59] A few months later, American papers shared the first published photograph of Hitler, 'probably Europe's most famous camera dodger'. Whatever his aversions to publicity might once have been, Hitler would soon get over them.

Hitler

This is the first photograph of Adolphe Hitler, leader of the German national socialist party, to be published. He is probably Europe's most famous camera dodger.

Next to the photo of Hitler was a report complaining that, as foreign policy, 'America first' was meaningless. 'The cry "America

First" is used in Europe as in America more as a camouflage to disguise an utter lack of foreign policy,' an indecision that was 'very detrimental' to American prestige internationally.[60]

Just before Hitler had made his debut in the *New York Times* in 1922, a *Washington Times* columnist asked his readers: 'Has it occurred to you that our American Fascisti are the gentlemen of the Ku Klux Klan? This country has no conception of their power and growth.' The columnist had been told by a well-informed Washington insider that seventy-five members of the new Congress were also members of the 'Ku Klux'.[61]

A month later, the St Paul *Appeal* reported that a meeting of the majority of the governors of the United States had refused to denounce the KKK, leading to the conclusion that the 'silence of most of the governors on the Klan issue would appear to give weight to current rumors that most of them were elected by the Klan'.[62]

The governor of Oregon warned that the Klan could lead America to another civil war, as it was 'gaining an amazing grip' across the country. The problem was that 'the tolerance with which the Klan was at first regarded was due to the belief that it was merely anti-Negro and not anti-anybody else'.

It was one thing to be 'anti-Negro': evidently the white citizens of Oregon had no objection to that. But once they discovered the Klan was anti-others, including perhaps themselves, they began to protest. 'The same sort of outrages – committed by night riders, masked in white gowns and cowls – that have swept the Southland have repeatedly occurred in Oregon, so that law and order is as much usurped by the American fascisti as in Louisiana.'[63]

Across the country, from Philadelphia and Iowa to Montana and Oregon, American citizens were confronted with the Klan and the Italian Fascists marching across the front pages of the news, in seeming lockstep. No one missed the comparison.

At the end of 1922, the Klan decided to make it official, announcing its intention to create an 'alliance' with Mussolini's Fascists. The Imperial Giant of the Ku Klux Klan promised at the annual 'Klonvocation' in Atlanta that as part of the Klan's 'European expansion program', the 'Fascisti will join with us in establishing the klan in Italy'.

This 'expansion program' was usefully clarified by the Atlanta correspondent as 'the klan's plan to invade Europe and organize for the maintenance of white supremacy throughout the earth'.

Some prominent Klan members expressed shock that the Imperial Giant was prepared to allow Roman Catholics, their avowed enemy, to join the Klub. The Imperial Giant argued that all 'white Christian men' were welcome to become members. Jews and blacks, of course, were still right out.[64]

By the beginning of 1923, the links among 100 percenters, the Klan and fascism were so obvious that they began to parenthetically define each other. A reader wrote to the Des Moines Register objecting to the fact that the country was governed by an economic elite, the 'two per cent who rule this country'. These plutocrats had chosen to 'foster and encourage such organizations as the American fascisti (K.K.K.) and the so-called 100 percenters of capitalism's praetorian guard, the [American] legion. Both are "patriotic," "100 per cent Americans," ready to "Americanize" anything at the drop of a hat,' the writer noted, putting all of the phrases in sceptical scare quotes, while adding that 100 per cent Americanism kept allying itself to fascists and plutocrats.

'The purpose of these organizations was and is the suppression of free speech, free press, and free assemblage, unless such freedom is authorized by a "kunnel",' while their 'midnight parades in dunce caps and cotton nighties are preludes to arson, murder, and deportation'.[65] Two months later the St. Louis Post-Dispatch reported 'an open declaration of the American Fascisti, known as the Ku Klux Klan'.[66]

That summer reports began to circulate that the Klan was behind the bid for the presidency of Southern Democrat William G. McAdoo, the cabinet member (and son-in-law) who had urged Woodrow Wilson to institute federal segregation. The Texan farmers who joined the order of the KKK and supported McAdoo's candidacy were adamant in their claims that the Klan was not 'anti-Negro'. It was merely a wholesome 'American Fascism'.[67]

SEIBOLD ON TEXAS--SAYS K. K. K. BEHIND M'ADOO THERE FOR THE PRESIDENCY

Order Not Anti-Negro—Farmers Joined it in Belief it is American Fascism

To be sure, none of the Texan farmers insisting their group wasn't racist, just fascist, yet knew the horrors European fascism would perpetrate. What little they knew about fascism they would have gleaned mostly from celebratory editorials like the one offered by the *El Paso Herald* after Mussolini came to power, reporting that Il Duce had been greeted rapturously by 'Fascisti organizations' in London and Paris, and informing their readers that these groups were 'good organizations. Their existence is one of the most hope-inspiring things in the world today.'[68]

The editorial helpfully identified what was so inspiring about fascists: their public love of country, their opposition to radicalism, and their determination to uphold government authority. However, it went on to concede, fascists 'are not altogether good'. Sometimes 'they disregarded law and substituted force under the plea of necessity'.

The good news was that 'displays of violence by Fascisti have been rare, and sporadic'; it was mostly the discipline of 'a well-ordered military force'. In the end, 'Fascism is wholesome, good for those parts of the world that seem to need it, when it is an ordinary, law-abiding demonstration of patriotism. It is certainly an effective rebuke to radicalism.'[69] Nothing says 'rebuke' like the regrettable necessity of illegal violence.

Defences of Italian Fascism were not restricted to the south. The *Chicago Tribune* also cheered on Fascist 'rebukes' against radicals. 'We have no respect for the fuss made over Fascist violence directed against a body of revolutionists which had not hesitated to use violence in their own cause,' a 1922 editorial pronounced. 'It is easy for American ideologues and parlor pinks to condemn the Fascisti for the use of illegal force, but Fascism confronted conditions, not theories.'[70] Anyone objecting that the clue was in the word 'illegal' could look forward to being dismissed as just another parlor pink.

In fact, the American press offered plenty of examples of fascistic violence, evidence that many observers chose to ignore as they used it to justify their own ethno-nationalist positions. 'Everyone knows,' observed the *St. Louis Post-Dispatch*, that 'Italian workers under the Fascist Government do not dare to strike, having been completely cowed into temporary submission by Fascist violence.' 'Democracy,' it ended, at least for the time being, 'is dead in Italy.'[71]

'The Fascisti launched a campaign of destruction,' readers in Muncie, Indiana, were informed, and 'the program of violence continued until after the election in July, 1921', at which point the violence was 'somewhat diminished'.[72]

Somewhat.

* * *

As for home-grown American fascism, whatever the El Paso farmers supporting McAdoo wanted to tell themselves, any American alive in 1922 was well aware of the actual 'anti-Negro' activities taking place. Lynching was condemned in newspapers across the country, while throughout 1922, the Dyer Anti-Lynching Bill (first proposed in 1918) was debated in Congress.[73]

President Harding had spoken out against lynching in 1920. 'I believe the federal government should stamp out lynching and remove that stain from the fair name of America,' he announced, winning the approval of papers including the African-American *Buffalo American*, whose allegiances with the Republicans as the party of Lincoln were long-standing. 'I believe Negro citizens of America should be guaranteed the enjoyment of all their rights,' Harding stated, adding, 'they have earned the full measure of citizenship bestowed'.[74]

Harding spoke in favour of the Dyer Anti-Lynching Bill in 1921, which passed the House in 1922 before Southern Democrats in the Senate filibustered, killing it. Some threatened that they would not enact a single piece of legislation that year if the bill were to pass, effectively holding the Senate hostage to their extreme partisan position.

The *Buffalo American* ran an editorial on the Dyer bill, arguing that it should represent the principles of 'America first', and commending Representative Dyer for his battle on its behalf. 'Unless he had been a 100 per cent. American, who is interested in that doctrine, so familiar in campaign times but forgotten now, "America First," he would not have stood and fought, not for a race, but humanity and human rights.' It was vital that 'the Administration's slogan, "America first"',' not be forgotten along with 'the tenth part of the population'.[75]

The Dyer bill failed, as did the *Buffalo American*'s poignant effort to extend the principles of 'America first' to cover all Americans, including the 10 per cent who were black. In the first half of the twentieth century, nearly two hundred anti-lynching bills were introduced to Congress. None of them passed.

African-Americans staged a 'Silent March on Washington' in support of the Dyer bill on 14 June 1922, forty years before Martin Luther King Jr would make his voice – and his American dream – heard.

While the Senate was filibustering the Dyer bill, the *Boston Globe* wrote a scathing editorial called 'The Right to Lynch', which was reprinted in the African-American *Dallas Express*, along with several other national condemnations. 'The Democrats do not like the Anti-Lynching bill,' the *Globe* noted, 'and are willing to talk themselves hoarse in order to prevent a vote upon it.'

This was a surprising position for them to take, the *Globe*'s editors observed, 'for the Democrats have given up their traditional position in favor of States' rights on all issues save one. Time and again they have favored a strong central Government, but make an exception in reserving the right to burn Colored people at the stake.'[76]

Alongside a cartoon depicting 'Our Own Hooded Kobra', lurking outside the Government of Laws, the *Brooklyn Daily Eagle* ran an item entitled 'American Fascism', connecting the Klan to fascism and 100 percenters. 'One factor common in all countries is the appeal to a pseudo-patriotism. The Italian Fascista is extremely patriotic, after the manner of "100 percent" patriots everywhere.'[77]

OUR OWN HOODED KOBRA

Saying that the proto-Fascist dictatorship of Primo de Rivera in Spain (whose son would establish a Fascist Falange party ten years later that soon merged with Franco's), and Mussolini in Italy, were forms of the same '100 percent patriotism in Europe', it argued that America was also rapidly heading in the direction of ultra-nationalist violence, thanks to the KKK. 'There should be no misunderstanding about the Klan. It represents in this country the same ideas that Mussolini represents in Italy; that Primo Rivera represents in Spain. The Klan is the American Fascista, determined to rule in its own way, in utter disregard of the fundamental laws and principles of democratic government.'

If such people were allowed to take over the country, it cautioned, 'we shall have a dictatorship.'[78]

* * *

Meanwhile Italians in America, and Italian-Americans, were also joining Mussolini's Fascists. The 'New York Fascia' had been established as the 'parent body' for local groups of Mussolini supporters around the United States, including the 'Baltimore Fascia'; all were taking 'instructions from Premier Mussolini'.[79]

Ironically enough, one of the concerns created by American fascists who followed Mussolini was that they were, by definition, 'hyphenates', with allegiances beyond the United States. Newspapers around the country debated in 1923 whether American fascist movements posed a danger to the US. The name was against it, said the *Springfield Republican*, for its 'emphasis on racial solidarity – a pan-Italianism as it were', could only perpetuate 'hyphenism'. The *Tacoma Ledger* agreed, calling American fascism an 'affirmation by the Italian government' that an American citizen still retained allegiance to 'the mother country'. This would make fascism 'as great a menace to Americanism' as had been German support a decade earlier.[80]

Although both the Klan and the fascists liked to claim that their positions were purely ideological – and certainly they were willing to inflict violence on ideological grounds – they also had a tendency to conflate capitalism with white supremacy. In the spring of 1923, a Republican politician was urging the South to 'lead [the] fight on radicals', telling Arkansas farmers that 'Reds Are Inciting Negroes', and urging retaliatory 'action by pure American stock'. Warning of 'Communist efforts to incite the negroes to commit acts of violence', he argued that the South was 'the most natural and appropriate' place 'to start a counter-movement against radicalism in America', because of 'the racial purity and political traditions of the Southern people'.[81]

By a strange coincidence, people of 'racial purity' were the natural enemies of 'radicals', returning to the nativist associative chain that declared war on everyone who was not 'pure American', whether ethnically, racially or ideologically.

But not all Americans who called themselves fascists were supporting Mussolini. That spring papers around the country reported that 'what is believed to be the first American Fascisti organization' was being formed in Nebraska by a 'deposed Kleagle'. The 'American Fascisti', explained a spokesman, was 'a law-and-order society'. They would follow their Italian counterparts in opposing 'the Socialists, Communists and strong revolutionary labor groups' but 'it would be in no way an enemy or an imitator of the Ku Klux Klan'.[82]

Like the Italian Fascists, they would wear black shirts, but no masks; 15,000 shirts had been manufactured and 'a monster meeting' was planned. 'It would not mix in political or religious disputes,' the spokesman said — except against socialists, communists and labour organisers, which evidently didn't count as 'political disputes'.[83] This 'non-political' organisation would 'oppose the "Reds" and the Klan', according to the former Kleagle who established it, but would 'embody all the good features of the latter organization'.[84]

The ex-Kleagle neglected to specify those good features, but many Americans picked up on the idea that American fascists would be less dangerous than the KKK if they were less secretive. It would not be surprising if 'the fascisti movement' spread rapidly throughout the United States, predicted one Nebraska paper; there were said to be some 20,000 American fascists already. 'In some respects the American fascisti resemble the ku klux, but are apparently not cursed with the degree of secrecy that makes the hooded riders a menace to public safety.'[85]

It seems unlikely that the thousands of Americans being intimidated, press-ganged, branded, tarred and feathered, assaulted, terrorised, tortured, hanged and even publicly burned at the stake in broad daylight would have agreed that secrecy was what made the Klan a menace.

7

THE AMERICAN DREAM 1924–1929:
A Willingness of the Heart

The American dream appears to have vanished into thin air in 1924; no one seems to have mentioned it at all that year. Perhaps it is no coincidence that the American dream went quiet just then, as if silenced by the noise of the boom as it took off: between 1924 and 1929 the Dow Jones industrial average increased by 216 per cent. Perhaps Americans were too busy dreaming of easy riches to have time for dreaming of anything else; a euphoric faith that endless prosperity was at hand took hold of much of the United States during those years. In so far as the American dream had been conjured in the first place to express progressivist ideals, it seems to have been partly eclipsed along with the progressivism it had championed.

But there is also a sense in which the expression was gathering its forces. There remained writers thinking about the ideas already associated with the American dream that year, including one who would finish a novel at the end of 1924 that is now widely hailed as one of the greatest articulations of the American dream ever written.

In *The Great Gatsby*, F. Scott Fitzgerald never uses the phrase 'American dream', but his novel is full of dreams of America. The story takes place on Long Island, between Manhattan and the village of Great Neck (which Fitzgerald calls 'West Egg'), where Fitzgerald had lived for eighteen months, from the autumn of 1922 to the spring of 1924. Much of the action occurs in the area between those two locations, in Queens, where the novel's plutocratic villain, Tom Buchanan, has a mistress named Myrtle Wilson. The Buchanans live on Long Island – where, as Fitzgerald was well aware, the Klan was busily burning crosses to terrorise African-Americans when the action of the story takes place.

Tom Buchanan is a white supremacist, spouting eugenicist nonsense he's learned from books about Nordicism. 'The idea is if we don't look out the white race will be – will be utterly submerged. It's all scientific stuff; it's been proved … It's up to us who are the dominant race to watch out or these other races will have control of things.' Mocked by his dinner companions, Tom tries to defend his 'scientific' theories. 'We're Nordics. I am, and you are and you are … and we've produced all the things that go to make civilization – oh, science and art and all that.'[1] He trails off in confusion, unable to defend the inanity of scientific racism. By the end of the novel, Fitzgerald has underscored Buchanan's stupidity: 'There is no confusion like the confusion of a simple mind.'[2]

Fitzgerald's allusion to an 'American dream' arrives primarily in the novel's famous concluding passage, as Nick Carraway looks out over the Atlantic and becomes

> aware of the old island here that flowered once for Dutch sailors' eyes – a fresh, green breast of the new world. Its vanished trees, the trees that had made way for Gatsby's house, had once pandered in whispers to the last and greatest of all human dreams; for a transitory enchanted moment man must have held his breath in the presence of this continent, compelled into an aesthetic contemplation he neither understood nor desired, face to face for the last time in history with something commensurate to his capacity for wonder.[3]

Gatsby had 'come a long way' to get there, the passage goes on, 'and his dream must have seemed so close that he could hardly fail to grasp it. He did not know that it was already behind him, somewhere back in that vast obscurity beyond the city, where the dark fields of the republic rolled on under the night.'[4]

The concept of the American dream of individual aspiration and its diminution into materialism could be said to emerge at last here, in Fitzgerald's novel – many have argued that it does. If so, then at the moment the American dream we know is intimated, it has already vanished back into the past, into the rolling fields of a dark republic.

Fitzgerald was responding to a culture that had, for twenty years at least, been arguing for a larger American dream, one that protected the American creed against the encroachments of the mechanistic spirit that was overtaking the country. Fitzgerald captures a moment when materialism was taking hold of the dream – he registered it, and saw what its costs would be: the death of hope, and endless disappointment; the loss of wonder, not the realisation of it.

Gatsby's famous ending, in other words, describes the narrowing of the American dream, from a vision of infinite human potential to an avaricious desire for the kind of power wielded by stupid white supremacist plutocrats who inherited their wealth and can't imagine what to do with it beyond using it to display their dominance.

Without quite using the phrase 'American dream', Fitzgerald evoked the trajectory it had begun to follow nationally: from a dream of justice, liberty and equality, to a justification for selfishness and greed. The American dream was emerging as a way to describe what the country was betraying: namely, its ideals.

This is why it is a dream Fitzgerald carefully connects not to the religious beliefs of the Puritans but to the commercial ambitions of Dutch merchants – because the novel is suggesting that economic opportunism is what will destroy the 'capacious' American dream, not what will realise it. Idealism is killed by unrestrained capitalism: Jay Gatsby's potential for greatness is corrupted by a nation that teaches him only to desire the trappings of wealth and luxury, while Tom Buchanan's inherited capital grants him virtually unlimited domination, which is indistinguishable from white supremacy.

In other words, Buchanan's white supremacy is no passing detail: it is central to Fitzgerald's conception of how power in America works, his clear recognition that American industrial capitalism was built on the immoral inheritance of slave labour (a point he had already made explicit in his 1922 story 'The Diamond as Big as the Ritz').

Jay Gatsby swallows wholesale the religion of pure capitalism, as Fitzgerald suggests in another famous passage, calling his protagonist 'a son of God, [who] must be about His Father's Business, the service of a vast, vulgar and meretricious beauty'.[5] Gatsby is the quintessential, symbolic American, absorbing all of its doctrines, including self-invention, the ability to become whoever you will yourself into being. But the son of a 1920s American God would necessarily interpret his father's business literally, crassly, as commercial business, one in the service of the 'meretricious' – superficial beauty that is worthless and lacking integrity, glitzy but trashy. That is the gospel of wealth.

When *The Great Gatsby* appeared in the spring of 1925, it sold only modestly, its ambivalent anti-capitalist message unsurprisingly rejected or overlooked by Americans in the midst of the boom. By contrast, one of the most successful books of the same moment was Bruce Barton's *The Man Nobody Knows*, which was published exactly a month after *Gatsby*.

The Man Nobody Knows celebrates Jesus Christ as the model of the perfect businessman, and it was one of the bestselling (supposedly) non-fiction books in America between 1925 and 1926. Jesus, Barton explains, was not only 'the most popular dinner guest in Jerusalem', and 'an outdoor man', but a 'startling example of executive success'.[6] The apostles were his employees: Jesus 'picked up twelve men from the bottom ranks of business and forged them into an organization that conquered the world'.[7] His parables were 'the most powerful advertisements of all time'.[8] If Jesus were alive in the 1920s, he 'would be a national advertiser ... as he was the greatest advertiser of his own day'.[9] The insights just keep coming.

Making Jesus sound indistinguishable from George Babbitt, Barton informs his reader that the son of God was 'the founder of modern business', glossing the story of the Feast at Jerusalem as 'the big national vacation', at which the young Jesus went missing. When his parents find him, Jesus gets snippy.

> 'How is it that ye sought me?' [Jesus] asked. 'Wist ye not that I must be about my father's *business*?' ...
>
> He thought of his life as *business*. What did he mean by business? To what extent are the principles by which he conducted his business applicable to ours? And if he were among us again, in our highly competitive world, would his business philosophy work?
>
> On one occasion, you recall, he stated his recipe for success ...[10]

And so it goes, as Barton turns the New Testament into a business self-help manual, complete with italicising 'business' when Jesus happens to say it in translation. It is no coincidence that both Fitzgerald and Barton lit on the same biblical phrase, 'His Father's Business' – albeit from opposite perspectives – to discuss the worship of business in modern America.

A bestseller that calls Jesus the first great businessman is the *reductio ad absurdum* of America's long conflation of business with religion, its veneration of success, and its degraded Calvinist idea that personal wealth must mean God loves you more.

* * *

In January 1925, President Calvin Coolidge declared in a famous speech: 'The chief business of the American people is business. They are profoundly concerned with producing, buying, selling, investing and prospering in the world.'[11] Commerce was always an

American value, but during the brief years of the so-called Coolidge prosperity, the nation accepted almost without question that the days of boom and bust were over, that everyone could get rich on the stock market.

In truth, between 1923 and 1929, 93 per cent of the country experienced a drop in per capita income, while throughout the 1920s, monopolies and corporate mergers were once again in the ascendant, as six thousand independent companies merged, leaving only two hundred large corporations in control of over half of American industry. By the end of the decade, 1 per cent of the American population owned 40 per cent of the nation's wealth.

Calvin Coolidge was well named, for Calvinism, in a mass-market sense, was his basic creed. Coolidge was widely quoted for declaring that 'the man who builds a factory builds a temple; the man who works there worships there, and to each is due, not scorn and blame, but reverence and praise'.[12] His faith in the market was literal, and the stock market began to surge, while experts promised that stocks would continue to rise. 'Coolidge prosperity' was deeply unequal, however: wealth was largely concentrated at the top, while the poor continued to be left behind. But that faith in prosperity soon started to feel like a promise, even a guarantee.

It is also in 1925 that descriptions of the American dream start to sound increasingly familiar, as when one widely reprinted article hailed the city of Miami as 'the minting in America, in one fine, shining piece, of the substantial compound of that very American dream of freedom – opportunity and achievement'.[13] In the mid-1920s, Florida was enjoying a real estate boom that was, in fact, a bubble; the idea of a get-rich-quick scheme was starting to turn up alongside the 'American dream' more frequently. As American dreams of individual wealth grew, so did the American dream increasingly converge with ideals of 'freedom – opportunity and achievement' over ideals of equality.

We have seen the American dream of freedom before, when it was marshalled during the First World War against the forces of imperialism. It would be mobilised again to fight totalitarianism, but that was yet to come. Different contexts could still shift the implications of the phrase, reframing it in terms of one value in the American creed or another.

It could still be associated with internationalism, as when the League of Nations' agreement to establish a World Court was called the realisation of 'an American dream' by different journalists from Los Angeles to Iowa,[14] while readers were assured that 'the World Conference on Faith and Order, the fulfillment of an American dream of 17 years, will be an unparalleled council of churches'.[15]

The attachment of the American dream to pioneers and immigration was also strengthening. A 1925 book was described as 'evoking American dream towns of the early days', when the goals of pioneers still shaped the land.[16] The *Milwaukee Journal* shared a reprinted portrait of a group of Jewish junk peddlers living on the south side of Chicago, who prospered. 'That American dream seemed to be coming true.'[17] But it is still only 'that American dream', suggesting the availability of others.

Such passing references as 'the American dream of beautiful womanhood' at a beauty pageant or 'the American dream of "impregnable defense"' show that although upward social mobility was converging with it, 'the American dream' had some way to go before it would narrow down to our very specific, limited meaning.[18] In 1925 a minister assured his congregation that 'our American dream of a Christianized individualism, our principles of a Constitutional republic and the Christ-like spirit of brotherliness' would triumph over 'Russian Bolshevism and the futility of European Socialism'.[19]

Individualism was starting to push ahead of other values symbolised by the American dream, but it had not yet left behind the principles of constitutional democracy and equality.

A question over the right of a House representative to take his seat prompted a congressional minority to issue a report arguing against setting a precedent in which corrupt politics could 'select anyone they need for any special purpose, and the House would be powerless to resist it'. This would effect no mere erosion of the Constitution, they warned, but 'a frontal attack on it, a blasting process which is to weaken the foundation of the great American dream of "representative government"'.[20]

Meanwhile, even when individual dreams were affiliated with the national dream, they continued to be modest, and secured to the myth of the country's founding as a golden moral age. 'The "little farm well tilled" was the average American dream,' said the *Miami News* in 1927, its use of the past tense suggesting that the days of this Jeffersonian yeoman dream were seen as numbered.[21]

The bull market, having lasted a mere four years, was galloping to breaking point. Coolidge decided not to run again in 1928; supposedly he said in private that he thought a correction was coming. His vice president, Herbert Hoover, however, promised America that prosperity was never-ending. He would put a chicken in every pot, two cars in every garage, and on the campaign trail he promised that America was closer to the 'final triumph over poverty than ever before in the history of any land'.[22]

* * *

On 19 October 1929, Fitzgerald published a story called 'The Swimmers', about an American named Marston working for the ironically named 'Promissory Trust' Bank, and his realisation that his nation's ideals have been corrupted by money.

Early in the story Marston's unfaithful wife, who is French, complains about the American women she sees on the Riviera:

'How would you place them?' she exclaimed. 'Great ladies, bourgeoises, adventuresses – they are all the same. Look! ...'

Suddenly she pointed to an American girl going into the water:

'That young lady may be a stenographer and yet be compelled to warp herself, dressing and acting as if she had all the money in the world.'

'Perhaps she will have, some day.'

'That's the story they are told; it happens to one, not to the ninety-nine. That's why all their faces over thirty are discontented and unhappy.'[23]

The American dream comes true for just 1 per cent: for the other 99 per cent, only discontent and bitterness await. The idea that the richest 1 or 2 per cent of the population was controlling the nation had become axiomatic. The 'American dream' as a dangerous delusion of wealth that writers like Dreiser and Anderson had warned against is here recognisably shifting to the 'promise' implicit in twenty-first-century meanings of the American dream, and the bitterness that ensues when that promise is – all but inevitably – broken.

The villain of 'The Swimmers' is a rich, vulgar banker who preaches an updated version of the Gilded Age's gospel of wealth. 'Money is power ... Money made this country, built its great and glorious cities, created its industries, covered it with an iron network of railroads.'[24] The banker is wrong, the story makes clear, but his vision of America is winning out.

Feeling increasingly alienated, Marston finds himself musing on the meanings of America, and especially its eagerness to forget history. 'Americans, he liked to say, should be born with fins, and perhaps they were – perhaps money was a form of fin. In England property begot a strong place sense, but Americans, restless and with shallow roots, needed fins and wings. There was even a recurrent idea in America about an education that would leave out history and the past, that should be a sort of equipment for aerial adventure, weighed down by none of the stowaways of inheritance or tradition.'[25] The buoyancy of modern America depended on its being unanchored by history or tradition.

Marston eventually decides that there is no place for him in the profiteering society symbolised by his rival, but he will not relinquish his faith in the ideals that America can represent. As Marston sails for Europe, watching America recede into his past, Fitzgerald offers a closing meditation nearly as incantatory as the famous conclusion of *Gatsby*.

> Watching the fading city, the fading shore, from the deck of the Majestic, he had a sense of overwhelming gratitude and of gladness that America was there, that under the ugly débris of industry the rich land still pushed up, incorrigibly lavish and fertile, and that in the heart of the leaderless people the old generosities and devotions fought on, breaking out sometimes in fanaticism and excess, but indomitable and undefeated. There was a lost generation in the saddle at the moment, but it seemed to him that the men coming on, the men of the war, were better; and all his old feeling that America was a bizarre accident, a sort of historical sport, had gone forever. The best of America was the best of the world … France was a land, England was a people, but America, having about it still that quality of the idea, was harder to utter – it was the graves at Shiloh and the tired, drawn, nervous faces of its great men, and the country boys dying in the Argonne for a phrase that was empty before their bodies withered. It was a willingness of the heart.[26]

Wall Street crashed ten days later.

8

AMERICA FIRST 1923–1929:
A Super Patriot, Patriot

'"America First!" How many times have we heard it in the years since the war,' sighed a syndicated columnist named Prudence Bradish on 2 July 1923. It reminded her of what 'we used to hear the Germans say – what no doubt they are still saying: "Deutschland über Alles!" That old "my country, right or wrong" tone, which is just the tone we want to get out of the whole world, as we get, or try to get, weeds out of a garden. It's a bad tone, and a bad thought.'

On the other hand, the whole point of the Fourth of July was to celebrate patriotic loyalty, which created a conundrum. Perhaps the solution, Bradish mused, was for everyone to say 'America first! … First before myself.'

Later that year a letter signed 'America First' was sent to the *Chicago Tribune* by a citizen demanding that all Americans with 'foreign names' Americanise them. Even second-generation immigrants, the writer alleged, 'cannot free themselves from the badge of foreign allegiance as long as they retain their old names. They herd as foreigners, vote as foreigners, and talk as foreigners. In my opinion they never become 100 per cent Americans and never can until they drop their foreign names for American names that harmonize with our language.'

The letter prompted a blistering response from another reader, accusing 'America First' of a 'pitiful exhibition of ignorant bigotry'. The writer began by pointing out that 'unless "America First" is a native Indian, he is not such an "American" as he believes'. Wondering 'what "America First" considers a strictly "American" name', he remarked that even the name of America itself is not American, but Italian, courtesy of Amerigo Vespucci.[3]

An irate reader in Baltimore similarly objected to a recent correspondent who 'speaks of the patriotic zeal of the Ku Klux Klan and makes the assertion that "They put America first and all other nations second"'. How could anyone urging the 'persecution of Jews, negroes and Catholics truthfully say that he is 100 per cent American?'[4] 'America first' was never far from the idea of 'one hundred per cent Americanism', and wherever those two mottos were to be found, the Klan had a nasty habit of popping up as well.

In October 1923, Hiram W. Evans, the Klan's 'Imperial Wizard' from 1922 to 1939, gave a speech in Texas called 'The Menace of Modern Immigration', in which he adduced the Klan's ideas about the 'polluting streams of population from abroad', immigrants threatening the 'native Anglo-Saxon stock' ('no mercenary motives brought *them* to our shores', he added, with awe-inspiring inaccuracy). 'Eugenics entered into it, not here and there, but everywhere,' Evans made clear, because intermarriage with 'bad results' was imperilling 'real Americanism'.[5]

By 1923, the KKK had achieved a frightening degree of political influence. That November, the *New York Times* ran a big article with a striking graphic, showing the states whose elections were being determined by the Klan, with headlines reprinted from Klan papers around the country.[6]

The journalist had travelled throughout the Klan-dominated states, investigating the rise of 'the forces of so-called "pure Americanism"'. The Klan was in control of local governments in Texas, Arkansas, Oklahoma, Indiana and Oregon, with even non-Klansmen in Indiana conceding a state membership of around 500,000, and the Klan claiming 700,000. No candidate in Indiana was likely to win local elections without Klan support that year, while Oregon, 'the first state to bend to the Klan yoke', had been in its control since 1922.

Meanwhile Ohio appeared 'ready to join the masked parade, and California is said to be coming fast'. After that, the Klan – which campaigned for state control in stages – was targeting Michigan, Kansas and West Virginia, followed by Kentucky, Illinois and Missouri. Their goal was to make each state 'safe for the hooded and pure Americans' who live there, the journalist added acidly; they sought political control by dictating nominations, and otherwise made their influence felt, so that 'the Klan is no longer a thing to joke about.'[7] It may once have struck some Americans as absurd, but fears that the Klan might gain control of government, even of the White House, were growing.

'Senators, Representatives, Governors, legislators, State officials, county and local officers in these States are silent' in the face of the

Klan's onslaught, the reporter added. In the upcoming Democratic National Convention, eyes were on William G. McAdoo, whom the Klan was said to support. McAdoo was resisting pressure to repudiate the endorsement, trying to remain 'a noncommittal recipient of the Klan's good-will'.[8]

Such silence, whether craven or complicit, would prove endemic, the *Times* reporter predicted. Anyone who doubted the Klan's power in the upcoming elections 'should try to get an old-line politician to denounce the Klan in any of these States. To denounce it, that is to say, for publication.'[9]

Part of the reason that attentions were fixed unusually on elections a whole year away, was that the summer of 1923 had brought an abrupt end to the easy promises of President Warren G. Harding, who died suddenly that August under the pressure of a mounting bribery scandal known as the Teapot Dome Affair, in which it was revealed that Harding and his cabinet had most certainly not been putting America first before themselves. In fact, Harding's cabinet was about to prove the most crassly corrupt in American history (although it may be worth noting that American history isn't over yet).

The Teapot Dome scandal erupted when Harding's Secretary of the Interior, Albert Fall, was revealed by the *Wall Street Journal* to have leased federal oil reserves (including Teapot Dome, Wyoming) to private oil companies without competitive bidding. It was done with the assistance of the Secretary of the Navy, Edwin Denby. In return Fall received over $400,000 – well over $4 million today – in 'personal loans'. Fall was the first US cabinet member in history to go to jail, but he wasn't the last. Harding's Attorney General, Harry Daugherty, was later forced to resign for receiving bribes, but managed to escape a jail sentence. A year after Harding's death, the government was suing to retrieve over a million dollars that had been appropriated, demanding back the 'stolen property, and its emoluments'.[10]

The Harding administration was defined by crony capitalism and corruption on an epic scale: it wasn't merely the Ohio Gang, old pals of Harding's, who were involved in myriad kinds of graft (and flagrant flouting of the Volstead Act, the law that enacted Prohibition). As a senator, Harding had met a man named Colonel Charles Forbes on vacation in Hawaii, and in 1921 decided to hand the newly created Veterans Administration Bureau over to him. Forbes engaged in mass fraud at the Bureau, taking bribes from contractors and selling off medical supplies for personal profit while leaving soldiers without proper medical care. Senate testimony subsequently revealed that he had left 200,000 unopened pieces of mail from veterans at the Bureau. Forbes went to jail, too.

'America first', however, emerged from Teapot Dome relatively unscathed, as did the Republicans in general, in part because of the famous probity of Calvin Coolidge, who pursued the corrupt members of Harding's administration when he became president, instead of pardoning them. Coolidge was widely admired as a frugal, modest, unpretentious businessman who espoused old-fashioned Puritan values. But it is also true that no one seemed concerned enough by the corruption that had been disclosed to blame the Republicans for it: they would return to the White House with formidable majorities in the next two elections.

When Coolidge ran for re-election in 1924, one of his slogans was 'America First'; thousands of 'placards' were printed with his name and that of his running mate, Charles G. Dawes, and both of their biographies, along with 'America First'. The placards were 'designed for framing'.[11] (Coolidge had another, more surprising, slogan: 'Keep Cool with Coolidge'.)

The keynote at the 1924 Republican National Convention continued to emphasise 'America first', proclaiming the Republicans as the party that 'are yet frank and unashamed, yes, proudly insistent, to put America first, and who decline to merge into a weak and precarious internationalism the loyalty and enthusiasm which they cherish for America alone'.[12]

That year the industrialist Henry Ford was also urged to run for president. A survey in the mid-1920s asked Americans to rank the greatest people in history; Ford came in third, after Jesus and Napoleon. He was the epitome of the self-made man, the quintessential American success story, and by the early 1920s he was immensely popular; he was also intensely anti-Semitic. In the end, he didn't run.

Seeking his party's nomination at the 1924 Democratic National Convention, McAdoo suggested that 'America first' was beginning to be tainted by its association with the corruptions of the Republican Party. When a supporter shouted, 'Don't forget Teapot Dome,' McAdoo promised, 'we won't let the Republicans forget that dirty scandal from now until election day ... We all hope that the deliberations of this convention will result for the benefit of the American Republic, for there can be no success unless democracy survives America first.'[13]

But McAdoo's candidacy had created a bitter struggle within the Democratic Party, after he was accused by a Chicago politician of depending on the support of the Klan. The story rapidly spread around the country, prompting a proposal for an 'anti-Klan' plank in the Democrats' national platform, seeking to force the entire party of the Southern Democrats to officially repudiate the KKK.

That year, the Klan succeeded in engineering the elections of officials from coast to coast, from Portland, Maine, to Portland, Oregon. In some states, such as Colorado and Indiana, they placed enough Klansmen in positions of power to effectively control the state government. Some 25 per cent of the Klan's national membership in 1924 was located in Indiana and Ohio.[14] The Klan's version of 'one hundred per cent Americanism' was clearly defined by an interest in wealth as well as power – an interest not lost on contemporary observers.

Colonel Simmons, whose lighting of a bonfire in 1915 on Stone Mountain had launched the Second Klan, resigned that year as 'Emperor' 'in consideration of receiving $20,000 in cash'. Then he launched a new organisation, called 'Knights of the Flaming Sword'. A reporter predicted 'that the Knights and the Ku Klux Klan may later dispute supremacy for the leadership of the American Fascisti'.[15]

A Colorado judge fought a bitter campaign against a Klan-supported opponent in the 1924 election, and wrote a letter shared in the press about his experience, which included a woman who

> screamed in my face, 'You are not one hundred per cent American, you are against the Klan.' It was utterly useless to reason with such people. They had paid $10 a head to hate somebody and they were getting their money's worth ... In no campaign have I ever seen such stark madness, such bitterness, such hatred ... They are the ready victims of that inferiority complex which gives them the feeling of exaltation with its accompanying delusions of grandeur when they read the Klan literature and are called 'men of the most sublime lineage the world has ever seen,' – the only Simon pure one hundred per cent Americans ... That enabled the charlatans to capitalize their ignorance into money and political offices.[16]

'Klan Plank is Big Party Issue,' reported an upstate New York paper with marked understatement, adding, 'So fierce has become the battle between the forces contending for and against an anti-Klan plank' that it had overwhelmed all other aspects of the Democratic platform, including their stand on the League of Nations, Prohibition, 'and other controversial issues'.[17] Later known as the 'Klanbake' because temperatures soared as high as tempers, the convention was so acrimonious that reports noted many of the 13,000 gallery spectators spitting on the screaming delegates.[18] The attempt to add a plank condemning the Klan was ultimately defeated by just one vote.

'McAdoo is Silent on Klan,' announced a *New York Times* headline as the convention began, reporting that his campaign manager refused to put questions to McAdoo regarding his position on the KKK.[19] Having denounced one of his primary opponents as the 'Jew, Jug and Jesuit' candidate, the Klan endorsed McAdoo at the convention. Repeatedly pressed on where he stood, McAdoo stayed silent or offered weak evasions, to widespread criticism.

In the end, McAdoo declined to disavow the Klan's endorsement. It was widely held to have cost him the presidential nomination.

* * *

A month before the conventions, Coolidge had signed the largest, and farthest reaching, anti-immigration act in American history. The Johnson–Reed Act of 1924, also known as the National Origins Act, introduced a quota system based on the nation of an immigrant's origin. It cut immigration by over 90 per cent, allowing visas to just 2 per cent of the total number of each nationality in the United States according to the 1890 census – a deliberate choice to skip the censuses of 1920, 1910 and 1900, to return the American population to a demographic before the 'Great Wave' of largely unrestricted immigration.

Republican Senator David Reed (not to be confused with Democrat James Reed, although there wasn't always much to choose between them), one of the authors of the act, told the Senate that earlier legislation was insufficient because it 'disregards those of us who are interested in keeping American stock up to the highest standard – that is, the people who were born here'.

Lawmakers were seeking actively to return to a nativist, 'whiter' past, when more immigrants were 'Nordic', establishing quotas based on earlier numbers to encourage migrants from Northern Europe and discourage or prevent migrants from anywhere else. They excluded Asian immigrants altogether, based on the geographically defined 'Asiatic Barred Zone' from a 1917 immigration act.

This effectively created categories of racial superiority, in which the percentage of visas available to those from Western and Northern Europe increased, while Eastern and Southern Europe and Asia were sharply restricted or fully barred from entry – a decision that severely strained America's diplomatic relationship with Japan. Altogether, the Johnson–Reed Act was a clear effort to create a definable American identity by controlling the racial composition of the United States, advocating an ideal of homogeneity that was fundamentally eugenicist in its ethos.

That this was no coincidence, if it were in doubt, was clear from the national conversation leading up to the passage of the Johnson–Reed Act. Throughout the 1920s, the nation's most popular magazine, the *Saturday Evening Post*, ran a series of prominent articles promoting Nordicism. In January 1922, for example, an article called 'Shutting the Sea Gates' had informed its readers of 'certain biological laws which govern the crossing of different breeds, whether the breeds be dogs or horses or men. These laws should be of considerable interest to a great many citizens of the United States for so many millions of non-Nordic aliens have poured into this country since 1880 that in several of America's largest cities these foreign born and their children far outnumber the native Americans.'[20]

A few months later, in response to a Minnesota mayor proclaiming 2 July 1922 'America First Day', a local minister called for 'The Americanization of America'. Spelling out what Americanisation meant in eugenicist terms lifted straight from Madison Grant's *The Passing of the Great Race*, he similarly specified 1880 as a watershed (as Grant had also done), after which America had begun to racially degenerate.

'Before 1880,' the minister told his congregation, 'most of our immigration came from the great Nordic race, that is from the northern countries of Europe – Sweden, Norway and Denmark; from England and Scotland and Ireland; from Germany, Belgium, France and Holland. These people possessed to a remarkable degree the power to govern themselves and others.' They were the world's aristocrats, the 'voluntary explorers, pioneers, soldiers, sailors and adventurers', he added, quoting Grant's description of Nordics almost verbatim. These superior Nordic types were the early settlers of America, he claimed; they were the framers who 'shaped the nation'.

'Since 1880', however, things had gone rapidly downhill. 'The bulk of immigration to the United States has been composed of people from the other two main races of Europe – the Alpine and the Mediterranean groups.' The Alpine were (all) 'the Slav peoples'. The Mediterranean were Southern Europeans (Italy, Greece and Spain were named) as well as North Africans. These people had never succeeded at 'governing themselves or anybody else', he pronounced, apparently unfamiliar with Alexander the Great, the Egyptian Empire, the Roman Empire, the Ottoman Empire or the Spanish conquest of the Americas. Such people's 'low standard of living' forced out higher types of people whenever they came among them. 'It is no wonder that Americans all over Europe who are familiar with this type of immigrant are sounding the alarm.'[21]

And then there were the socialists, who augured nothing less than 'the rule of the underman'.[22]

America was not 'a dumping-ground for criminals and paupers and incompetents', the minister railed, echoing Coolidge's language from 'Whose Country Is This?' The great majority coming to the US in recent years were, he complained, 'the weakest and poorest man materials of Europe – the defeated, the incompetent and unsuccessful, the very lowest layer of European society'. America should not be 'the melting-pot for elements that will not melt'. The nation had finally learned that you cannot 'make Americans out of any sort of racial scrap-heap'.[23]

This kind of social Darwinism espoused in honour of 'America First Day' reflected the widespread sentiments behind the Johnson–Reed Act. The effort to turn the racial and ethnic clock back – as if in 1879 everyone in the United States had been 'pure' – was no less consequential for being sheer fantasy. Arguably it was more so, for the futility of trying to restore a mythic phase in American history, and return to a moment before the original sin of racial affront, led not to reconsidering the myth, but instead to violent efforts to make the impossible come true.

Purity remained, much of the time, little more than a pious code for vicious ideas. In 1923 former Senator James K. Vardaman of Mississippi, popularly known as 'the Great White Chief' (his campaign slogan was 'A vote for Vardaman is a vote for white supremacy'), edited his own newspaper, *Vardaman's Weekly*, in effect an early version of social media. That May *Vardaman's Weekly* proclaimed its editor a man who had 'fought the battle to make America pure, free and safe'.[24] That may sound unobjectionable, but in practice, the battle to make America pure had included Vardaman's notorious declaration, 'If it is necessary every Negro in the state will be lynched in order to maintain white supremacy.'[25]

The National Origins Act, codifying the idea that a person's ethnic and racial 'origins' measured their potential value to American society, was associated with 'America first' throughout the political debates surrounding it. When objections were made to the exclusion of the Japanese, a Republican congressman announced on the House floor that 'the party does not want the support of those who do not believe in the doctrine of America first for Americans'.[26] In an October 1924 speech, Coolidge defended the immigration curb by telling 'voters of foreign birth' to serve America first. 'Those who cast in their lot with this country can be true to the land of their origin only by first being true to America.'[27] 'America must be kept American,' Coolidge proclaimed on 26 May 1924, as he signed the Johnson–Reed Act into law.

In other words, they wanted to make America great again.

 * * *

In the autumn of 1924, a correspondent wrote in to the *Detroit Free Press* to ridicule the idea that the Klan represented 'one hundred per cent Americanism'. 'Join the Ku Klux Klan and be one hundred per cent American,' the letter began – but what did that mean in practice? First, 'you must be native born', although 'that's an accident'. Second, you must be Protestant, although most people follow the religion they were raised in.

After accidents of birth came the Klan's self-contradictory definitions. 'You must be loyal to the Constitution, and in the next breath you must hate Catholics, Jews and Negroes. Loyalty to the constitution and breathe hate for your fellow citizens can't be done. Once you are a klansman you violate the first amendment.' Next, 'You must be a Christian! How can you and subscribe to the klan doctrine?'

Finally, the correspondent prophesied that if America ever did need defending in battle, Klansmen would be nowhere to be seen until the fight was over. But once 'the days of peace and plenty are restored, then the cohorts of intolerance' would rise again 'with their cry of one hundred per cent Americanism and down with Catholic, Jew and Negro'.[28]

Calvin Coolidge delivered a speech before the American Legion in 1925 that was widely reported throughout the country, assuring listeners that 'America first' was still the nation's goal.

> The generally expressed desire of 'America first' cannot be criticized. It is a perfectly correct aspiration for our people to cherish. But the problem which we have to solve is how to make America first. It cannot be done by the cultivation of national bigotry, arrogance, or selfishness ... We can only make America first in the true sense which that means by cultivating a spirit of friendship and good will, thru [sic] progress at home and helpfulness abroad standing as an example of real service to humanity. It is for these reasons that it seems clear that the results of the war will be lost and we shall only be entering a period of preparation for another conflict unless we can demobilize the racial antagonisms, fears, hatreds, and suspicions, and create an attitude of toleration in the public mind of the peoples of the earth.[29]

It was a laudable ambition, but 'America first' may not have been the best way of going about it, not least because 'America first' continued to be associated with groups entirely driven by national bigotry, arrogance, selfishness, racial antagonisms, fears, hatreds and suspicions – including the American Legion itself, which had formally adopted a guarantee 'to foster and perpetuate a one hundred per cent Americanism' into its constitution, and was regularly accused of being a fascist organisation.[30]

By 1925, national membership of the Klan was estimated at anywhere between three million and eight million; most historians assume it was around five million, in a nation of 115 million, or about 4 per cent of the entire population of the United States.

The African-American *Buffalo American* was losing hope by 1925 that Republicans would use 'America first' for the betterment of all Americans, not just the white ones. 'To awaken interest in "America First" there should be a colored contact officer appointed in each of the federal departments to interpret the government to the people, and them to the government. That these things have not been done is regarded by the Negro as indifference of a party to which he has long been loyal.'[31] But the party of Lincoln's indifference to the cause of civil rights would only harden as the twentieth century wore on.

* * *

As the Klan began to face electoral failures and scandals in 1926, Hiram Evans promoted the organisation again, in a pamphlet called 'The Klan's Fight for Americanism'. It sought to explain 'the character and present mind of the mass of old-stock Americans. The mass, it must be remembered, as distinguished from the intellectually mongrelized "Liberals." ... Liberalism is today charged in the mind of most Americans with nothing less than national, racial, and spiritual treason.'

Having called liberals traitors (and by definition not 'old-stock Americans', although plenty of liberals could, of course, trace their ancestry back to the *Mayflower*, some of them just chose not to), Evans went on to enumerate the grievances of 'Nordic Americans' like himself.

Nordic Americans for the last generation have found themselves increasingly uncomfortable, and finally deeply distressed ... We are a movement of plain people, very weak in the matter of culture, intellectual support and trained leadership. We are demanding, and we expect to win, a return of power into the hands of the everyday, not highly cultured, not overly intellectualized, but

entirely unspoiled and not de-Americanized, average citizen of
the old stock. Our members and leaders are all of this class –
the opposition of the intellectuals and liberals who held the
leadership, betrayed Americanism, and from whom we expect to
wrest control, is almost automatic.

What Evans cast as their anti-elite populism was also motivated,
he insisted, by economic anxiety – or, as he called it, 'economic
distress': 'the assurance for the future of our children dwindled.
We found our great cities and the control of much of our industry
and commerce taken over by strangers, who stacked the cards of
success and prosperity against us.' Evans reiterated their allegiance
to 'the basic idea of white supremacy', encompassed in 'the Klan
slogan: "Native, white, Protestant supremacy"'.[32]

The problem, if it needs stating, was that the Klan felt
'uncomfortable and deeply distressed' because their old sureties of
power and dominance were, indeed, being eroded – by the progress
of the people they sought domination over, the 'strangers' who took
over the commercial power they believed was theirs by entitlement.
And they responded by terrorising those people – blacks, Jews,
labour unionists, radicals, the foreign-born and uppity women –
who were considerably more 'uncomfortable and deeply distressed'
than the Klansmen.

Threats against their once unquestioned political and economic
hegemony made the Klan cast themselves as victims, as they offered
any number of justifications for their violent reassertion of a
diminishing privilege. Increasingly, the Klan viewed any government
intervention on behalf of the citizens whose equality they denied
as an act of oppression. Before long they would cast themselves as
freedom fighters against a fascist state.

That year a new word entered the English language:
'totalitarianism', coined by the writer Luigi Sturzo to describe
Mussolini's Fascism.[33] Within two years, American lecturers were
debating the consequences of totalitarianism, defined for local

audiences as the 'theory which holds that the dominant party is the state and can do no wrong', and that anything critical of the state 'is rank treason'.[34]

But at the same time 'America first' was also beginning to be pushed beyond what such a vacuous slogan could bear. In 1927 Chicago Mayor 'Big Bill' Thompson created an 'America First' movement as part of an anti-British campaign that was treated with much derision by the national press. Thompson promised he'd 'crack King George one in the snoot' if he ever came to Chicago, and began a campaign to root out pro-British literature from the public library, insisting that the British were spreading colonialist propaganda. To some extent, his anti-British pronouncements were doubtless calculated to curry favour with Chicago's large Irish-American population.

Papers around the country ridiculed these preposterous claims. In 'Big Bill's Superpatriot Society' the *St. Louis Post-Dispatch* noted the relationship between Thompson's club and the KKK. Like the Klan, the America First Foundation cost $10 to join, it observed. 'Its platform resembles that of the Klan in that it professes high purposes – better citizenship, loyalty' and other civic virtues. But its true purpose appeared to be 'appeals to ignorance and prejudice to stir up racial and national hatreds for political purposes'.

The editorial proposed that Thompson's America First should adopt as its anthem a verse recently written by the satirist Alec Woollcott.

> I'm a one hundred per cent American
> I'm a super patriot, patriot
> A red, red, red, red, red, I am
> A red-blooded American.
>
> *Chorus:*
> I'm a one-hundred per cent American,
> I am, goddam, I am.[35]

Thompson had 'aroused some interest and much amusement by his cry of "America First" and his book-burning, British-baiting campaign in the city of gang shootings, street murders, and corrupt elections', the *New York Times* agreed, while also noting the campaign's implicit association with the Klan. The America First Foundation had appealed to Klansmen in Georgia, who were 'hot for Mayor Thompson and his anti-English slogan'.

But soon this had set all their bigotries into conflict, when 'some literate Klansman made the discovery that the Klan was backing the Nordic against all comers, and that it was the Nordic English who settled Georgia; and here was the Mayor of a city full of hated immigrants trying to shoot up the Nordic cradle'.

So how could they know which Nordics to support, when the America First Foundation was attacking the English? Klansmen were happy to be anti-British until someone told them that the British were 'Nordic', and that the people attacking the British were immigrants in Chicago. Suddenly they had to be on the side of the 'Nordic English' and against Thompson's 'America First', which instead of being a wholesome group for 'real Americans' was allied with the hated 'unreal' cities. It was all very confusing – which is what comes of trying to take seriously anything as asinine as scientific racism.

'The disillusionment was instantaneous,' the *New York Times* correspondent mockingly wrote, 'but it would have come along sooner or later. For when Mayor Thompson selected $ 10 as the fee for joining his hate society, this struck at the heart and soul of the Klan – their purse.'[36]

'America first' organisations, whether Thompson's foundation or the Klan, were all in the business of selling hate, as the Colorado judge had noted. They even priced it the same.

In addition, the association of the increasingly discredited Klan with 'America first' was beginning to cause trouble for its followers. In 1928 the *Chicago Tribune* reported that the Republican governor of Illinois had been forced to deny 'affiliations with the Ku Klux Klan', rumours which had created a new slogan: 'One Hundred Per Cent Americans First'.[37]

* * *

The Democrats, meanwhile, continued to be troubled by infighting and charges that they were failing to unite around a single issue that voters could believe in.

'Irresistibly the question presents itself,' wrote an irate Missouri editorial. 'Must the Democratic party be an ass?'[38]

McAdoo was still on the scene, urging Democrats to define themselves around support of Prohibition, a platform favoured by many of the Southern Democrats whose religious fundamentalism aligned them with the ideas of America first. Governor Albert Ritchie of Maryland, by contrast, wanted to appeal to the urban, ethnic voter who hated Prohibition, and saw in it the ideas of a rural evangelical minority being allowed to dictate the laws governing the populations of America's big cities.

The Missouri editorial was unimpressed by both arguments, suggesting that, as it was now law, the Prohibition ship had sailed; Democrats should move on and unite against Republicans. 'The United States still needs government by the people and for the people,' and it needed a party to stand up for ordinary Americans against the big-business oligarchs and crony capitalism that controlled the Republican agenda in the 1920s.[39]

'No observing citizen can fail to see how hard and fast the lines are being drawn between a democratic government of the United States and an oligarchical government,' it added, 'between government by the people and government by a small and powerful and privileged class. The future not alone of this republic but of the whole of civilization depends upon whether American democracy or American fascism wins this war.'[40]

'For the Democratic party to refuse to unite,' the editorial concluded, 'to fight a great battle for the Jeffersonian theory and to challenge the rule of Mellon and Morgan; for it to insist rather upon an internal feud ... to which all the beneficiaries and organs of special privilege are urging it,' would be 'not only recreancy to a great trust; it would be fat-headed stupidity – which is even worse'.[41]

Although this editorial may well be the earliest use of 'American fascism' to describe corporate oligarchy and the risks Wall Street could pose to democratic government, it was far from the nation's only confrontation with the spectre of American fascism that year. It appeared six months after the Memorial Day parade riots in New York, when the Ku Klux Klan and self-proclaimed American fascists clashed with onlookers in Manhattan and Queens, and seven men were arrested, one of whom was twenty-year-old hyphenate German-American Fred C. Trump. The 'C' stood for Christ.

PART THREE

1930—1940

9

THE AMERICAN DREAM 1930–1934:
Das Dollarland

Two years after the Wall Street Crash, America was in the grip of the Great Depression, thanks at least partly to the 'businessmen presidents', whose radically laissez-faire policies had driven American economics for a decade. Believing that the budget needed to be balanced, Hoover was reluctant to fight back: in 1931, his administration passed no major legislation to confront the Depression, while in 1930 the passage of the Hawley–Smoot Tariff had raised American import duties to their highest level in history, an act of protectionist nationalism that only made a bad economic situation worse. But the Democrats were also in disarray, most of them agreeing with prevailing fiscal wisdom that balancing the budget was the only way to emerge from the crisis. The gross national product continued to plummet as unemployment rose: by 1932 it would hit 23 per cent, while more than two thousand bank failures in 1931 alone led to millions of Americans losing homes, farms, businesses and life savings. Hoover's response was nationalistic: he maintained that the Depression had been caused by the economic instability of post-war Europe, rather than by any fundamental unsoundness in the American system.

Millions of Americans were unemployed, and politicians seemed unwilling or unable to remedy the situation. Although the supposed epidemic of suicides following the Wall Street Crash was greatly exaggerated, business leaders were getting panicky and demanding governmental action, while ordinary Americans were also making their anger felt.

It was in 1931, when the Depression was still deepening, that the phrase 'American dream' finally began to dominate the national conversation. It all started with a book called *The Epic of America*, by historian James Truslow Adams. (He had fought to use 'The American Dream' as his title, but his publishers were adamant that readers 'would never pay $3 for a dream', and insisted he change it.)[1]

The book was published in October 1931 and became an instant sensation, giving the nation a way to discuss the catastrophe that had befallen it, and reclaim a lost purpose. For Adams, the country's failures were primarily spiritual, rather than financial. It was a message that resonated across America.

Arguing that chasing the spectre of commercial success was precisely what had mired America in the Depression, Adams urged the country to repudiate its focus on material things, and recall its higher ideals, what he termed 'the American Dream of a better, richer, and happier life for all our citizens of every rank ... That dream or hope has been present from the start. Ever since we became an independent nation, each generation has seen an uprising of the ordinary Americans to save that dream from the forces which appeared to be overwhelming and dispelling it.'[2]

It's an often quoted definition, without much attention paid to the clear warning embedded in it: the American dream would come under threat, and need to be revitalised, every generation. Adams doesn't spell out the forces that oppose it, but the enemy of democracy ('for all our citizens of every rank') is authoritarianism in the many guises Americans had been discussing for the previous thirty years: tyranny, yes, but also special interests, corruption, plutocracy and oligarchy, crony capitalism and corporatism, and the various forms of rising totalitarianism, as tyranny went corporate.

Every generation, Adams observed, would have to fight the battle anew; every generation would find ordinary Americans called upon to resist the impact of authoritarianism, to reclaim the democratic dream of liberty, equality and justice. 'Possibly the greatest of these struggles lies just ahead of us at this present time,' he added.

But for Adams, democracy had another clear foe: materialism itself. Throughout *The Epic of America*, he hammered home the message that acquisitiveness was destroying the American dream. 'It is not a dream of motor cars and high wages merely, but a dream of social order in which each man and each woman shall be able to attain to the fullest stature of which they are innately capable, and be recognized by others for what they are, regardless of the fortuitous circumstances of birth or position.'

The American dream, according to Adams, was about the power of character, not purchasing power. And it was firmly opposed to nepotism and inherited privilege. It was a return to the old American creed, to principles of democracy and equality, of agency and self-determination, of justice and generosity. A desire for personal wealth and the accoutrements of luxury wasn't the solution to the American crisis, according to Adams, it was the problem. America was losing sight of its soul, of the democratic ideals that defined it, settling for chasing after shiny objects instead.

In one sense Adams was returning the American dream to a Jeffersonian faith in the 'common man', as opposed to Walter Lippmann's scepticism towards such mystical populism. But Adams also had some trenchant words for the supposedly pragmatic populism of Jacksonian democracy. Under Jackson the 'American doctrine' that 'anyone could do anything' took hold. As every ordinary American had learned he could put his hand to any job and 'become a Jack-of-all-trades himself in his daily life, without special training, he could see no reason why public office called for particular qualities or experience'.[3]

But, as Adams also observed, the quality of work produced by a Jack-of-all-trades may not be the best the country has to offer. The law of averages means that 'mediocrity is one of the prices paid for complete equality, unless the people themselves can rise to higher levels'.[4]

Like the Progressives thirty years before him, Adams held that 'the American dream' required the energetic maintenance of a social order dedicated to values beyond individual affluence. Americans had been remembering the cost of everything and the value of nothing: 'size, like wealth, came to be a mere symbol of "success," and the sense of qualitative values was lost in the quantitative, the spiritual in the material'.[5]

Sharing the blind spots of his time, Adams saw American history in terms of the European migrations and the actions of white men, calling indigenous people 'savages', barely noticing the presence of 'negroes', and ignoring all but a few white women. But Adams was also describing a national ethos that had been defined by these white male European settlers. And the principles he was excavating of the dream of self-realisation applied to all, even to the many Americans men like him tended to forget – as those overlooked Americans were pointing out with ever increasing force.

Much of the *Epic* was devoted to a cultural history of 'rugged individualism', explaining that the American dream was shaped by the brutal realities of wresting life from a wilderness, creating a national economy and ideology to support it. Early settlers got into the habit of deciding for themselves which British laws they would obey, which instilled a culture of autonomy bordering on autarchy. Throughout American history we can hear, Adams wrote, 'the *stroke, stroke, stroke* of the ax on trees, the crash of the falling giant – advancing woodsmen making their clearings; Democracy; "business"'.[6]

It was in the nineteenth century, he added, that Americans began to convince themselves that the accumulation of wealth was a patriotic duty, pursued for the mutual benefit of individual and the nation, that indeed it was citizens' moral obligation to develop and build the country. The fallacy took hold. 'If the making of a hundred thousand was a moral act, the making of a million must be one of exalted virtue and patriotism,' no matter how immoral the means by which the money was made.[7]

Being rich had become taken for a virtue, so much so that people might one day believe a man was good merely because he was rich, rather than viewing obscene wealth as just that – obscene. Vast fortunes have always been more likely to signal moral turpitude than rectitude.

American individualism had enabled 'an extraordinarily rapid economic exploitation and development', but individual competition for 'dazzling prizes' was destroying 'both our private ideals and our sense of social obligation'. The wealthiest remained unconcerned about privilege, 'because privilege was to their advantage', while the majority 'rebelled, about once a generation, against the accumulated abuses' of this radically individualist system.

But individualism was always restored as America's 'working theory of government', because the nation's deep resources meant that individuals continued to glimpse personal opportunities, and resented a government interfering with them.

There was only one way, Adams held, that the American dream of equality and opportunity could become abiding reality. Trusting 'the wise paternalism of politicians or the infinite wisdom of business leaders' would never work – but Adams was not demonising the wealthy. He saw that they represented the values of their culture; by definition the ambitious strove to attain what their society taught them to respect. As long as wealth and power remained 'our sole badges of success', they would continue to shape national aspirations, 'unless we develop some greatness in our own individual souls'.[8]

It was ludicrous to expect people with wealth and power to 'abandon both to become spiritual leaders of a democracy that despises spiritual things'. By the same token no politician would ever 'rise higher than the source of his power'. There was no point in looking to leaders, therefore, 'until countless men and women have decided in their own hearts, through experience and perhaps disillusion, what is a genuinely satisfying life, a "good life" in the old Greek sense'.[9]

This genealogy of America's value system made *The Epic of America* a bestseller. Adams's ideas were welcome to a nation that was trying to survive a crisis by changing its rules; a renewed sense of mutual obligation and commonweal, in the old sense of common well-being, rather than commonwealth, seemed the obvious answer to many, an ethos that they used the 'American dream' to indicate. Economic and moral failures were intertwined, they concluded, and set about restoring the nation's moral economy.

Selfishness had failed, spectacularly. It was time to focus on the greater good.

* * *

The Great Depression provoked a national identity crisis; James Truslow Adams gave the country a way to reclaim that identity in the name of the 'American dream'. After the publication of his book in 1931, the saying suddenly exploded into the national archives, its appearances increasing exponentially. Within a matter of weeks, it started making its way into the national press, as writers and politicians began debating its evolution.

'It is idle now to deny the dream, as many of us do, or to say there was nothing in it,' declared a January 1932 essay in the *Saturday Evening Post*. 'And of all our dreams so far, or any installment of the serial American dream, this one with which we fell in 1929 would be the most difficult to externalize in reality, because of its magnitude, its complexity and the strangeness of its parts.'[10]

Those years also saw a surge of other books about the meanings of America, including *The American Ideal*, *Who Owns America?: A New Declaration of Independence*, *The Decline of American Capitalism*, *Pursuit of Happiness: The Story of American Democracy*, *American Saga: The History and Literature of the American Dream of a Better Life*, *The Awakening of America* and the like, as America struggled to understand where it had gone wrong, turning to history to make sense of its failures.

In November 1932, Franklin Delano Roosevelt was elected president on a Democratic platform that promised Americans 'a new deal', offering a 'contract' with America that included job growth, national old-age insurance, agricultural relief and repeal of Prohibition. In his second inaugural address as governor of New York in 1929, Roosevelt had outlined his political philosophy: 'Our civilization cannot endure unless we as individuals realize our personal responsibility to and dependency on the rest of the world,' he had declared. 'It is literally true that the "self supporting man" and woman has become as extinct as the man of the stone age. Without the help of thousands of others, anyone of us would die, naked and starved.'[11] On the presidential campaign trail Roosevelt also consistently promised to cut back government spending, a promise he would comprehensively break.

More than 11,000 banks had failed, losing the life savings of millions of Americans. Unemployment was approaching a staggering 25 per cent, as currency values continued to plummet in a deflationary spiral, and national income had more than halved. The environmental catastrophe of the Dust Bowl, the worst drought in the history of the American continent, was creating the migrant crisis that John Steinbeck would depict in his two classic novels of the 'American dream', both written during the Depression, both concerning the desperation and dreams of migrant workers, *Of Mice and Men* in 1937 and *The Grapes of Wrath* in 1939.

It might seem that Adams's 'American dream' of a spiritual greatness that was explicitly opposed to material prosperity was a perverse reassurance to offer a nation facing real destitution, with widespread homelessness and hunger. Surely dreaming of spiritual betterment is a luxury for the affluent; starving people dream of food.

A more cynical view, by contrast, might suggest that such evanescent dreams would take hold precisely during times of national deprivation, that it might make good political sense to urge citizens to focus on 'higher ideals', to distract them from economic conditions that cannot be wished away.

But the Progressive Era that had given birth to the saying twenty years earlier was in fact one of relative prosperity, in which living standards were on the rise, even as many Americans watched the accumulation of wealth among some with great unease, wondering at its moral costs – not for the individual, but for the nation.

The meaning of the American dream that Adams was popularising had, in fact, been lurking in American conversations for decades, as we have seen: he was returning to a belief that the democratic experiment would fail if equality and social justice were not protected, a proposition that amounted to the American dream for the vast majority of the people who used the phrase in the first decades of its currency. The Depression didn't create this idea as a palliative: it rediscovered it as a solution.

Similar diagnoses of the toxicity of materialism were offered by other influential writers. In *Only Yesterday*, the first history of the 1920s, also published in 1931, Frederick Lewis Allen remarked upon the previous decade's misplaced faith in wealthy businessmen. 'It was no accident that men like Mellon and Hoover and Morrow found their wealth an asset rather than a liability in public office, or that there was a widespread popular movement to make Henry Ford President in 1924. The possession of millions was a sign of success, and success was worshipped the country over.'[12]

But America's heedless pursuit of 'success' had become self-destructive; at a time of profound national crisis, the 'American dream' became a way to articulate the path America needed to rediscover: a path away from materialism, not towards it. The American creed – of liberty, justice, equality, democracy – had to be recovered first; economic dreams of prosperity for all could only be achieved in a society that prioritised those principles.

Culture and cultivate come from the same root; values do not just sustain themselves. Any ethos has to be cultivated; America had stopped conserving democracy, and started conserving money. The costs were immediately apparent.

Suddenly, Americans were making ironic comments about 'the nightmare of the 1920s', and the previous decade's 'poverty', reversing the truism that the jazz age was a delirious era of prosperity and riotous boom. In retrospect, they saw a spiritual poverty at the heart of recent times. In 1933 Adams looked back on the 'sudden expansion of trade, our huge profits, the end of immigration and the whole of the jazz age', when 'the American dream was changed into a nightmare of gambling and corruption and mad spending'.

The moral poverty of the 1920s was widely blamed for the economic poverty of the 1930s, and it was clear that education was necessary to uphold the American dream of spiritual and personal fulfilment. In 1930, Adams had written: 'There are obviously two educations. One should teach us how to make a living and the other how to live. Surely these should never be confused.'[13] Americans were starting to see the distinction.

Many educators began to admit that public schools had contributed to the current 'social confusion and uncertainty', as one put it; 'they, like the rest of our philosophy, have overemphasized material success'. Schools had been reinforcing 'the average American dream of getting rich quickly', without teaching students 'to appraise America critically'.[14] Too much attention had been 'given to preparation for making money and too little to training for the abundant life' that money was supposed to create. 'The rich man and the go-getter were the idols of the school house as well as the market place.'[15]

By 1933, local debates were asking: 'Can the Junior High School Contribute to Social Planning for the Attainment of the American Dream?' A school principal argued that America had been teaching its children 'a wrong slant' on 'the pursuit of happiness', encouraging them to accumulate wealth to enjoy in a putative retirement, instead of creating the 'incentives to fine and constructive interests' that contribute 'to our children's physical, moral and spiritual welfare'.

Schools might prove their worth in an age of austerity 'only by establishing higher ideals of success and by stimulating a broad social consciousness'.[16]

Another article deemed education a 'manifestation of the American dream of which James Truslow Adams writes, a longing for things of the mind and the spirit denied us in our preoccupation with the humdrum and the material, a step along the way in our search for a fuller and richer life'.[17] Ordinary citizens argued explicitly against the idea that education should train people to be docile wage slaves so that they could become consumers, providing the wealthy with both its labour and its markets. By 1934, the educational reformer John Dewey was declaring: 'Public education is the soul of the American dream, the very core of its central idea. Whatever we are, of strength or weakness, we have been shaped by that dream.'[18]

The expression was becoming a truism, fusing with foundational national beliefs to articulate an American dream that begins to sound ever more familiar. One of the nation's historic experiments, a graduating class was told, was the invention of 'the American dream – that this is a land of opportunity for every man, woman and child to accomplish the best that is in him or her'.[19]

The 'heart's desire of the typical American', an economist told a lecture hall in Illinois, was 'to preserve this country as the land of opportunity, of economic freedom and of individual enterprise and initiative. This is the American dream.'[20]

But over the last seventy-five years, he added, American society had been moving against defending that dream, thanks to 'the concentration of financial control', and the 'increasing power of a few great financial and industrial leaders in our social political life'. Under America's new system of 'corporationism', a group of 'comparatively few men have become the self-elected, self-perpetuating, largely irresponsible trustees' of national resources, including the savings and investments of their fellow citizens. This economist was, as it happens, arguing from a conservative standpoint, 'attacking as radical New Deal efforts' to create state monopolies. Conservative and liberal alike saw the concentration of wealth and power in the hands of the few as an authoritarian threat to the American dream.

Health care also joined the American dream: as cities began experimenting with public health systems, and found they paid 'public dividends', they argued that universal health care contributed to 'what J.T. Adams has called "the American dream," the dream of equal opportunity for every child in the community'.[21] Safeguarding the American dream meant protecting the health of children, not the wealth of individuals.

As early as 1932, the press was reporting that populist Louisiana Senator Huey Long's favourite phrase was 'the American dream', and that in order to make that dream come true, he was arguing for the confiscation of 'all incomes in excess of $5,000,000 per annum, if such still exist'.[22]

'Every man a king,' Long famously promised, even as he began displaying authoritarian tendencies, and populism once again seemed to pull towards tyranny. Many observers concluded that the only king Huey Long really cared about seeing crowned was himself.

* * *

The American dream as a promise of social justice against the self-interest of material gain meant that to some it also suggested the case for internationalism and against isolationism, as when an Oklahoma minister said that 'the American dream', requiring that 'the moral law must be at the heart of any stable social order', also meant that 'isolation is impossible for us practically and wrong for us morally'.[23] The American dream was ready to go international, just as it had in the countdown to the First World War, becoming a symbol for protecting the dream of democracy worldwide – paving the way for the meaning of the expression that would one day define the Cold War and shape the post-war order.

In the autumn of 1932, an American historian went to the
University of Berlin, where he gave an inaugural lecture on the
'American dream'. It must have been one of the first international
talks on the topic, introducing the phrase to the rest of the world.
The 'American dream' was still an unfamiliar enough term that the
New York Times ascribed it to Dr Norlin and shared his definition: it
was 'at once an aspiration, a principle and a practice', a foundation
of 'American character "in self-reliance, self-respect, neighborly
cooperation and vision of a better and richer life, not for a privileged
class, but for all"'. So the country liked to tell itself – but Dr Norlin
also shared his rueful discovery that in Germany, America was
known as 'das Dollarland'.[24]

Two days later, Franklin Delano Roosevelt was elected
president, announcing in his inaugural address in March 1933
that it was time to confront 'our common difficulties. They
concern, thank God, only material things.' Throughout the
address, in which he famously told Americans they had 'nothing
to fear but fear itself', Roosevelt also stressed that America had
gone astray in chasing material prosperity to the exclusion of
anything else.

The 'unscrupulous money changers stand indicted in the court of
public opinion, rejected by the hearts and minds of men', Roosevelt
charged. Lacking true values, these 'false leaders' of business and
finance had failed to restore confidence because 'they know only the
rules of a generation of self-seekers. They have no vision, and when
there is no vision the people perish.'

Instead of 'the mad chase of evanescent profits', Americans
needed to recognise both 'the falsity of material wealth as the
standard of success' and the equally 'false belief that public office
and high political position are to be valued only by the standards of
pride of place and personal profit'.

It was, to put it bluntly, time for 'changes in ethics', as the nation
acknowledged a newly chastened spirit. Whether it was true that
'the money changers have fled from their high seats in the temple

of our civilization', as Roosevelt also assured the American people, was, however, another question.

In its first weeks, the Roosevelt administration passed a raft of sweeping reforms, including finance regulations, relief programmes, pensions, unemployment insurance, welfare benefits, medical entitlements and tax reform. And it created the Public Works Administration, which invested billions of dollars in American infrastructure over the next decade. Roosevelt's New Deal reforms effectively introduced social democratic policies into American society for the first time, as his administration created the welfare state and began spending its way out of depression. By the time the United States entered the Second World War, the New Deal had more than doubled federal spending.

At first many Americans, liberals and conservatives alike, saw in the New Deal a grave overreach of the federal government, many viewing Roosevelt's arrogation of executive power as dangerous, even immoral. His critics called him a dictator; his defenders, the nation's saviour. Republicans would spend the rest of the century and beyond adamantly determined to reverse these reforms – a position they would later take in the name of realising the 'American dream'.

Throughout the 1930s, the 'American dream' was already giving a language and history to national debates about the principles of the New Deal – socialised education, health care, housing, inequality – but also to other conversations about the evolution of American society. James Truslow Adams himself had begun as a supporter of FDR, but staunchly opposed Roosevelt's economic reforms. Complaining in a 1929 letter to a friend that he could no longer afford domestic help or a house big enough for his library, Adams had added: 'That is merely the working of democracy the world over, and I am rapidly becoming an anti-Democrat.'[25] It is one thing to have lofty principles, quite another to live by them; but it is also true that humanity's perennial failure to live up to its ideals does not make the ideals less worthwhile.

Adams continued to offer prophetic warnings about what would happen to the nation if it lost sight of the American dream, even as he griped in private about having nowhere to put his heirloom furniture. In May 1933, for example, he cautioned that giant corporations 'seem destined to rule the land'. If corporate plutocracies came to control the American political economy, then the American, once defined as a free citizen, would soon 'be rated as a consumer' only. Commodity fetishism would take over; the 'flood of new goods', 'discoveries and applications' that had been promised would 'profoundly alter the material bases of our lives'.

If America entered a technologically advanced era 'with no philosophy of life' other than 'getting and spending to the utmost limit of our power', then the American dream would be fatally 'warped', promising only that every American home might become 'an up-to-date department store'.[26]

The nation had passed through 'three emotional states' since the crash, he added: bewilderment, fear and resentment, 'directed against the bankers and other leaders who have betrayed their trust'. But now the nation seemed 'merely to be waiting' for prosperity to return, 'for the chance to begin over again'. The country needed 'a saner philosophy. Without such a philosophy the American dream is doomed', and the nation would 'go spiritually bankrupt'.[27]

Americans had rediscovered that there should be a moral to the story, but the nature of that moral was still unclear.

AMERICA FIRST 1930–1934:
The Official Recognition of Reality

While America was confronting its spiritual failures in 1933, Europe was confronting the Nazis' consolidation of power: Roosevelt was sworn in as president almost exactly one month after Hitler became chancellor. Three weeks after that, the *Chicago Tribune* was reporting that he had ceremoniously opened his first concentration camp, 'at Dachau, near Munich', on 22 March 1933.[1]

Two years earlier, the journalist Dorothy Thompson had interviewed the chancellor, calling him 'inconsequent and voluble, ill-poised and insecure. He is the very prototype of the little man.'[2] In *I Saw Hitler*, her 1932 book based on the interview, Thompson noted that *Mein Kampf* was 'eight hundred pages of Gothic script, pathetic gestures, inaccurate German, and unlimited self-satisfaction'.[3]

Perhaps the most extraordinary part of Hitler's rise, she thought, was its very premise: 'Imagine a would-be dictator setting out *to persuade a sovereign people to vote away their rights.*'[4] She would later be mocked for having 'dismissed' Hitler in this first assessment, but although she underestimated dictators, she also overestimated voters.

When Hitler took control, Thompson was aghast at his electorate's self-deception and self-destruction, writing that Hitler had not been 'thrust upon' the German people; instead 'dictatorship was accomplished by popular will … He recommended himself to them and they bought him.' More than 50 per cent of German voters 'deliberately gave [up] all their civil rights, all their chances of popular control, all their opportunities for representation'. In sum, 'they bought the pig of autocracy in a poke'.[5]

Hitler came to power 'largely because so-called civilized people did not believe that he could', Thompson warned. The problem was that they complacently assumed that their idea of civilisation was 'greatly cherished by all men', who agreed that their culture, a 'complex of prejudices, standards and ideas', had been 'accumulated at the cost of great sacrifice' over centuries.

Instead, the intellectual elite needed to understand that 'this culture is, actually, to the vast masses no treasure at all, but a burden'. And if economic conditions deteriorated, leaving those people resentful, 'hungry and idle', they would only view such 'civilization as a restraining, impeding force'.[6]

At which point, they would identify smashing that system as freedom.

* * *

As European fascism was taking serious hold, the one hundred per cent American kind found itself in increasing trouble. The Klan was in decline by 1930, its political influence waning after electoral failures, while financial and political scandals, including accusations of election fraud, graft and bribery, further undermined its leaders. The *New York Times* had declared 'The Klan's Invisible Empire is Fading'[7] as early as 1926, and by the late 1920s estimates of national membership dropped down to a few hundred thousand. After the 1929 crash, many rural farmers found themselves no longer in a position to pay $10 for membership.

Klansmen were also, some historians have suggested, at least partly a victim of their own success: having driven out the African-Americans they feared were economic competitors, they found themselves without an economic minority to exploit, no one to press-gang into picking their cotton for them.[8] They may have found themselves with less spare time for inflicting violence.

As the Klan declined, however, more groups of self-styled 'American fascists' began to take its place. In the summer of 1930, papers around the country reported with some anxiety that for two months Atlanta had been 'seething over the activities' of a new group called the 'American Fascisti', who in practice preferred to call themselves simply 'Black Shirts'. Although it promised to combat the spread of Communism, in reality, as reports soon showed, its members were targeting African-Americans. 'Membership is restricted to native-born white Americans.' Black shirts were the official insignia, and its sponsors denied 'any connection with the Ku Klux Klan', calling it a 'spontaneous movement'.[9]

'Born out of the throes of unemployment and the canny exploitation of what its leaders term a Communistic threat to white supremacy, the organization claims to have enrolled 27,000 members,' reported the *Baltimore Sun*.[10] They were not Italian-American followers of Mussolini; they were nativist supporters of a home-grown American fascism. The main leader of the American Blackshirts, unsurprisingly, was a former member of the KKK.

Along with the 'American Fascisti', two other groups were 'stirring racial agitation' in Atlanta, reported an Illinois paper in 1930: 'the White Band of Caucasian Crusaders, and the Ku Klux Klan. For the moment the American Fascisti appears the most active. The White Band perhaps is next, and the Ku Klux Klan seems but a shadow of its former self, although no one is exactly certain as to its exact strength.'[11]

That summer, around seven thousand 'American Fascisti' paraded in Atlanta, carrying banners, one of which read: 'Back to the cotton patch, Nigger – it needs you; we don't!'[12] Threatening Atlanta employers with boycotts and violence if they didn't fire their African-American workers, the 'American fascist association and order of the black shirts' soon found itself facing Grand Jury indictments.[13]

In the spring of 1930, an Oakland newspaper ran a section of ads for fraternal societies that were seeking membership, among them the Klan, which was struggling to recruit new members.

'All Native Born Protestant Americans are invited to join the KU KLUX KLAN. This all American organization is now conducting a vigorous drive for fifty thousand new members. We are after the state convention for 1932. Now is the chance to join the fraternity that has the backbone to stand for America FIRST, LAST and ALWAYS.'[14]

But even if the Klan was disintegrating as an organisation, its former members had not suddenly renounced their beliefs – or their willingness to use peremptory violence to impose them. Ten days after the Oakland Klan sought to recruit new members, the Negro Labor Congress announced a campaign against 'lynching and other forms of white terrorism'.[15]

It was none too soon. August 1930 brought the notorious double lynching in Marion, Indiana, of Thomas Shipp and Abram Smith, whose dangling bodies were photographed over grinning and pointing white crowds. Such photographs had long circulated, but now they were making their way into the papers. The photograph of Shipp and Smith, which rapidly became iconic, inspired the anti-lynching lament 'Strange Fruit', originally sung by Billie Holiday.

The *Evening Press* of Muncie, Indiana – about forty miles south of where the lynchings occurred – published the photo on its front page.

When Lynchers Became Law at Marion

This remarkable picture—gruesome as it may be—was taken at Marion last night just a few minutes after two negroes, who admitted killing a white man and attacking a white girl, were hanged from trees in the courthouse yard. They had been badly beaten, stabbed and dragged across a cement walk—all this the picture shows. Only a small portion of the milling mob is shown in the photo.

The caption reads: 'This remarkable picture – gruesome as it may be – was taken at Marion last night just a few minutes after two negroes, who admitted killing a white man and attacking a white girl, were hanged from trees in the courthouse yard. They had been badly beaten, stabbed and dragged across a cement walk – all this the picture shows. Only a small portion of the milling mob is shown in the photo.'[16]

Gruesome was one word for it; neighbouring Muncie was not, it seems, prepared to use a stronger one. Next to the photo of two men dangling from trees, the editors, stupefyingly, printed a column with the subhead 'It's In the Air', which opened: 'When times are really getting better you can feel it in the air.'

The lynching of Thomas Shipp and Abram Smith has sometimes been identified as the last public lynching in the United States. Sadly, it was not. Spectacle lynching was still active enough in 1934 to provoke a blistering *New Yorker* cartoon from the artist Reginald Marsh, of a white woman holding up a small blonde girl in an excited crowd, happily telling her neighbour: 'This is her first lynching.'[17]

"This is her first lynching."

Less than two months after Marsh's cartoon appeared, Claude Neal was lynched in Marianna, Florida, in front of an estimated crowd of five thousand, accused of raping and murdering a white woman. It was 'advertised hours in advance', reported the *New York*

Times, 'bringing together thousands of men, women and children eager to witness the spectacle'. The lynching itself was 'marked by unspeakable torture and mutilation'.[18]

The torture and mutilation that papers at the time would not name were itemised by a white undercover investigator for the NAACP, to whom an eyewitness boasted ten days later:

> 'They cut off his penis. He was made to eat it. Then they cut off his testicles and made him eat them and say he liked it. Then they sliced his sides and stomach with knives and every now and then somebody would cut off a finger or toe. Red hot irons were used on the nigger to burn him from top to bottom.'... From time to time during the torture [the investigator continued] a rope would be tied around Neal's neck and he was pulled up over a limb and held there until he almost choked to death, when he would be let down and the torture begun all over again.[19]

After Neal's body was cut down, the mob stamped and urinated on it, drove cars over it, and small children stabbed it with sticks.

Some local papers had announced in their morning editions the imminent 'lynch party' later that day. The *Dothan Eagle*, from neighbouring Alabama, had explained in an afternoon headline on the day of the lynching exactly what was planned: 'Florida to Burn Negro at Stake: Sex Criminal Seized from Brewton Jail, Will be Mutilated, Set Afire in Extra-Legal Vengeance for Deed'.[20]

Another headline informing locals of the lynching to come had read: 'Ku Klux Klan May Ride Again'.[21] The Klan was down, but it wasn't out.

* * *

As the Klan found its grip on reactionary sentiment in America slipping, 'America first' continued to be brought into disrepute by others using it as well. When Big Bill Thompson tried to rally support once more for his faltering America First Foundation, he generated more ridicule than riches.

Increasingly it looked spent as a political force, as even Thompson was forced on occasion to concede. When asked in 1930 about 'the "America First Foundation," his child in 1927', the blustering Thompson replied with an uncharacteristic sigh, consigning it 'to the past tense: "America first went along and did a lot of good," he said. "The results of it can be found in the United States senate."'[22]

But then Mayor Thompson gave it another shot, inviting William Randolph Hearst to help celebrate 'Chicago Day', commemorating the great Chicago Fire of 1871. The theme of the day was 'America first'. '"America First" Hearst,' read the headline.[23]

"America First" Hearst
Welcomed by Chicagoans

A few weeks later, in Marion, Ohio, the home of Warren G. Harding, another politician took the stand with 'America first'. Seeking re-election in the midterms, Senator Roscoe McCulloch returned to the oldest version of the slogan, insisting, 'we must think of America first and the rest of the world afterward'. 'The issue is clearly drawn,' he asserted: 'Americanism against internationalism; expatriated capital against American capital, invested in home industries; American working men against foreign workmen. And the protective tariff is all that will save us.'[24]

Local politicians were also still adopting the 'America first' slogan, combining it with other coded claims about one hundred per cent Americanism: a platform of 'America First' and 'America for Americans' should 'make it clear to the world that America's door is open only to those who come with the declared intention of becoming loyal American citizens', contended state representative Virgil A. Fitch, running for re-election in Michigan; his campaign advertisements promised 'Economy with Efficiency, Immigration Restriction to Reduce Unemployment, Old Age Pensions, "America First"'.[25]

During the 1932 presidential campaign, 'America first' briefly revived again – this time, swinging back to the Democrats. In a report on FDR's presidential hopes, the *New York Times* mentioned his 'progressive principles', as well as 'his unflinching stand for the interests of America first, as against the policy of helping Europe at the expense of American taxpayers'.[26]

Meanwhile William Randolph Hearst was actively campaigning on an 'America first' platform in 1932, having manufactured a presidential campaign for Democrat Speaker of the House John Nance Garner, in order to oppose the candidacies of Roosevelt and Al Smith, both of whom Hearst detested. He attacked them for their association with Woodrow Wilson, whom Hearst accused, somewhat forgetfully, of not being in favour of 'America first', despite the fact that Wilson was widely credited with having invented the phrase. As one 1930 article put it, 'America first has become the property of the whole nation since Wilson first used it in a speech in New York in early 1915, but its misuse as a slogan by demagogic politicians has detracted sadly from its significance as a patriotic plea.'[27]

For Hearst, Garner's opponents were 'internationalists' who had 'fatuously followed Woodrow Wilson's visionary politics of intermeddling in European conflicts and complications'. The American people needed to get 'back upon the high road of Americanism', Hearst maintained. 'Unless we American citizens are willing to go on laboring indefinitely merely to provide loot for Europe, we should personally see to it that a man is elected to the Presidency this year whose guiding motto is "America first."'[28]

Hearst's campaign for Garner prompted outright derision from Walter Lippmann in his national column. 'Mr. Hearst said with great fervor that Mr. Garner stood for America First,' as if, Lippmann added, the other candidates stood for 'America Second, Third or Fourth'. Garner's opponents were 'tainted', Lippmann gathered, by a common recognition that America's security and welfare are in certain vital respects related to the security and welfare of other nations. They are 'internationalists' because they all believe that in the world today there are problems which have to be dealt with by international action. This, I take it, is what Mr. Hearst would like to deny.[29]

Sadly for Hearst, Garner had betrayed the great man's trust by committing himself to internationalist policies. 'This horrible experience ought to be a lesson to Mr. Hearst,' Lippmann concluded. 'It ought to teach him that there must be something the matter with his theories if nobody can stand by them.'[30]

Lippmann was not the only one to treat 'America first' with contempt. A Nebraska editorial, widely reprinted, suggested reconsidering its use as a motto. 'The full extent of the perfidy behind the slogan through which the Republican party regained control of national affairs in 1918 and 1919 gradually is dawning upon the American people,' it began, calling 'America first' the result of a 'subtle and sinister attack planned and executed by a group of Republicans under the leadership of the late United States Senator Henry Cabot Lodge of Massachusetts', an attack that appealed directly to xenophobia.

According to the editorial, Lodge deliberately popularised 'America First' because 'he wanted to destroy Wilson', and decided to exploit the fact that 'inbred in the average Yankee [was] a deep aversion to Europe and the rest of the world. Out of this recognition was born the phrase, "America First."' The isolationism it led to represented 'the real problem before President-elect Roosevelt. In some sections the cry of "America First" is heard still.'

'We might as well be honest,' the editorial finished. 'We started it. We have heaped fuel on the flames for 12 years, until virtually we have closed the doors of trade the world over.' If the United States had only followed Wilson's dreams of internationalism, it would have averted much. Instead, America had been swayed by Republicans' appeals 'to ancient prejudices, carefully nursing instinctive suspicion'. It would take 'stupendous sacrifice and Herculean effort' for Americans to emerge from the 'death valley' of protectionist isolationism it had entered.[31]

The *New York Times* agreed. 'The easiest way to get cheers is to wave the flag and shout for "America first,"' it wrote at the beginning of 1932. Clearly Americans 'are sick and tired of the company of the world', while 'the inconveniences of internationalism enrage every nation'. But this attitude could not last: the US was going to have to confront the international situation sooner or later, a reluctant, tacit realisation that had left Congress mired in 'gloom', 'a sign that Washington at last faces facts. Worthy of a headline is this hopeful event: the official recognition of reality.'[32]

If enthusiasm for 'America first' was beginning, in some quarters, to wane, it was by no means dead. The New York State chairman of the Republican National Committee gave a speech just before Roosevelt's inauguration in which he 'expressed the hope that President-elect Roosevelt would dedicate himself to a policy of "America first"'.[33]

Roosevelt seemed perfectly prepared to use the slogan if it appealed to voters, although he never campaigned on the basis of it. In an article about interventionism headlined 'Roosevelt Believes Public Backs "Sock in the Jaw" to Europe', the *New York Times* reported 'not only that [Roosevelt] is for "America first," but knows what that means and how to enforce it'.[34]

'America First Campaign Opens in Washington,' read the headlines in the summer of 1933, a few months into Roosevelt's first term. 'US No Longer World's Football,' a Pennsylvania paper announced, although failing to specify when, exactly, America had been kicked around so badly by the international community. 'A foreign policy based on the doctrine of "America First" was shaping up rapidly today as part of the "new deal,"' it added, without asking what was new about America first.[35]

That summer a journalist reported that 'America first is the slogan of our President', apparently unaware that it had also been the slogan of each of the previous four presidents before him. 'Let all of us take up the slogan,' urged a Kentucky paper, 'and in harmonious tones give it the power and volume it merits.'[36] Readers might have been forgiven for thinking it had been given quite a lot of volume already.

That volume was continuing to diminish, however, as voices were raised in warning against isolationism, which merely created 'emotional slogans and irrelevant catchwords', contended one lecturer. With such easy slogans 'demagogues could easily ensnare the votes of the yokelry', from 'William Randolph Hearst and his chain of newspapers' to '"Big Bill" Thompson, [who] won the Chicago mayoralty election on a platform of "America First," "Biff King George on the Snoot," and "No World Court"'.[37]

Isolationism 'reveals the emotional mysticism, the unshakeable irrationality, the almost unbelievable stupidity and provincialism of a large section of the American electorate', the professor added bluntly, if tactlessly. Isolationism was simply a 'popular patriotic mythology' that seemed to cling to American culture like a fog.[38]

More laconically, a Delaware paper observed: 'America first is a good slogan, but a more prosperous America is better.[39]

Another educator likened American isolationism on an international scale to individualism on a national scale. Domestically, 'the unsound foundation of rugged individualism' had simply resulted in inequality, giving more and more profits to 'the few, the owners', leaving the majority to low earning and purchasing power, while an increasing number had no earning power at all, and no chance to acquire it. The only way to get out of the mess America was in, at the nadir of the Great Depression, was to socialise 'the vast resources' of the nation, and distribute the wealth 'to give to the whole public the earning and buying power essential to prosperity'.[40]

In terms of foreign policy, the teacher added for good measure, this individualism had expanded into an unworkable isolationism. 'Nor can we continue to say: "America first, and the rest of the world go hang."'[41]

One Ohio correspondent wrote to his local paper in protest against the position taken in a previously published letter signed by 'A Republican'. 'If the Republican party ever comes back or deserves to,' he commented, 'it will be by disavowing and discountenancing such deplorable partisan ideas.' They had best reverse their old motto and 'adopt the slogan "America first, the Republican party afterward," for there are times in a nation's life when unthinking partisanism is responsible for more sins than charity can cover'.[42]

* * *

On 17 May 1934, 20,000 members of a group called the 'Friends of New Germany' held a rally at Madison Square Garden in New York City. The Friends of New Germany had been authorised by Rudolph Hess in 1933; officially recognised by Hitler, it was described by American papers as the 'American subsidiary of the Nazi party'.[43]

They gathered that night, they said, in part to protest against a boycott of German goods. Such rallies were becoming more and more common; only a month earlier a correspondent had written to the *New York Times* to protest the mixing of 'Stars and Stripes with Swastikas' when both flags were hung together at meetings of the Friends of New Germany.

Newspapers did not give the American Nazi rally at Madison Square Garden that May much space. 'Hitler Cheered at N.Y. Rally,' read a small headline on page 4 of the Allentown *Morning Call*. 'Chancellor Hitler was cheered and boycotters of German goods were booed tonight as 20,000 Nazi sympathizers packed Madison Square Garden in a rally under the watchful eye of hundreds of metropolitan police.' There were also 'eight hundred members of the German "Ordnungs Dienst"' there to help 'preserve order'.[44] The *Brooklyn Daily Eagle* told its readers of clashes among protesters in the streets after the 'Nazi rally', putting the story on page 3.[45] The *Chicago Tribune* called it a 'demonstration', relegating it to a few lines on page 6.[46]

The pictures taken that night in Madison Square Garden, however, suggest that more attention should have been paid; the

New York Times reported it on the front page, reprinted a chilling photograph on page 3, mentioned it again the following day, and then never returned to the story again.[47]

Two months earlier, the German Consul General in New York had assured Americans that there were 'only a few hundred national socialists in this country'.[48] Ten days after 20,000 American Nazis gathered at Madison Square Garden, a welterweight boxing match there garnered more national coverage than the massive Nazi rally had. By the end of 1935, the Friends of New Germany would briefly dissolve – only to re-form almost instantly in early 1936, as the (ironically hyphenate) German-American Bund.

'Americans, awake!' wrote a correspondent to the *Brooklyn Daily Eagle* a few months after the rally. 'Your indifference to this Nazi menace might result in almost anything'; the Friends of New Germany was 'spreading Hitler doctrines in America under the cloak of Americanism'. The writer, self-proclaimed president of the 'America First and Always Society' of Brooklyn, was writing to 'protest strenuously against those un-American methods of making bigots' in America.[49] But rejections of bigotry in the name of 'America first' were becoming harder and harder to find.

In September 1934 a man named James M. True founded 'America First!, Inc.', which promised to 'give the New Deal an X-ray exposure' and 'restore the Constitution'.[50] 'America First, Inc.' (variously printed with or without the exclamation point), would 'combat and expose the propaganda and subversive activities originating within the New Deal', reported the *Scranton Republican*.[51] True's charge that the Roosevelt administration had 'Communist affiliations' with Russia made it into newspapers around the country, including the *New York Times*.[52] In October, America First, Inc. announced that credit unions were 'tax spies' who were being used in a federal surveillance system against American citizens.[53] Then it alleged that 'all Congressional candidates by the New Deal and the Federal Government have violated the Corrupt Practices Act of 1925'.[54] True began giving speeches on behalf of America First, Inc., again claiming that Roosevelt's administration was 'controlled largely by Communists'.[55]

'America First, Inc.' had 'succeeded in creating something of a stir' that year, drily acknowledged one local paper, but only by 'distorting the news' with paranoid propaganda.[56]

That September, William Randolph Hearst visited Germany, where he met and 'chatted intimately' with Hitler.[57] Many American papers, noting Hearst's 'sympathetic attitude toward the Nazi regime', condemned his support of Hitler as 'unfair, prejudiced and harmful', the 'worst kind of war-time propaganda', a 'direct appeal to prejudice, ignorance, and hatred'.[58] These journalists did not think their job was merely to report the fact of Hearst's visit; they had an obligation to make judgements and draw conclusions, calling out sophistries and bigotries where they saw them.

Asked to share his conversation with the German chancellor, Hearst replied that it was not for publication. 'Visiting Hitler is like calling on the President of the United States,' he said.[59] Reporters did not hide their contempt at the idea of suggesting an American president could ever resemble a fascist.

The amount of
increasing maturity.

THE AMERICAN DREAM 1934—1939:
The Pageant of History

'Did anybody ever see an American Dream walking?'

This question, put to its readers by the *New York Times* in a 1934 essay called 'The American Note', may seem a trifle difficult to answer.[1] But by the mid-1930s, the American dream had indeed become ubiquitous, roaming from lecture to sermon, from lunchtime talk to book review, and from feature essay to political speech. Almost anywhere you went, you were likely to encounter it.

As 'America first' seemed increasingly pushed to the margins where only cranks and zealots lurked, the 'American dream' continued to make its presence felt, still primarily to summon principles of liberal democracy and the dreams of the founders — but its relation to upward social mobility was strengthening as well.

'The American Note' had been described by a British guidebook as a national sense of boundless progress and possibility, an indifference to authority and tendency to innovation, and 'inextinguishable hope'. These forces had achieved in the United States 'a wider realization of human brotherhood than has yet existed' elsewhere in the world.

The *Times* essay quoted de Tocqueville's observation that although democracy is not the most efficient government, it produces what more efficient political systems cannot: 'namely, an all-pervading and restless activity', the turbulent energy that can 'produce wonders'. Americans might ask, the *Times* concluded, 'whether an American dream that has shown no change since de Tocqueville a hundred years ago, and has been traced back by James Truslow

Adams three hundred years, can properly be described as a dream'. The conditions of democracy were 'a popular state of mind' in America, and 'that which endures for three hundred years is as real and enduring as most things are in this transitory world'.² Like language, dreams can create truths, conjuring them into existence.

The dream seemed stable enough by 1934 to be called a reality – not because it had come true, but because the dream was so shared, so persistent, that it had made its presence felt, and was shaping American cultural reality.

Put another way, the American dream of democratic equality was kept alive by the sheer number of people who kept appealing to it, even as they acknowledged that it was far from being achieved. Hope and faith came from the commitment to the dream itself; they weren't dependent upon its realisation, but upon the effort to realise it.

That summer, a New Mexico paper defended Roosevelt's plan for social security in the name of the American dream of 'building a society here in which the common man would get a better break than he ever got elsewhere. Seeking to protect the common man against unemployment, against accidents, and against the traditional penury of old age, and trying to guarantee that he shall have a decent home to live in – what is this but an effort to make the old American dream come true?'³

'If the high hopes of the last 18 months are not to be dashed,' maintained a Pennsylvania editorial a few weeks later, it would be wise for the country to recall the ideas 'which helped, in the early years of the republic, to build that great American dream which has always dazzled our eyes just beyond the horizon', namely, 'that the rights of the humblest man could be made as sacred as the rights of the mightiest, and that progress should mean nothing at all unless it means a better life and a truer freedom for the fellow at the bottom of the heap'. This 'noble dream' may have become 'stained and frayed' over time, 'but it remains our finest heritage; and if the confusion of this era is to mean anything at all, it must mean a revival of that dream and a new effort to attain it'.⁴

Earlier that spring, James Truslow Adams had similarly claimed that the democratic American dream was itself the greatest intellectual contribution America had made to the world. In an essay called 'Rugged Individualism' (using Theodore Roosevelt's famous phrase), Adams argued that the United States had not, in fact, produced markedly unique thinkers, but rather innovators and inventors: America bred not Einsteins, but Edisons.

'Perhaps our most notable contribution has been what I have called the "American dream,"' Adams concluded (with a little flourish of self-promotion), 'that belief in the right and possibility of a better life for all, regardless of class or circumstance.' Americans' faith in individualism, Adams held, meant that neither communism nor socialism would ever take hold of the country, for both were fundamentally authoritarian. It was not capitalism that would safeguard America, but individualism. And that individualism needed to be protected by a democratic government from the giant corporations that would otherwise suffocate it.

As lectures, articles, speeches and books on the American dream started springing up across the country, the phrase's meanings soon diverged, although it was still widely adduced to describe ideals of social justice and the problems created for democratic self-government by economic inequality.

Those focused on safeguarding individual rights and freedoms against what they saw as the illegitimate encroachments of the Roosevelt administration were also working to reclaim the American dream, however, as its meaning was contested. When the New Deal placed pressure on the national value system, liberty tilted upward on the scales of the American dream once more. For example, in a widely reprinted radio address, the president of the California Institute of Technology warned against the 'danger of dictatorship' as a menace to the 'American Dream of liberty and progress'.

'Stateism': this 'new and useful term', coined in Dr R. A. Millikan's broadcast, incorporated 'Communism, Socialism, Fascism, bureaucracy and paternalism', the *Los Angeles Times* told its readers. It constituted the 'greatest menace to the American ideal of a land of freedom and opportunity for each individual to rise to the position to which his merit and character entitle him'. If Americans accepted 'too much paternalism', it would lead the country 'from freedom into despotism'.[5]

'Excess government may spoil the American dream,' Dr Millikan warned. But even a conservative arguing against state intervention still accepted the basic premise that the government should be 'regulatory'; his speech only resisted the idea that government should be too 'operative' or invasive. An overly active government might create problems, but in the 1930s the idea that government had a proper regulatory role was not disputed by any serious public voice, even the ones on the right arguing against excessive government intervention. That's one of the things government was for: to protect individuals from forces beyond their control.

'The American dream' could only be realised, Millikan concluded, by 'the wide distribution of power and opportunity among [American] citizens, not by the concentration of it either in the hands of necessarily politically minded officials, or in the hands of despots'.[6]

Both free-market capitalists and liberal democrats found in the 'American dream' a way to describe their – increasingly divergent – ideals for the nation, but neither found the American dream compatible with the concentration of large amounts of wealth and power in the hands of politicians or autocrats, and neither believed that free markets were the same thing as political freedom – or that one led to the other.

Indeed, the American dream remained firmly associated with democracy and liberty across the political spectrum. A sermon delivered to the American Legion, called 'The American Dream', was reprinted in New Jersey; it began with a biblical text: 'Ye are called to liberty.' Noting James Truslow Adams's definition of the American dream, as most still did, the sermon claimed that the dream was 'challenged', and would only come true if people 'wake up and make it true ... If not, we may witness the failure of democracy, the failure of the common man to rise to full stature, to the fullness of all that the American Dream has promised of hope for mankind.'[7]

* * *

Throughout 1935, a Pulitzer Prize-winning liberal historian and journalist named Herbert Agar was publishing widely syndicated columns arguing that the majority of the country was still 'in favor of what has been called the American dream. This dream is not merely of a nation in which all men have a high standard of living. There is nothing natively American about that; the desire is common to the whole human race.'

For Agar, freedom was inseparable from equality. 'The American dream is of a nation where men are free,' he explained, 'in the true sense that they have the maximum of independence, that their fate is just so far as possible in their own hands. It is a dream of a nation where men are equal,' not only under the law, 'but in the sense that they all have a chance to make themselves a dignified and worthy life.'[8]

Everyone wants to live in comfort; what made the American dream exceptional was not a promise of individual success but a promise of self-determination. Yet that still left open the question of whether self-determination was best achieved under a laissez-faire government, or under one that intervened to prevent larger cultural or economic forces from interfering in individual sovereignty.

At the end of 1935 Agar published a book called *The Land of the Free*, in which he argued counter-intuitively that 'the failure of Americanism' was 'its failure to exalt the right of private property' – not for the few, but for the many. 'The betrayal of Americanism came with the increasing concentration of wealth, privilege, power in the hands of a few people', which was contrary to 'the American dream ... of a free nation of free men, enjoying the final fruits of freedom in a firm stake in the land and the machinery of production'.[9]

This idea of the American dream always stretched backwards, invoking an originary value system that many Americans feared was being lost. Although it may look at first glance like a nostalgic appeal to a golden moral age, it was more of a bracing reminder – not that America used to be better, but that it used to dream bigger.

Soon this idea of the American dream as a constant urge to national improvement had merged with broader ideas about American history, as an avalanche of talks, plays and pageants were produced by local citizens on the theme of the American dream. The tenor of the vast majority of them was not triumphalist, but meliorist, as a kind of moral optimism began to reassert itself.

An attorney in Portland, Oregon, spoke on 'The American Dream' at a local election and picnic, focusing on 'the dream of freedom and equality for the common man'.[10] High-school students in Allentown, Pennsylvania, presented a pageant entitled 'The American Dream Unfolds', which told the history of America from colonial settlement to 'The Melting Pot' of 1935. Valedictorians gave speeches about the American dream, talks that 'traced from the early colonies the ever westward industrial expansion of this country in which the ideal of physical growth and the profit motive ran amuck in the wave of wild speculation until the crash of 1929', and ended with 'recognition of the growing materialism in American life', urging the nation to 'recover the human side of American life'.[11] 'The "American Dream" – the doctrine embodied in the Declaration of Independence, "life, liberty, and the pursuit of happiness," was being forgotten and blanketed by a stormy search for wealth.'[12]

In Binghamton, New York, a minister preached on 'The American Dream versus The Religion of Nationalism', arguing that patriotism was different from 'destructive' nationalism, 'which some of our brethren refer to as "hundred per cent"'. Such white nationalism was 'out of harmony both with the Declaration of Independence and with the Preamble to the Constitution, with the American dream'.[13] It had not taken long for the American dream, clearly defined as the

framers' ideas of democratic equality, to become a rebuke to the
'one hundred per cent American' nationalist discourse.

The point of the American dream for many was that it was not
something that the nation gave to its citizens – it was something
they would have to make, and remake, for themselves. An editorial
in Ithaca, New York, lamented the loss of a sense of civic duty,
observing: 'When the naturally-equipped leaders of any society
decline to lead, then the door is open to the leadership of the unfit.
That is the history of human society. Dictators arise when the
intelligent people abdicate their role of guidance. There must be
a feeling of civic responsibility if the American dream is to come
true.'[14]

At a Flag Day ceremony in Williamsburg, Virginia, a speaker
observed that the colonial setting of Williamsburg should remind
the audience that 'certain concepts of the 18th century philosophy
in the Declaration are eternal. If the American dream is to become a
reality we must evaluate today in the light of our past', remembering
that the flag represents the 'spirit' of that American dream, namely
'Liberty and Justice for all'.[15]

None of these invocations presumed that the American dream
was supposed to have already come true. It was a national aspiration
to which ordinary Americans were renewing their commitment,
not a complaint that promissory notes had not been redeemed. If
the dream were to ever come true, it would be up to all Americans
to make it so.

Mark Schorer, who would later write the authoritative biography
of Sinclair Lewis, published his first book in 1935, a memoir of
growing up in Wisconsin. A review described what had gone wrong
in his small Midwestern town: 'having ignored the American dream,
[it] slowly proceeded to disintegrate spiritually as it advanced
materially, a process we are all familiar with in life and in novels
on the American Scene, as it used to be called'. The American
dream remained a shorthand for defending transcendent ideals
against materialism: focusing only on material advancement meant

'ignoring' the American dream, a choice that would inevitably lead
to spiritual disintegration.[16]

A school superintendent in Tucson, Arizona, spoke to a conference
of teachers on the difficulty of reconciling liberty with equality.
'The trouble is that the American Dream is double,' he explained,
as it was both 'conceived in liberty' and 'dedicated to equality'.[17]
The conflicts built into the American creed between freedom and
equality, between liberty and justice, were becoming clearer as the
nation grew and industrialised, and as more and more Americans,
including the disenfranchised, were insisting that the national value
system applied to them, too.

The popularity of the expression 'American dream' served to
focus national attention on the fact that principles of democracy were
often in direct conflict with corporate capitalism, a system which –
if unchecked – would reflexively tend towards authoritarianism and
plutocracy, in the shape of a powerful business elite.

A political science professor in Iowa predicted that the
'horoscope of the moment seems to point to the coming of a
dictator' in America, because 'if threatened with defeat' capitalism
would 'accept his rule', preferring a dictator who supported
Wall Street to a socialist who regulated it. The nation needed to
'stand firm in support of our American dream' to ensure that
'our democracy shall not fail'.[18] The association of the American
dream with democracy would only strengthen as the shadow of
totalitarianism spread across Europe.

That the problem was how to reconcile liberty with equality was
becoming clearer, but it was also exposing a growing rift over the
meanings of liberty itself. In Eugene, Oregon, a rotary club address
warned that Americans had 'come perilously close to wrecking our
National Dream. All because we have not seen the inner relationship
that exists between liberty and equality! We have worshiped at the
altar of liberty and at the expense of equality. The only possible
way to restore and recover the American Dream is to see again the
inherent value of equality in our social scheme of life.'[19]

It was not hard to see, argued a 1936 essay, that the principles of liberal democracy had been 'used obscenely by the patrioteers, and neither was it hard to see that they were fast becoming principles in name only. Yet they were not to be discarded lightly; they were not, if the future held a ray of hope, to be discarded at all. For they represented something more than personal liberty and freedom of speech. They represented all that was dynamic in the American dream, the vigor and eternal freshness of the democratic ideal.'[20]

Equality was not merely economic; it was political, too. This crucial understanding, shared by ordinary American citizens debating the meanings of their national value system, presages the shift that the 'American dream' would eventually take, as the citizens defining it gradually abandoned the language of equality in favour of the liberty that was meant to underwrite individual success. Increasingly, the only freedom that mattered in the post-war discourse of the American dream would be the freedom of free markets.

'Basis of Social Democracy is Destroyed' ran a headline in Baltimore that year. An economist and author had given a lecture arguing that 'industrial capitalism has destroyed the basis of the "American dream" of liberty, equality, and social democracy'.[21]

Today, many American political commentators regularly claim that the American dream is antithetical to social democracy. But as the phrase took hold of the national imagination, the American dream was all but synonymous with social democracy: it was authoritarianism, whether on the right or the left, that was antithetical to it.

* * *

The New Deal was starting to pull America out of depression by 1935. Unemployment had nearly halved, from 23 per cent to 14 per cent, while the GDP rose just as steeply, going up 11 per cent in one year, and bank failures had slowed to a trickle. Home ownership was growing, too.

In Pittsburgh, a small notice observed that the New Deal's
Federal Housing Administration, though barely a year old, was
'doing more to crystalize the American Dream of A HOME OF
ONE'S OWN than any provision yet made'. In 1935, the American
dream was just starting to be linked with home ownership, still
by no means a common association.[22] In 1936 Herbert Agar edited
What is America?: A New Declaration of Independence, which reacted
to the housing crisis by calling for state-sponsored guarantees to
home ownership. Without 'genuine property, genuine competition',
Americans would be better off with an economy planned for the
good of all, 'rather than a State planned by robber barons for the
good of one another'.[23] It was clear that risk had been socialised, but
profit remained privatised; without the moral hazard of capitalism,
there would be no morals in capitalism at all.

The idea that the American dream would be under threat if
capitalism were set above a moral economy was not limited to
progressives like Agar. In the spring and summer of 1936, former
President Herbert Hoover appealed to the American dream in
urging fellow Republicans to rally against Roosevelt's New Deal in
the upcoming election. Hoover's language anticipated the arguments
that Republican opponents to government welfare supports
would use for the best part of the next hundred years. Reporting
on Hoover's speech at the Republican National Convention, the
New York Times headline declared: 'Hoover Excoriates New Deal
as Fascism, Demanding a "Holy Crusade for Freedom"' of the
individual.[24] But a month earlier, Hoover also repudiated as 'fascist'
a nation in which 'big business' ran the country for individual profit.

The grim danger that confronts America is the destruction of
American freedom. We must fight again for a government
founded upon ordered individual liberty and opportunity that
was the American vision. If we lose, we will continue down this
new deal road to some sort of personal government based upon
collectivist theories. Under these ideas ours can become some

sort of Fascist government. In that case big business manages the country for its financial profit at the cost of human liberty. Or we can become some sort of Socialist state. In that case everybody gains as much as his greed for political power will bring him at the total loss of his liberty. I do not know whether Socialism or Fascism is the greater evil. I do know they are not the American dream. They have become the world's nightmare.'[25]

No one – not even a former Republican president who had written a book called *American Individualism* – was arguing that corporate plutocrats should run the country. 'Stateism' was a growing concern on the right, but conservatives also recognised that human liberty was threatened by big business, as well as by totalitarianism.

On the eve of his second election, at the end of October 1936, Roosevelt delivered a speech at Madison Square Garden, in which he declared open war on big business. 'We had to struggle with the old enemies of peace,' he said: 'business and financial monopoly, speculation, reckless banking, class antagonism, sectionalism, war profiteering.' The financial forces of America 'had begun to consider the government of the United States as a mere appendage to their own affairs'. But 'government by organized money is just as dangerous as government by organized mob'.[26]

Two years later, even *Fortune* magazine was making a similar argument to criticise both Republicans and Roosevelt's New Deal. The editorial roundly condemned the avarice enabled by previous Republican administrations. 'There is little that can be said for the previous practices of the republican party, which had consistently identified itself with the use of federal power for private enrichment,' it began.

But *Fortune* also objected to Roosevelt's 'reactionary restrictions and interferences, designed for the public benefit in the reiterated name of democracy, but falling like a shadow across the American dream'.[27] The line between liberty and regulation would continue to be contested.

The economy severely restricted again in 1937, falling back into recession. Perhaps relatedly, associations of the American dream with material plenty also began to reappear. At Franklin Roosevelt's second inauguration, in January 1937, he spoke of the return of national prosperity, famously telling the American people: 'the test of our progress is not whether we add more to the abundance of those who have much; it is whether we provide enough for those who have too little'.

Roosevelt's words reminded one reporter of the speeches about '"the abolition of poverty" and "two chickens in every pot" uttered by "Herbert the Unhappy" on the eve of the collapse of 1929. The words were similar because prosperity is still our national goal,' the journalist wearily remarked, 'material plenty still the American dream, the promised land of which we are striving.' Whatever idealists tried to maintain, 'no high dream of ardor, or spiritual experience, of intellectual achievement has yet become good politics in these United States'.[28]

Material insecurity was beginning to shake the nation's faith in the larger American dream, argued an Indiana editorial. Where once Americans trusted in self-determination, believing that whatever deprivations they faced were largely of their own making, the Depression had ended 'this comfortable conception'. As Americans realised that their prospects depended not only upon themselves, but also 'on forces which [they] cannot hope to understand or foresee', a different kind of insecurity was created, around national identity. The country had to make itself 'depression-proof, not only because we must save people from actual want, but because this feeling of uncertainty and doubt is clouding the American dream itself'.[29]

President Roosevelt urged Congress in 1937 to grant federal aid in order to 'save the American dream' of individual farm ownership, promising 'the American dream of the family-size farm', the earliest use of the phrase by a major political leader, and one that instantly associated the American dream with property ownership.[30] (Roosevelt would never use the phrase again in public speeches.)

It was the same year John Steinbeck published *Of Mice and Men*, in which migrant workers Lennie and George dream of owning their own farm, so they can 'live off the fatta the lan''. Steinbeck contrasts this pastoral dream of reclaiming the Edenic abundance of the American landscape against the tragic alienation of modern American life, the failure of the common man to achieve self-determination or self-sufficiency.

Of Mice and Men was the first of the novels now considered a classic examination of the 'American dream' that was written when the phrase was in widespread national use. But it is yet another American dream novel that never uses the words 'American dream' – indeed, it never uses the word 'dream'. Although associating the protagonists' desires with property ownership and prosperity, Steinbeck's story also connects their hopes to equality and collective social justice, the more prominent meanings of the 'American dream' at the time.

By the end of 1937, a syndicated editorial was writing of 'the American dream of "a home of one's own"', an association that – primarily thanks to Roosevelt's promise – suddenly burst into the national conversation, from Utah to Arkansas to Alabama.[31] A small feature in Reading, Pennsylvania, told its readers in 1938: 'For many years we have cherished the "American dream" of a home for every family – and a garden.'[32] The association of a white picket fence with the phrase 'American dream' was still some way off, however. (White picket fences were iconic enough: they just weren't connected to the 'American dream' until after the Second World War.)[33]

Horatio Alger and the success story, however, had at last arrived. A 1937 article on the Guggenheim brothers held that their story was 'the stuff of the American dream, a Horatio Alger story if there ever was one'.[34] Two years earlier, a widely reprinted *Fortune* magazine article on 'American Communism' had argued that 'the American dream of Poor Boy Makes Good' formed a bulwark against the rise of communism in America. It led 'even the most underpaid drudge to consider himself a potential millionaire. This makes it hard to arouse him to a Marxian class consciousness. The American proletarian, someone has wittily remarked, is a capitalist without money.'[35]

Not until 1943, however, does the *New York Times* seem to have put Horatio Alger and the American dream together – and ironically, it was in an article assuring its readers that the nation was 'getting back to the Horatio Alger feeling about the American Dream', although it was the first time the national paper of record had ever mentioned that feeling about it.[36]

Ideas of self-determination are never far from personal ambition; symbols of individual success like Horatio Alger and the presidency were increasingly coming into the orbit of the expression. 'The American "dream" that every boy has a chance to become President has vanished,' a Pennsylvania article reported, quoting an English author visiting the United States in 1937. 'Englishmen have long regarded the American idea that every boy may become a millionaire as a fundamental concept of your country,' he explained. But 'most Americans now believe such an idea far-fetched'.[37] (Not as far-fetched as a girl becoming president, clearly, as that idea wasn't even considered.)

By 1938, the idea of 'free enterprise' – itself a reframing of the increasingly discredited older notion of 'private enterprise' – was also becoming popularised, and joined forces with the 'American dream' to begin to shift the meanings of the phrase further. Debates on 'whether the American dream of unlimited progress for the individual is over' started springing up, although the idea of infinitely progressing personal success had not been very visibly associated with the American dream since 1914, when Lippmann argued that the nation's 'dream of endless progress' would need to be curbed, because it was just as foolish, and as dangerous, as dreams of a glorious past.[38]

But now instead of a foolish illusion, dreams of endless progress were being represented as central to the American dream even as the phrase captured the nation's imagination. The Secretary of Commerce gave a speech in early 1939, widely circulated, in which he stated that 'the preservation of our system of free enterprise is no longer simply the American dream; it is the American imperative. It is imperative that freedom of opportunity be maintained for all who can contribute to our national well-being.'[39]

The foundations for the American dream of endless individual progress through free enterprise were being laid; but they would not take hold until after the savage conflagration that was waiting just beyond the horizon.

* * *

Perhaps the one thing that has always remained consistent in appeals to the American dream is that it is supposed to apply to ordinary citizens from all walks of life – whether the dream of becoming president, or rich, or the dream of liberty or equality, or the dream of education or justice. The American dream returns to the discussion whenever the forces of inequality and oligarchy seem to be limiting the opportunities of ordinary Americans.

Throughout the 1930s, many of the debates revealed a tacit belief, widely shared, that the American dream relied upon regulating big business for the sake, not of consumers, but of small business. An editor in Hartford, Connecticut, insisted that it was the 'small businessmen', Americans 'with small properties and a heavy sense of democratic responsibility, that Jefferson and Jackson, the presidential models, had first in mind when they attempted in their various ways to realize the American Dream'. Returning to Theodore Roosevelt's progressive Republicanism, he argued: 'The nation cannot do without its big business, but it ought to realize that a nation consisting entirely of big businesses is a nation that will finally have to accept a high degree of planning and regimentation, whether by public or private agencies. If the nation wants to keep its democratic soul, it will have to see to it that the little businessman is kept alive, flourishing and kicking.'[40]

The prolific Herbert Agar published another book in 1938, *Pursuit of Happiness: The Story of American Democracy*. In its review, the *New York Times* highlighted Agar's attack on 'the poverty of rich nations'. There was a bitter irony to the fact that the inequality in America meant a widening gap between the average income and the mean income: the rich were so rich that they skewed the average. 'Our rich men are richer than those of any other nation. The proportion of our population that is really well off is larger than that of any other nation. And the proportion of our population which lives in want is so large that it should make us bow in shame.' Such inequality, the reviewer remarked, 'is clearly contrary to "the American Dream" promulgated by Jefferson'. For Agar, economic inequality was the inevitable consequence of 'the Hamiltonian partiality for commerce, industry, and high finance'. 'Very few' Americans, the reviewer added, 'will demur at his plea that vast fortunes are contrary to the spirit and intent of the wiser Fathers'.[41]

It's startling today to read an article in the nation's leading paper which assumes that 'very few' American readers would dispute the premise that the accumulation of vast fortunes is *contrary* to the American dream, that it is contrary to the spirit and intent of the Founding Fathers. But as we have seen, this was far from an idiosyncratic position, even if its claims about the founding fathers were largely mythical.

The point is that Americans across the political spectrum were still broadly agreeing in 1938 that inequality would destroy the American dream, because the American dream was of equality – both democratic and economic – which would measure collective, not individual, success. The dispute was about how best to achieve that equality.

* * *

Meanwhile, just as it had been conjured to fight the forces of imperialism during the First World War, so in the countdown to the Second did the American dream of democratic liberty quickly emerge as a way to articulate opposition to European fascism.

At the beginning of 1938, the *Los Angeles Times* urged Americans to be more vigilant in defending democracy. Liberal governments risk being too tolerant of the forces that seek to destroy them, it warned: 'liberty will destroy itself if it permits its enemies to assail it in the name of liberty'. Because most people spend little time analysing political events or studying history, democracy will always risk being shaped by voters' feelings rather than analysis. If feelings overruled reason, it could 'convert our country from the most advanced in the world to one of the most hysterical, irrational and backward nations in a short period of time'.

'We need a more aggressive democracy in this land,' the *LA Times* leader insisted. 'If our descendants are not to be deprived of their birthright; if the American dream is not to burst like a bubble', Americans must realise that 'liberty must be safeguarded. It was given us as a gift, but through fighting, and it can only be retained by fighting.' That fight would include teaching all Americans not merely to salute the flag, but to 'cherish the ideals symbolized by that flag'. Children should be 'instructed how to analyze propaganda', and helped to become better judges of character. 'They should be schooled in the causes and results of persecution.' Finally, the editorial warned in prescient terms:

Unless we rid ourselves of our sectionalism and political corruption, unless we bury our narrow hatreds and prejudices, unless labor and capital learn to get together for the good of all, unless we abolish poverty and insecurity and at the same time leave sufficient freedom for the individual to develop his abilities, unless we clamp down on the traitors within and build up our own power against the poisonous propaganda coming from without, America and her ideal of democracy will disappear from off the face of the earth.[42]

The American dream was a way to differentiate American democracy from totalitarian or authoritarian projects – and from the prejudice and racism that propelled fascism. Implicitly, the American dream was coming into conflict with some of the tenets that had long been associated with 'America first'.

'The best in the "American dream" is as broad as America itself,' asserted a 1938 Maryland paper. 'Americanism does not rest upon a narrow racial base.' The nation needed to appeal to 'the breadth and generosity in the American character, not to that which is bigoted and hateful'. Instead of defining itself as either 'anti-Communist' or 'anti-Fascist', the United States should protect democracy by 'remedying abuses and making liberty so fruitful in spiritual, intellectual, and economic wealth that Communism and Fascism alike will appear only as an impoverishment to all free men'.[43]

That autumn, a Philadelphian named Baruch Braunstein gave a speech called 'The Great American Dream – How Can Jews Strengthen It'. Raising money for 'an organization devoted to obtaining funds with which to settle Jewish refugees from Europe in Palestine', Dr Braunstein was interviewed about his thoughts on the plight of the Jews in Europe, and on anti-Semitism at home.

Braunstein saw 'unmistakable evidences of increased anti-Semitism' across the United States, and cautioned America against imagining 'that a form of Fascism here would be different from the European variety'. That would be 'madness, for it certainly can happen here'. That said, it didn't have to: 'The Great American Dream does not consist of wearing down the cultures of various racial groups to a common uniformity. The true democracy of Jefferson and the founders of this republic was based on the theory each single group has much to give out of its own special tradition and culture.' Pluralism was the answer, and it was an answer consistent with the American dream.

Braunstein urged American Jews to pursue 'alignment with the forces that make for peace, for equitable distribution of wealth and income, for political rights and freedom for all groups, and with all groups and forces that help strengthen the "Great American Dream" of a free and tolerant America'.[44]

An editorial from the *Christian Science Monitor* on the rise of the pro-Nazi German-American Bund (the former Friends of New Germany) was reprinted from South Dakota to Maryland. Joining forces with 'thirteen other nationalist forces', the Bund's platform, 'inspired by tenets of national socialism', consisted of 'Americanism' and 'anti-communism', as well as 'hostility to the Jews' at its forefront. 'Americans today are being confronted with many and varied organizations claiming to sell a brand of superior Americanism,' the editorial cautioned, but 'genuine Americanism does not include racial animosity and does not ground its action upon hatred and antagonism for groups'.[45]

To be sure, the editorial did not pause to admit that in the United States this principle, historically speaking, was clearer in the breach than in the observance; counter-arguments such as the Chinese Exclusion Act, or the history of elite institutions that disbarred Jews, let alone the highly conspicuous examples of slavery, segregation or the continued affliction of lynching, did not cross the editor's pen.

But the point is that ordinary Americans of all colours and creeds could see clearly, and were not afraid to admit, that the scourges of racism and anti-Semitism were fundamentally inimical to the American dream – and in 1938 the editor of the *Christian Science Monitor* was Roscoe Drummond, a Republican journalist who would later help found the democracy watchdog Freedom House.

Again, the ideal was being reaffirmed through what were less assertions than exhortations, to themselves, as much as to anyone else. 'Americanism does not rest upon a narrow racial base. The best in the "American dream" is as broad as humanity itself,' the editorial concluded.[46]

Even if it was a fantasy, it was a necessary fantasy, a national imaginary that was continually reconsecrating the principles of democratic equality as a creed, and making it ever more possible for the people excluded from the fantasy to assert their equal right to its principles. Broken promises may gradually defeat a civilisation, but it is only when it has no promises to offer that it dies.

Put another way, part of the eternal vigilance that is the price of
liberty includes a basic recognition of its fragility, and singularity.
Take a 'prayer' written by a sixteen-year-old Jewish refugee who had
arrived safely in America that was shared in an editorial reprinted
around the country. 'I am thankful I live in a country governed
by democracy rather than by force,' the letter began simply. 'I am
thankful I am happy and free.' The editors added a gloss to the
refugee's message.

> We forget to be thankful for the American dream – the American
> reality. And yet is anything more important to us than the
> American dream? If we lose that dream have we not lost everything
> most worthwhile? If we forget that long-held ideal of freedom
> and liberty, have we not forgotten that force which has built our
> country into a great country? If we abandon tolerance, which
> grants to others the same liberty of thought and expression that
> we reserve for ourselves, have we not betrayed our forefathers?[47]

The jump from the dream to the reality was not as unearned as
it might appear. Once more, words shape cultural reality; assert
the right to a dream often enough, and it persists through the
shared beliefs of the people who live by it. And collective liberty,
the item pointedly observed, does not survive without tolerance;

an ideology emphasising liberty alone might easily forget that
crucial qualification, especially in a country that so highly valued
individualism as a proxy for equality. Liberty requires tolerance of
others' liberties.

The 'American dream' was both a way to talk about how to
reconcile the problems of equality and liberty, and a way to avoid
doing so, by mixing freedom, equality and democracy together as if
they were synonymous. The 'American creed' had long been another,
as we have seen – and one 'small-town businessman' put them
together, writing a letter to his local paper that circulated around
the country in the final weeks of 1938, from Santa Cruz, California,

to tiny Hope, Arkansas (pop. 7,475). Patriotism was not mere 'blind loyalty', the anonymous businessman wrote. 'It was something that men have struggled hard for and died for unhesitatingly, something that has been worth all of the blood and tears and toil that went into the building of this nation.'

That intangible something had nothing to do with prosperity, which, crucially, was never mentioned (and would have been easy enough to identify, had it seemed important). It was, rather, the 'American's creed', which the writer had been taught in school – the very one that had been composed in 1918, popularised in the 1920s, and inculcated in citizens like this man, who invoked it twenty years later to enlist the American dream in the fight against fascism.

Any person who understood the American creed, and the American dream that represented it, he believed, 'will insist that today's problems be solved in such a way that those priceless elements in the American heritage are not destroyed or weakened'. The whole country was 'based on an understanding that there is something unspeakably precious wrapped up in the American dream'.[48]

And that precious, unspeakable something belonged to every single American citizen.

* * *

How to identify that unspeakable something began to present more and more of a problem, however. Was it social justice and equality, or was it liberty and opportunity? *Fortune* magazine published an influential editorial in the last weeks of 1938, which circulated around the country. Officially called 'Business-and-Government', its subtitle announced the essay's contention: 'The Essence of the American Dream is Liberty and Revolution'. Perhaps unsurprisingly, the version of the American dream favoured by a magazine called 'Fortune' emphasised individual opportunity, the 'American dream' as a way to encode personal success pushing its way more forcefully into the national argument.

But even *Fortune* was perfectly ready to admit the premise of government regulation – that was a given. The question was not whether, merely how much. Although the New Deal had done much good for the country, *Fortune* maintained that it was also overextending the state and risking the principles of liberty and individualism.

'The American Dream was the product of the great revolution in the Western world,' the editorial began. 'Liberty, to its creators, meant individual opportunity.' This 'libertarian revolution, epitomized in the American Dream, was a turning point in the history of man, an irreversible experience. With regard to it, all subsequent movements have been counter-revolutions' while 'any doctrine that advocates a return to institutionalism is a counter-revolutionary doctrine', namely, fascism or communism.[49] 'Libertarian', originally a theological word from the doctrine of free will, had very occasionally been used in an American political context since the turn of the century; by the late 1930s, as debates about freedom and free enterprise accelerated, it began to gain purchase.[50]

Fortune went on to argue that liberty – a 'highly particularized word' favoured by the framers – 'has been supplanted recently by the generalized word "democracy," a word that the founders used sparingly'. And then *Fortune* made its central claim clear: 'The concept of democracy, to be sure, was a component of the American Dream; but it was not the most important.' Democratic government was merely a means to the ultimate end, namely, 'the emancipation of the individual'.

'The spokesmen of the present Administration almost never mention liberty,' the *Fortune* editorial ended, criticising Roosevelt's New Deal. 'They talk democracy, and they talk as if democracy were the core of the American Dream' rather than liberty.[51]

The problem with *Fortune*'s assertion that the highly particularised word liberty was the core of the founders' American dream is the founding documents' highly particularised protections of slavery. The fact that those documents do enshrine both liberty and democratic equality (even if they sparingly use the word 'democracy') has been the basis for all claims to equal civil rights under the law, from the antebellum period to the present. But *Fortune* saw no contradiction in its assertion that American democracy was only created to support the emancipation of the individual, and its blindness to the need for regulations that would protect the equality of all those emancipated individuals.

As if that discordance weren't obvious enough, *Fortune* chose the word 'emancipation' to describe American liberty – the word most associated with the freedom of black Americans, used at a time when former slaves and their descendants were still so far from enjoying the full political or economic freedoms that emancipation was supposed to entail.

This essay was by no means the first, or only, moment in the national conversation during the 1930s when the meaning of liberty was contested. It is, rather, highly representative of the way the debate was unfolding. *Fortune* was bringing the libertarian fight to the forces of social democracy. The proper meaning of the 'American dream' became one of the cultural battlegrounds in that long struggle, one which isn't over yet.

That *Fortune*'s argument glorified liberty over principles of equality and social justice wasn't lost on the editorial's first readers, as a letter from Tennessee makes clear. 'The ideal of liberty is identified by *Fortune* with "the American Dream." And so it is,' the correspondent agreed. 'But if a threat to the Dream exists it arises not from any disaffection from the ideal of Liberty, but from a feeling of the inadequacy of our socio-economic system to supply the basic human needs.'[52] The question wasn't the value of liberty; it was how to survive it.

In moments of crisis, the tension among the ideas encompassed in the American creed has on occasion reached breaking point – and the combination of economic depression with the rise of totalitarianism certainly constituted a crisis. But it's also worth noting that although *Fortune* and the many American papers circulating its case were ready to fight in 1938 for the centrality of liberty to the American dream, not even *Fortune* was arguing that making a fortune was central to it.[53]

Moreover, the effort *Fortune* put into rebutting the idea that the 'American dream' meant democratic equality is just one of many examples affirming the traction that sense must have had at the time (or they wouldn't have put up such a fight against it). A speech in Cincinnati declared: 'Everywhere lip service is given to the American dream. This is not enough – to hate despotism is not to guarantee freedom – to be anti-Fascist is not equivalent to being pro-democratic.'

We can infer from such statements that the American dream was not only ubiquitous, but widely tantamount to supporting anti-fascist democracy. That speaker was urging Americans to do more to fight fascism than merely refer to the American dream as democracy, while *Fortune* was arguing that the American dream meant more than democracy; but if there was one thing they all agreed on, it was that the American dream signified democracy, and was opposed to autocracy.[54] And, increasingly, the American dream was accruing explanatory force.

From the American dream's inherent hostility to authoritarianism it was a short associative step to the question of racial equality that arguments like the *Fortune* editorial were so blatantly sidestepping. And once again, hindsight is not required to see this. For Memorial Day in 1939, a minister in Sheboygan, Wisconsin, delivered an address that suggests plenty of people recognised that racial equality and tolerance were always bound up in the principles of the American dream – just as they were in claims about the American creed stretching back to the nineteenth century and beyond.

The address, commemorating soldiers lost in battle – who represented all races, heritages and beliefs – began by noting that the military draft was one aspect of American life that had never discriminated against those who were not white Christians.

Thousands of Jews and Negroes have died to create this American dream, but they certainly cannot sleep. Not as long as we treat them as outlanders, close the doors of opportunity to their children, believe every unfounded and prejudiced story which discredits them. There are Americans whose dust lies in this cemetery – they came from England, Germany, France, and Holland, because they wanted religious tolerance, political liberty and economic opportunity. They do not want us here speaking about Americanism if we deny these distinctly American privileges to people because of color or race.

Americans needed to 'keep faith' with those who had died for the nation's ideals, the minister concluded, and promise that 'we will maintain the American ideals of liberty and justice' in order to support 'the defense and rich realization of the American dream'.[55] Ordinary citizens around the country, black and white alike, long recognised that universal principles of democratic equality and individual liberty were incompatible with racial and ethnic discrimination.

Thus two months after the Sheboygan minister gave his address a reader wrote to a St Louis paper to suggest that 'race prejudice' was one of America's greatest problems, but it could be solved by making the 'American dream of a nation in which men of all nations, creeds and denominations can live in peace and work for the common good' come true.[56]

The point is not merely that principles of social justice are far from recent inventions; it is, rather, the number of ordinary Americans who once viewed the 'American dream' specifically as an egalitarian principle that was fundamentally opposed to bigotry.

The friction between social justice and individual dreams was the subject of another classic 'American dream' novel that focuses on the dream as a betrayed promise that destroys the people who believe it, John Steinbeck's *The Grapes of the Wrath*. Published in March 1939, once again it is a book held to exemplify the phrase that never actually uses it; but this novel, like *The Great Gatsby*, also uses the symbolism of dreams to insinuate the idea into the reader's awareness. When the Joad family reluctantly decides to leave home and head west to the 'promised land' of California, Steinbeck describes the moment of departure in terms of the dream of America.

> They were afraid, now that the time had come – afraid in the same way Grampa was afraid. They saw the shed take shape against the light, and they saw the lanterns pale until they no longer cast their circles of yellow light. The stars went out, few by few, toward the west. And still the family stood about like dream walkers, their eyes focused panoramically, seeing no detail, but the whole dawn, the whole land, the whole texture of the country at once.[57]

Later, when the Joads join forces with other migrant families, Steinbeck reinforces the idea that they are being lured by a collective dream of hope and plenty in the west. 'In the evening a strange thing happened: the twenty families became one family, the children were the children of all. The loss of home became one loss, and the golden time in the West was one dream.'[58]

* * *

Two months before *The Grapes of Wrath* was published, as the march of European fascism grew too loud to ignore, the *New York Times* reviewed a book called *American Saga: The History and Literature of the American Dream of a Better Life*. The review opened by making an explicit allusion to the current political situation. 'It is no accident that Americans today are showing more interest in their own history and its meaning than at any previous time within the memory of the living,' the reviewer began. 'We are asking ourselves, as our ancestors did three-quarters of a century ago, what is meant by the American kind of democracy. We ask that question because we know that it is threatened,' he added. 'And we are now, beyond doubt, at one of our turning points, and should be acutely conscious of the pageant of history.'[59]

Ever Hear of the American Dream?

history show

hotme of someroll

equaity, greg..., and

future,

12

AMERICA FIRST 1935—1939:
It Can Happen Here

The American dream was grabbing hold of the national conversation, but although Big Bill Thompson's campaign had done much to bring 'America first' into disrepute, William Randolph Hearst and its other champions had no intention of relinquishing it without a fight.

On 29 January 1935, the Senate rejected a proposal that the United States join the Permanent Court of International Justice, otherwise known as the World Court, ambitions for which had long been referred to in the press as an 'American dream of international justice'. The Senate's vote was largely in response to a media campaign orchestrated by Hearst and Father Charles E. Coughlin, the influential and rabidly anti-Semitic spokesman for the 'Christian Front'. The fight against the World Court had begun hard on the heels of the attack on the League of Nations, and its final defeat, a full fifteen years later, was nearly as consequential. In particular, Midwestern isolationists were held to have ended the measure; its defeat was pronounced another triumph for 'America first'.

The *Brooklyn Daily Eagle* responded with acid sarcasm in an editorial headlined 'America First!' At last, the leader began, 'visionaries and "internationally-minded" folk' who had been trying 'to entangle us in foreign affairs' had been vanquished. 'We have been told a hundred times that this was a great victory for Americanism and that henceforth and forever we must put America first.'

The *Eagle* was ready, it promised; 'duly contrite', it would endeavour to get in line behind the new isolationism. Pledging itself 'from now on to work unceasingly for the upbuilding of America, leaving the rest of the world more or less to shift for itself', the editorial asked the prime question: 'In what way can this newspaper promote the America First doctrine?'

If the best way to contribute to a stronger, more prosperous international order was to protect America first, then it followed that 'we might contribute to this cause of a stronger, more prosperous America by doing what we can to advance the interests of Brooklyn. How can we best serve Brooklyn, now that we are done with internationalism and are determined to put America first?'

For a start, all the international shipping in New York would need to stop, so that Brooklynites were not forced to handle tainted foreign goods. This would save money, as neither a new subway system nor a new park on Jamaica Bay would now be required: once the international industries had disappeared, there would be plenty of room along the waterfront. That was fine, for clearly the docks, warehouses and factories that currently lined the harbour had no role in the new scheme of things; the government could also gradually phase out the Navy Yard, for 'ultimately as a hermit kingdom the United States will not need a navy'. As there was no need for international trade, they could focus domestic activities in the Middle West, which was now dictating the nation's interests.

'The task of making Brooklyn over so that this community will conform to the America First program will not be easy,' the column conceded. 'The Federal Government must help if Brooklyn is to reach the new patriotic heights.' It would have to build farm homesteads in the Midwest 'to accommodate the two million people from this neighborhood who will have to move into the interior or starve'. And to conserve money, they should probably 'put out the light on the Statue of Liberty'.[1]

Not everyone appreciated the '"smart aleck" editorial', it should be said – and several people did so, including one who usually liked the *Eagle*'s columns, and for whom that 'spleenful tirade [had] come therefore as a shock'.[2]

That the forces of 'America first' nativism were not going anywhere soon was made clear by letters such as the one sent to the *Pittsburgh Press* a month later. 'Being an American, I believe in America first and that it takes one generation of people to make a good American citizen.' Just the one was sufficient, evidently.

Therefore the correspondent was advocating 'a law that would require all public officials in any capacity whatever to be a native-born American. It certainly hurts to try and transact business in any department of the City and County and come in contact with people of a foreign accent [*sic*] telling us how to run our government.'[3] Nativism was nothing new, but by 1935 'America first' had become the most obvious way to express it – to the point of arguing that being born in the United States naturally made you a better person.

By August 1935, papers around the country were reporting that 5,000 members of the Friends of New Germany had gathered at Camp Siegfried, near Yaphank, Long Island, 'to renew their allegiance to the political and economic creed of Nazi Germany.' As part of the camp's 'summer festival', they marched with Swastikas mixed with American flags, giving the Nazi salute; photographs circulated around the country.[4]

* * *

That September, a month after announcing he would run for president, Senator Huey Long was assassinated by the son-in-law of a political opponent. Called 'America's first dictator' more than once, Long had worried many observers with his blend of populism and authoritarianism; after his death, profiles weighed his penchant for invoking the American dream against his predilection for American fascism.[5]

'His promise of a house, a car, a radio, as well as $5,000 a year for all families, with education for deserving young people thrown in, sounded in the ears of many like a new version of the American Dream,' noted one assessment soon after Long's death.

What Long's supporters did not at first see, the profile went on, was that ultimately he had chosen 'fascism of the most rigid sort' to solve the problems he had identified. That fascism was what Long had enabled 'was sharply revealed in the blaze of guns in the corridor of the Capitol the other night'. Although the spaces were dedicated to democratic principles, 'their spirit had fled'. Under Long, Louisiana's government had become so 'Balkanized' that for the young doctor who killed him, 'a Balkan solution' – i.e. assassination – seemed the only alternative.

This was the true 'menace of the Kingfish', the profile concluded, using Long's self-appointed nickname. His goal was not mere political gain. Instead, he was 'an ambitious demagogue', 'who knew how to capitalize the discontent' of various groups for his own advancement. Had Long lived, he might 'have created an American Fascism. The moral of his career is that the United States is not of itself proof against fascism', and unless democracy were safeguarded, fascism's 'head may rise again'.[6]

A biography of Long published a few weeks after his death was more succinct: 'Kingfish may be the Mississippi valley rendering of Il Duce'.[7]

Despite many Americans' assurance that 'it can't happen here', the rise of Huey Long had shown worried observers just how it could. It was so clear that at the end of 1935 Sinclair Lewis published a novel with exactly that title, inspired by the career of Huey Long (but written before his assassination), in which he imagined what American fascism would look like. The title was 'ironical', Lewis told reporters. 'I don't say fascism will happen here,' he added, 'only that it could.'[8]

It Can't Happen Here suggests that in America, fascism's most dangerous supporters would always be those 'who disowned the word "fascism" and preached enslavement to capitalism under the style of constitutional and traditional native American liberty'. American fascism would necessarily be shaped by capitalism – or, as

Lewis all too prophetically put it, 'government of the profits, by the profits, for the profits'.

A furious satire of the idea that American exceptionalism might insulate it from fascism, It Can't Happen Here was one of Lewis's most successful novels, attacking the 'funny therapeutics' of trying to 'cure the evils of democracy by the evils of fascism'. Senator Buzz Windrip, obviously modelled on Huey Long, runs for president on a populist campaign of traditional values, making simplistic promises about returning prosperity ('he advocated everyone's getting rich by just voting to be rich'). A newspaper editor issues futile warnings: 'People will think they're electing him to create more economic security. Then watch the Terror!'

Once in office, Windrip makes good his authoritarian threats, creating a private security force called the Minute Men and imprisoning his political enemies in 'concentration camps', as Hitler had been doing in Germany since 1933.

When President Windrip is informed that resistance is beginning to foment – 'bubbles from an almost boiling rebellion in the Middle West and Northwest, especially in Minnesota and the Dakotas, where agitators, some of them formerly of political influence, were demanding that their states secede … and form a cooperative (indeed almost Socialistic) commonwealth of their own' – he rails at his cabinet: 'You forget that I myself, personally, made a special radio address to that particular section of the country last week! And I got a wonderful reaction. The Middle Westerners are absolutely loyal to me. They appreciate what I've been trying to do!'

Windrip's administration agrees to 'hold all elements in the country together by that useful Patriotism which always appears upon threat of an outside attack', and so they immediately 'arrange to be insulted and menaced in a well-planned series of deplorable "incidents" on the Mexican border, and declare war on Mexico as soon as America showed that it was getting hot and patriotic enough'.

No longer did governments, Windrip's cabinet understands, have to 'merely let themselves slide into a war, thanking Providence for having provided a conflict as a febrifuge [remedy] against internal discontent'. Instead, 'in this age of deliberate, planned propaganda, a really modern government like theirs must figure out what brand of war they had to sell and plan the selling-campaign consciously', using modern advertising.

Windrip grows increasingly narcissistic, in love with his own cult of personality; he 'amuses' himself by shocking the country with his capricious, irresponsible acts. 'Was he not supreme, was he not semi-divine, like a Roman emperor? Could he not defy all the muddy mob that he ... had come to despise?'

A revolt begins – but then it stalls, because in America, 'which had so warmly praised itself for its "widespread popular free education," there had been so very little education, widespread, popular, free, or anything else, that most people did not know what they wanted – indeed knew about so few things to want at all'.

So they return to doing what Windrip tells them, and the novel ends with America's third dictatorship in place, a false war with Mexico, a state-run media in which every newspaper is called 'The Corporate', and the resistance made up primarily of old reporters.

* * *

In October 1935, the same month that Lewis's novel was published, another pro-Nazi rally was held at Madison Square Garden. Again, it garnered very little national coverage, most of which made it sound benign. 'German Ambassador to the United States criticized the Versailles Treaty,' reported the *Cincinnati Enquirer*, 'in an address tonight before 15,000 German-Americans celebrating German Day in a mass meeting at Madison Square Garden.'[9] And once again, photographs tell a rather more sinister story.

Sinclair Lewis and Dorothy Thompson had married in 1928; both his biographers and hers agree that his novel was primarily influenced by her circle's conversation about the situation in Europe. As Lewis began writing *It Can't Happen Here*, Thompson had just become the first American foreign correspondent to be ejected from Germany by Hitler, making her an international celebrity. 'Whatever else the

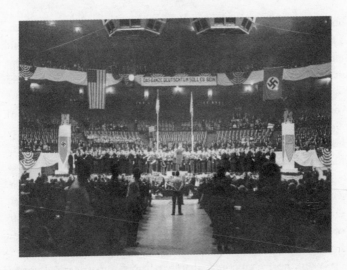

Hitler revolution may or may not be,' she wrote, 'it is an enormous mass flight from reality.'

In a letter, she commented that 'most discouraging of all is not only the defenselessness of the liberals but their incredible (to me) docility. There are no martyrs for the cause of democracy.'[10]

Thompson returned home from Europe raging and worried. Within months, Lewis had finished his anti-fascist satire and soon after that Thompson was given a nationally syndicated column: 'On the Record' began in March 1936, positioned in the *New York Herald Tribune* opposite Walter Lippmann's column, 'Today and Tomorrow', and it continued three times a week, for the next twenty-two years. Syndicated by more than 150 newspapers around the country, 'On the Record' was read by 10 million Americans; in the summer of 1936, Thompson was given her own national radio broadcast, which ran until 1938. By 1939, she had been named by *Time* magazine the second most influential woman in America, after Eleanor Roosevelt.

Two months after she began, in May 1936, Thompson published an 'On the Record' column titled 'It Can Happen Here', discussing the emergence of 'bands' of loosely organised fascists around America. A man from one group calling itself 'Christian Vigilantes' had sent her a letter sharing their 'motto': 'Please learn by heart: Christian Nordic white America will, in the spirit of Hitler, keep the Jews and Negroes in their place of Jim Crow inferiority.'[11]

Several of these extremist groups appeared to have banded together into 'a fantastic organization, running across state lines', Thompson explained, of self-proclaimed '"white male Protestants," pledged to "defend the United States and the Constitution"'. They were also determined 'to exterminate Anarchists, Communists, Catholics, Negroes, and Jews; to restrict immigration and deport all undesirable aliens; to support and participate in lynch law; to arm its members for civil war ... and eventually to establish a dictatorship in America'.

One of the organisation's members had summarily shot another (in a fit of impatience, he said, not in a dispute) and the homicide investigation had uncovered the existence of this shadowy, underground affiliation. This band of far-right hate groups making common cause didn't appear even to have a name.

'Whom do they hate?' Thompson asked. 'Life, which has treated them badly. Who is to blame? Some scapegoat is to blame. The Negroes working in the fields that should be theirs? Or the Jews? Do they not keep the prosperous shops? Or the Communists ... or the trade unionists ... Or the Catholics who have a Pope in Rome? Or the foreigners who take the jobs? These are to blame. Therefore exterminate them. We are poor and dispossessed. But we are white, Anglo-Saxon, Protestant. Our fathers founded this country. It belongs to us.' Protesting they were being replaced, they responded with violence.

These people, she noted, were 'the poor, the credulous, the violent; little men, full of confused hatred. They are gullible. The organization, they are told, dates back to Revolutionary days. It has 13 officers representing the 13 original colonies. They have a direct link with the Ku-Klux Klan and its old night riders.'

J. Edgar Hoover's FBI professed itself unable to pursue the group across state lines, while 'states reserve to themselves, under the Constitution, the right to lynch their own minorities'. Thompson concluded by declaring that everyone who listened 'tolerantly to intolerant expressions of racial prejudice, without registering our own indignation against such un-American ideas' was equally to blame. 'All of us who sit smugly by and think that It Can't Happen Here!'[12]

Three weeks earlier, the *Oakland Tribune* had reprinted a poem called 'America First', written by thirteen-year-old Elaine Erickson.

> America First in every American heart
> To do his share
> And to do his part;
> Every American should care
> For the right and not for wrong;
> As you go about your work,
> Sing your song –
> 'America First.'
>
> America First in your song
> But do not hold yourself high up
> And far above those not of your race,
> Think of them and with them sup.
> And help them in time of need.
> Do not be too full of greed.
> But down inside you think
> 'America First' with me.[13]

It's a startling final sentence, suggesting as it may that the poem is urging its readers to pay lip service to tolerance of other races, but all the while deep 'down inside you think "America First" with me' – as if by 1936, even children could see that 'America first' had become a code for secret racism.

In early 1936, James Waterman Wise, a popular author, lecturer and anti-fascist campaigner who was also the son of a nationally renowned rabbi, gave a series of talks on the probable characteristics of American fascism. At the John Reed Club in Indianapolis, he was reported to have included Father Coughlin in his description. (Father Coughlin delivered radio broadcasts that denounced 'Jewish bankers' and their cabbalistic control of world finance and media, ideas taken straight from the notoriously anti-Semitic forgery *The Protocols of the Elders of Zion*.) Both Coughlin and William Randolph Hearst, Wise held, represented a distinctly American fascism, which, when it appeared, would 'probably be "wrapped up in the American flag and heralded as a plea for liberty and preservation of the constitution"'.[14]

This famous image of a fascism camouflaged by the American flag ('When fascism comes to America it will be wrapped in the flag and carrying a cross') would later be widely attributed to Sinclair Lewis (and indeed to *It Can't Happen Here*) but Lewis never said it.

Instead, it probably came from Wise, who repeated the image in another lecture, from which he was quoted slightly differently: 'There is an America which needs fascism,' he said in this version. 'The America of power and wealth' depended on 'enslaving the masses' to endure. 'Do not look for them to raise aloft the swastika,' Wise warned, 'or to employ any of the popular forms of Fascism' from Europe. 'The various colored shirt orders – the whole haberdashery brigade who play upon sectional prejudice – are sowing the seeds of Fascism. It may appear in the so-called patriotic orders, such as the American Legion and the Daughters of the American Revolution' or 'it may come wrapped in a flag or a Hearst newspaper' – preaching 'America first'.[15]

The 'haberdashery brigade' was a reference not only to the Blackshirts of Mussolini and the Brownshirts of Hitler, but also to the so-called 'Silver Shirt Legion', which had been formed in 1933 by William Dudley Pelley in Asheville, North Carolina. The Silver Shirts were an avowedly white supremacist, anti-Semitic, paramilitary organisation, and by 1936 just one of many groups declaring support for a fascist regime in America. That year Pelley ran on the presidential ballot as a candidate for the 'Christian Party' in Washington State, while rumours that he had called for 'an American

Hitler and pogroms' were active enough to prompt the Hollywood
League Against Nazism, headed by popular Jewish comedian Eddie
Cantor, to send a telegram to President Roosevelt demanding an
investigation into Pelley's 'secret pro-Nazi organization'.[16]

It was just weeks after Wise's lectures that Fritz Kuhn, who had
fought in the Bavarian infantry in the First World War and become
an American citizen in 1934, formed the German-American Bund.
Within months, a 'Union Party' assembled to unite the right,
creating an affiliation of white supremacist fascist organisations.

Dorothy Thompson went after them all in the summer of 1936
in a two-part column called 'The Lunatic Fringe'. The Union Party
represented, Thompson charged, 'a nearer approach to a national
fascist tendency' than anything yet seen in America. 'The Union party
says America shall be self-contained and self-sustained', attacking
'the moneyed interests of Wall Street', as well as the '"reactionaries,
socialists, communists, and radicals," but they reserve their greatest
vituperation for advanced liberalism which they lump with socialism'.

Thompson was distinctly unimpressed by those conflating
liberalism with socialism. 'So', she remarked, 'did Mr. Hitler.'

Their followers, too, resembled the followers of Nazis: 'the
dispossessed and humiliated of the middle classes, bankrupt
farmers, cracker-box radicals, and the "respectable" but extremely
discontented provincials'.

And because of the group's opposition to all forms of socialism,
'powerful industrial and conservative interests would secretly
support them, and certainly tolerate them, in the hope of bringing
down a program like that of President Roosevelt', the New Deal's
social welfare system. Some conservatives and capitalists, she
warned, would make cynical alliances with fascism rather than
tolerate liberalism.

'The combination of monetary radicalism, plus hundred percentism
and hatred of so-called alien ideas, plus the belief in the capitalistic
system of production,' she went on, 'were all characteristic of the
Nazi movement before it came into power. And anti-socialist and

anti-liberal, scripture-quoting and anti-alien leadership, which makes its appeal not to the well-to-do, but to the discontented and indebted lower middle classes,' as well as to the 'incredibly numerous' 'so-called patriotic groups of Ku Klux Klan mentality'. Whether such a group could consolidate power would depend in part on whether a leader emerged who could catalyse these movements.

And it would depend, too, she added, 'on how enlightened American conservatives prove themselves to be', how willing they were to fight such a leader. If extremist groups formed on both the left and the right, as they had in nearly all European countries, 'and men who call themselves conservatives' began helping far-right groups in order to defeat liberals, 'then we will be well started on the road over which much of Europe has gone', namely, the road to fascism.[17]

In the follow-up column, 'The Lunatic Fringe II: "Saviors of Our Race and Culture"', Thompson listed dozens of anti-Semitic, pro-fascist fringe organisations in the United States, including not only the Silver Shirts, but also the 'Crusader White Shirts', the Black Legion, the 'World Alliance Against Jewish Aggressiveness', any number of 'Christian' organisations ('Loyal Aryan Christians', the 'Defenders of the Christian Faith') and the Ku Klux Klan, all busily circulating *The Protocols of the Elders of Zion* and denouncing Roosevelt as 'Rosenfeld'.

But because people on the far left 'stupidly reply in kind, and label everybody who does not agree with them "Fascists"', left and right had combined to make 'the very word "patriotic" anathema to any upright and generous mind'. Invoking Samuel Johnson's famous quip about patriotism, Thompson charged: 'It is time for patriots to insist that patriotism is not the last refuge of a scoundrel, nor the monopoly of the ignorant, prejudiced and fanatic.'[18]

While it is true that not all those who disagreed with the hard left were fascists, it is also true that there were Americans prepared to make common cause with fascism while insisting they weren't fascists, ready to 'tolerate' it, as Thompson had observed in her previous column, to achieve their own political ends. Fellow travellers don't have to be the ones doing the navigating to end up in the same place.

That year William Faulkner published *Absalom, Absalom!*, his great meditation on the processes of mythmaking and how they intersect with national history, a Homeric epic of America that shakes off dreams of moonlight and magnolia to reveal the Gothic nightmare underneath. The plot of *Absalom* is driven by the proposition that what had defined Southern history was the fact that poor white people gained self-respect and racial pride from their belief in their inherent superiority to black people. If that sense of racial superiority were ever threatened, the story recognised, they would erupt in violence.

Just a year earlier, W. E. B. Du Bois had similarly identified the 'psychological wage' of whiteness, the recognition that 'white laborers were convinced that the degradation of Negro labor was more fundamental than the uplift of white labor'. Race had functioned to divide and conquer the workers, endlessly deferring revolution. (Many would argue, following Du Bois, that the question of why socialism never took firm hold in America can be answered in one word: race.) Although white labourers remained poor, Du Bois added, they were 'compensated in part by a sort of public and psychological wage', the wage of racial superiority.[19]

The past isn't dead, Faulkner famously said. It isn't even the past.

Meanwhile, 'America First, Inc.' was making some more noise. *Time* magazine picked up a story that had first appeared in the radical magazine *New Masses*, reporting that America First, Inc.'s founder, James M. True, told a journalist (who was pretending to be a Republican) that he was planning a 'national Jew shoot' in September.[20] True also boasted that he had patented (under the category 'Amusement Devices and Games') a policeman's club, which he referred to as a 'Kike Killer', two examples of which were sitting on his desk. Since 'for a first-class massacre more than a truncheon is needed', True was practising for his 'September pogrom' by shooting at soap, as 'the consistency of soap approximates Jewish flesh'.[21]

The *Time* journalist's tone in reporting all this seemed rather flippant. Four days later the *Wisconsin Jewish Chronicle*, sounding considerably less amused, named 'America First, Inc.' one of the country's 'leading anti-Semitic organizations'.[22]

In February 1937, Roosevelt made what many consider the greatest political mistake of his career, trying to expand the Supreme Court in order to counter its continued hostility to many of his New Deal reforms. Widely denounced at the time as an assault on the principle of the separation of powers in US government, Roosevelt's attempt to 'pack' the Supreme Court was strongly opposed by even his own vice president.

Across the nation, editorials called the president a 'dictator'. Dorothy Thompson, often a sharp critic of Roosevelt, warned that this was just how a Hitler would come to America. After some desultory resistance, 'the American people, who are seldom interested in anything for more than two weeks, will begin to say, "Oh, let the president do what he likes. He's a good guy."' Unfortunately, 'no people ever recognize their dictator in advance. He never stands for election on the platform of dictatorship.'

'When Americans think of dictators they always think of some foreign model,' she added, but as all dictators claim to represent 'the national will', an American dictator would be 'one of the boys, and he will stand for everything traditionally American'. And the American people 'will greet him with one great big, universal, democratic, sheeplike bleat of "O.K., Chief! Fix it like you wanna, Chief!"'[23]

In July 1937, the Bund established Camp Nordland, in Andover, New Jersey, where Kuhn told an audience of 12,000 that the organisation stood 'for American principles, America for Americans'.[24] On 4 July, standing before a giant swastika, Kuhn addressed an audience of 10,000 at Camp Siegfried, Long Island, promising that the Bund, 'which professes to be 100 per cent American', would 'save America for white-Americans'.[25] Photographs were carried from coast to coast of 'Fuehrer Fritz Kuhn's uniformed "one hundred per cent Americans"', some 25,000 strong, saluting Nazi and American flags on Long Island and in New Jersey, provoking outcries around the country.[26]

IT LOOKS LIKE BERLIN OR ROME—BUT IT'S YAPHANK, LONG ISLAND!

25,000 German-Americans Join in Nazi Salute

Italian Fascists on Parade

The Nazi swastika and the Stars and Stripes—symbols of conflicting principles of government—were mingled in the "German Day" parade at Camp Siegfried, Yaphank, Long Island, N.Y, where 25,000 persons heard Hitler and the Nazi government praised and the CIO attacked as evidence of "growing radicalism" in the United States.

"Black Shirt" formations, in uniforms derived from Fascist Italy, appeared on Long Island when the Circolo Mario Morgantine, New York Black Shirt organization, was the guest of the "Amerika-Deutscher Bund."

When a senator from Alabama named Hugo Black was nominated for the Supreme Court in the summer of 1937, questions were raised about his prior associations with the Klan. The confirmation committee was urged to inquire 'into the facts and implications of Senator Black's endorsement by the Ku Klux Klan at an earlier period of his career; into his silence as a political leader in Alabama on the issues raised by the Scottsboro case; into his attitude during the Hoover Administration toward equality of relief between white and colored victims of unemployment; and, above all, into his reported threat to filibuster against anti-lynching legislation'.[27]

A month later, Black was easily confirmed as a Supreme Court Justice. Just after his confirmation, the *Pittsburgh Post-Gazette* ran a week-long exposé, disclosing Alabama Klan records showing Black had become a lifelong member in 1926. Locals 'talk of the great days when the Klan ruled Alabama and Hugo Black journeyed up and down the state preaching the glories of the Invisible Empire'. A local Klansmen spoke to reporters, declaring, 'I am proud to be known as a Klansman.' That immense pride notwithstanding, he asked the reporter to withhold his name, before explaining that everyone knew Black owed first his Senate seat, and then his seat on the bench, to the Klan.[28]

In October, Black gave a radio address admitting to having been a Klansman, but claimed that he had resigned and repudiated his membership, and had had nothing to do with the Klan as a senator. Editorials around the country exploded in response, denouncing Black's 'confession' as 'a mess of factitiousness and inconsistency'. The Baltimore *Evening Sun* observed that 'since Hugo L. Black was a Southern politician of the cheaper sort, it was almost inevitable that he should have joined the Ku Klux Klan'. But as 'the fact that it was a racket became more and more apparent', 'even the most backward politicians could see the writing on the wall and publicly denied any connection with it'. Black differed from these only because he 'didn't see fit either to admit membership or to denounce the objectives of the Klan until public pressure forced him to do so'. A Virginia leader was equally biting. 'His repudiation of the poisonous Klan philosophies now does not wipe out the unwholesome record of the silence that was broken only after public clamor had become so great that he was compelled to break it.'[29]

The *Pittsburgh Post-Gazette* remained firmly unconvinced, reporting the words Black used in accepting his Senate nomination before the Klan, whom he called at the time 'representatives of the real Anglo-Saxon sentiment that must and will control the destinies of the Stars and Stripes'. Regardless of whether he had repudiated his former values, the editorial protested, 'no man with that record ought ever to sit upon the highest court in the United States of America'.[30]

Dorothy Thompson wrote several furious columns denouncing Black's appointment; in one, she imagined Senator Black cross-examining Justice Black about his Klan associations.

SENATOR BLACK: Mr. Justice, why … did you join the Klan?
JUSTICE BLACK: I don't recall.
SENATOR BLACK: What part did the Klan play in electing you to the Senate?

JUSTICE BLACK: I don't recall …

SENATOR BLACK: Didn't you receive this membership card at
    a meeting of the Klan, and didn't you publicly acknowledge
    your indebtedness to the Klan for your election, and didn't
    you in receiving the card again indicate your solidarity with
    the principles of its members?

JUSTICE BLACK: I don't recall …[31]

But Thompson was equally enraged by Black's partisan defenders. Because he was a Democrat appointee, progressives were justifying his record. She excoriated 'so-called liberals' who would not only 'stoop to making an apology for the Klan, but actually to justify any kind of personal behavior, if it is politically expedient'. Such amoral rationalisations meant abandoning 'the ground upon which you can attack most of the evil in the world', from 'the third degree in American police stations, to concentration camps in Germany and wholesale executions in Russia'. Moreover, she warned: 'If political expediency alone is to be the guide of men's conduct, it follows that politicians in the future will be justified in using the Klan, or any similar organization, as an instrument of political power. Do the "liberals" want to be responsible for a revival of the Klan and all its kindred organizations, such as the Black Legion and the Nazi organizations, on this soil?'

The Klan had already been revived once, she noted, transforming itself in the 1920s into 'a money-making racket for the men at the top, playing upon the prejudices of the ignorant'. Now, thanks to Black's confirmation and liberals' decision to defend it, the Klan 'can, and will, say to thousands of the same kind of men who joined it before, that the President appointed Mr. Black to the Supreme Court because he was a Klansman, and that the administration is behind the Klan'.

The Klan, she pointed out, was also a firm believer in 'political expediency'.[32] The example set by political leaders had enormous consequences for the nation; cynical justifications for immoral behaviour would seep down and poison the political system.

A sardonic joke began circulating in Washington: Justice Black wouldn't have to buy a new robe when he joined the bench, they said. He could just dye his white one black.

* * *

Meanwhile, the German-American Bund was holding rallies and picnics on the West Coast, as well. In Los Angeles the *News of the World* ('A Journal in Defense of American Democracy') revealed that for German Day in 1937 fascists had gathered for a 'Nazi-run picnic' in what was then called Hindenburg Park, the site of more than one American Nazi rally in the 1930s.[33]

Books began appearing that explained German fascism to American readers. One called *The Spirit and Structure of German Fascism* chronicled 'the most impressive contemporary experiment in social retrogression, an experiment frequently described as "industry feudalism"'. Robert A. Brady argued that fascism was 'the last stand of capitalism against its own inherent destructive forces', the '"corporate state" a final effort to insure the continuance of profits'. This was accomplished by means of 'a reorientation of popular beliefs and ideals, a tremendous emotional wave of personal loyalty to the fascist leader, and the whole counterfeit system of "blood-and-soil" mysticism'.[34]

That autumn a South Carolina paper shared a striking image of a crowd watching a parade on the far Upper East Side of Manhattan. 'Some Cheer, Others Hold Noses as Nazis Parade,' read the headline, and a caption added further bite: 'Here is a view of some of the spectators who watched the parade of the German-American Bund, Nazi organization in America, in New York's Yorkville. Less than a thousand marched in the parade, after publicity given by the Bund had placed the figure at ten times that number. Note that some of the bystanders are giving the Nazi salute, while others are delivering the Bronx Heil, or razzberry. Maybe they just don't like Nazis?'[35]

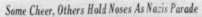

Some Cheer, Others Hold Noses As Nazis Parade

Here is a view of some of the spectators who watched the parade of the German-American Bund, Nazi organization in America, in New York's Yorkville. Less than a thousand marched in the parade, after publicity given by the Bund had placed the figure at ten times that number. Note that some of the by-standers are giving the Nazi salute, while others are delivering the Bronx Heil, or razzberry. Maybe they just don't like Nazis?
(Central Press)

Two months earlier, Roosevelt had given a press conference pledging to do everything possible to 'keep us out of war'; soon after, Hitler and Mussolini appeared together at a rally in Berlin. Their speeches were broadcast around the world, as Hitler affirmed 'the common ideals and interests inspiring Italy and Germany'. A week later, Roosevelt delivered his so-called 'Quarantine Speech', trying to shift America out of its determined isolationism, declaring that 'peace-loving nations must make a concerted effort to uphold laws and principles on which alone peace can rest secure', for fascism was creating 'a state of international anarchy and instability from which there is no escape through mere isolation or neutrality'. But Roosevelt's court-packing attempt had wasted nearly all of his political capital; Americans were listening to the isolationists, who insisted that FDR was trying for political reasons to force America into a foreign conflict.

In March 1938, the Nazis marched into Austria. A few weeks before the Anschluss, Thompson had written, in a column called 'Who Loves Liberty?': 'The very essence of American democracy is the protection of certain basic rights of individuals, groups and minorities against a majority of even 99 per cent.'

'Perhaps it is a personal prejudice,' she added, 'but I happen to dislike intensely "liberal" Fascists, reactionary Fascists, labor Fascists, industrial Fascists, Jewish Fascists, Catholic Fascists, and personal Fascists. When it comes to choosing the particular brand of Fascism, I'm not taking any.'[36]

America was certainly offering plenty to choose from. That spring, the *Brooklyn Daily Eagle* reported that William Dudley Pelley, head of the Silver Shirts, had recently painted 'an idyllic picture' of a meeting with James M. True, founder of 'America First!, Inc.', when they sat in 'comfortable chairs in the city of Washington, DC, and talked of many things that are good for the soul', such as their mutual determination to wipe out the Jews. True had 'a glint in his eye', Pelley rhapsodised, 'that means humor or battle, depending on your racial extraction, whether you're Gentile or Jew'.

As the *Daily Eagle* noted, True was 'not only anti-Semitic but anti-Roosevelt and anti-New Deal, pro-Japanese, pro-Nazi and pro-Fascist everywhere and even pro-Moslem [*sic*]'. According to 'the William Dudley Pelleys and the other native little American Hitlers', the journalist added, 'true Americanism' could only be 'based on distinctions of race, color, and religion. They talk, though guardedly, of "bloodshed" to bring these things into being. "Patriotism" consists of plotting, though ineffectually, for the overturn of the government.'[37]

Later that year, a Yale professor named Halford E. Luccock delivered a lecture, picked up by the *New York Times*, that gave voice to a sentiment increasingly expressed. 'When and if fascism comes to America it will not be labeled "made in Germany"; it will not be marked with a swastika; it will not even be called fascism; it will be called, of course, "Americanism."' He added: 'the high-sounding phrase "the American way" will be used by interested groups, intent on profit, to cover a multitude of sins against the American and Christian tradition, such sins as lawless violence, tear gas and shotguns, denial of civil liberties.'[38]

It wasn't a stretch – the simple fact, as we have seen, was that many Americans had long been associating 'pure Americanism' with bigotry, nativism, xenophobia and racial violence.

That autumn, reports grew of 'a "rising tide of anti-Semitism" in the United States', which seemed at least partly due to 'the large number of organizations in this country which agitate such sentiments and in part on the effects of "the situation in Europe"', noted the *New York Times*. Those prominent anti-Semitic organisations included 'America First, Inc.', along with 'American Aryan Folk', the 'American Gentile Protective Association' and 'American Fascists'.[39]

At the same time, William Randolph Hearst decided to put his considerable weight behind 'America first' once again, delivering a radio broadcast responding to Winston Churchill's request that the United States 'join forces with Europe's democracies'. Hearst insisted that 'America must not be drawn by unwarranted sentiment into the disasters of another foreign war'. The slogan 'America First Should Be Every American's Motto' now appeared on the masthead of all Hearst papers.[40]

That year the legal philosopher Jerome Frank published *Save America First: How to Make Our Democracy Work*, which was much in the news, arguing that isolationism was the only defence for American democracy and prosperity; to steer a course between communism and fascism, the 'profit system' of capitalism had to be saved.

Suddenly 'America first' was right back at the forefront of the national conversation, as Americans once more signed letters to their local papers 'America First', and editorials joined in, urging isolationism in its name. A Pennsylvania leader headed 'America First' endorsed the advice of an American Legion spokesman, who said 'that citizens of the United States would be "saps" if they embarked on a European war for the sake of England and France'.

The editorial wholeheartedly concurred: 'We have no place in these United States for Nazism, Fascism, or Communism. What we want, unadulterated by any foreign ideology, is Americanism.' Americans needed to 'guard the precious liberties we enjoy and improve our own lot while Europeans solve their own problems'.[41]

What they didn't do was acknowledge the rising threat of 'one hundred per cent American' fascism in the shape of the Bund and other self-proclaimed American fascist groups.

A South Dakota paper, also headlined an editorial in praise of 'America First': 'It is hardly short of axiomatic that our national interests will be made more secure if we maintain a program of serving America first ... It is practical sense to serve America first, and to keep out of foreign crises in which we are interested secondarily to our own security and well-being.'[42]

At a rally of the Bund in Queens in November 1938, Fritz Kuhn told his audience that Roosevelt's administration was offering not a New Deal, but a 'Jew Deal'. 'The Bund leader declared the American press and radio were controlled by Jews "who are trying to smash this country even as they tried to ruin Germany",' reported papers around America.[43]

That same day the American press also widely circulated a story about an inquiry being undertaken by 'the house committee investigating un-American activities' into the alarming increase in far-right, pro-fascist organisations. The chairman of the committee identified a long list of such groups, including 'America First, Inc.' in Washington, DC, as well as the 'American Aryan Folk Association' (Portland, Oregon), 'American Fascist Order of Black Shirts' (Atlanta), 'American Fascists' (Chattanooga, Tennessee), 'American Fascist Khaki Shirts of America' (Philadelphia), 'National Socialist Party' (New York), 'American Nationalists' (Washington, DC), 'American White Guard' (Los Angeles), 'Black Legion' (Detroit), 'Black Shirts' (Tacoma, Washington) and many others.[44]

On 30 September 1938, Neville Chamberlain signed the Munich Agreement trying to appease Hitler, who was so very appeased he promptly marched into Sudetenland and Czechoslovakia. Less than six weeks later, on the 'night of broken glass', Nazis and their sympathisers destroyed Jewish businesses, razed synagogues, arrested thousands and killed almost a hundred Jewish people. The excuse for Kristallnacht was the assassination of a German official in Paris by a young Jewish Pole, a refugee named Herschel Grynszpan.

Dorothy Thompson was outraged, writing passionate accounts of Grynszpan's desperation, describing the refugee crisis and raising money for his defence. In 'The Nature of "The Thing"', written a few days later, she warned America again. (Thompson was called an 'American Cassandra' more than once; she retorted that history always proved Cassandra correct.)

Part of the problem in the United States, Thompson observed, was that a certain type of 'industrialist leader' showed 'a natural subconscious affinity for what is presented to them as the concept of the Fascist state'. They were falling for what a later generation would call spin, which made fascism appear 'familiar and comfortable to them. It is – in the propaganda designed for industrialists – a large, efficient, monopolistic corporation, run by an efficient management.'[45]

European fascism was undeniably corporatist in certain respects, she explained: 'that is why Henry Ford likes Nazism, for which sympathy he has recently been decorated by the Nazi state. Nazism, in Mr. Ford's mind, is a Ford factory on a gigantic scale', one that 'has gotten rid of the "parasitic" Jews'.

But this airbrushed image of corporate fascism was a myth. In actuality Nazi leaders were not industrialists, but 'ruthless, third-rate, psychopathic, déclassé formerly unemployed intellectuals and soldiers'. Fascism whipped up mass support by 'a combination of propaganda and terror'. To do this it had to keep the masses 'aggressive – by working up continual internal and external enemies', posing as the people's 'defender against all the forces of privilege, against the richer nations and the richer classes'.

For democracy to defeat fascism, it would have to see clearly what it was fighting. It would need to create 'passionate solidarity for the things we all agree on'. And it would need to 'regard as treason any attempt to make one American detest another American on racial grounds'.[46]

Thompson was hardly the only fierce critic of fascism in the United States, of course. But thanks to her prominence, forcefulness and outspokenness, it is also true that for many Americans she was rapidly becoming the voice of the anti-fascist cause in the United States. 'It would scarcely be possible to exaggerate,' her biographer later observed, 'the extent to which she had become identified in the public mind with the struggle to preserve democracy.'[47]

* * *

In the first days of 1939, a flurry of reports appeared concerning Nazi intentions for the Bund. A story disclosing that 'German officials plan to create a "strictly American division" of the German-American bund' was reprinted around the country; the new division would entail the 'merger of a number of minor subversive forces' in America 'under the swastika leadership' of the Bund.[48] A separate item noting that 'about 25,000 persons are active members of the German-American bunds' was also widely reprinted on the same day, adding that 'about 100,000 persons are "willing to be seen" at public bund manifestations'.[49]

Throughout 1939, Dorothy Thompson continued to fulminate against the 'machine of Nazism', 'the strange rag-bag of nazi ideology'.[50] They were 'propagandists who have nothing even to propagate', 'revolutionists without a revolutionary idea; ideologists without an ideology'.[51] 'If Hitlerism spreads it is only because the peoples who already have all imaginable resources don't know what to do with them. They continue to cherish nationalism and to increase it, even as between each other, and to keep the world Balkanized as a matter of principle.'[52]

But Americans increasingly responded to a Balkanized world with cries of 'America first'. Letter writers insisted that the 'persecutions' in Europe were not America's problems: 'the sooner our American diplomats adopt the policy of "America First" the better off our grand country will be. It certainly doesn't make sense to me how any full blooded American can get riled up over the foreign persecutions.'[53]

Politicians once again began arguing that America should 'mind our own business and keep out of other peoples' troubles and other peoples' wars ... A sound "America First" foreign policy is the best of all defenses.'[54] Senator Rush Holt of West Virginia gave a radio address entitled 'Let's Look After America First': 'to become entangled in the controversies of foreign countries is a sure way to endanger our country'.[55]

On 20 February 1939, four days after Senator Holt's broadcast, the Bund held a rally of 20,000 supporters in Madison Square Garden, where they stood 'under the sign of the swastika to denounce "international Jewry," some members of the Roosevelt cabinet, and any American alliance with European democracies', as 'uniformed storm troopers marched intermittently inside the Garden'.[56]

A young Jewish hotel worker jumped on the stage to protest; he was beaten and kicked by Bund storm troopers before the New York police, on hand to maintain order, rescued him. The event was filmed and photographs circulated widely; large swastikas hung above the stage, while storm troopers in Nazi uniform (except for their white shirts) were lined up at attention in every aisle.

'Stop Jewish Domination of Christian Americans,' read one enormous banner, while papers reported that the stage was 'decorated with a gigantic picture of George Washington, standing between a mélange of American flags and Nazi swastikas'.[57]

Dorothy Thompson attended the rally to draw attention to it, loudly laughing and shouting 'Bunk!' and 'Stupid fools!' during the speeches (one of which jeered, as per, at 'President Franklin Rosenfeld').[58] When the Bund's storm troopers tried to remove her, she asserted her rights and promptly returned to the front row. Papers around the country shared with delight Thompson's 'eloquent rebuttal' of the fascist leaders' speeches: 'Bunk!'[59] (The *Chillicothe Gazette* declined to print the word 'bunk', primly reporting that she shouted 'nonsense!')[60] 'Dorothy Thompson in Gala Fight,' read one front-page headline, jokily comparing her

appearance to a prizefight.[61] 'Writer Given Rush by Nazis at Bund Meet,' reported another.[62]

Thompson responded directly to the Madison Square Garden rally in her next column. An open alliance had been formed, she explained, 'between the followers of Father Coughlin and the followers of Fritz Kuhn to abolish the American democracy'. Their alliance became plain at 'the meeting in the Madison Square Garden called by the German-American Bund under the slogan of "Free America"'. The previous day, Father Coughlin had distributed promotional materials and tickets for the rally at one of his own meetings. 'They enjoy the prerogatives of free speech, and with the instruments of democracy they intend to set up in this country a Fascist regime.'

'They do not, of course, call it Fascist,' she continued. 'Sinclair Lewis, when he wrote "It Can't Happen Here," foresaw with prophetic vision that when Fascism came to America it would present itself as "true Americanism."'

In the novel, she noted, Lewis had predicted 'almost exactly the meeting that was conducted in Madison Square Garden Monday night', at which there would be 'Storm Troopers' in place 'to deal with "unruly elements."Those unruly elements are you and I,' she added.

Thompson would continue to be defiantly unruly in her spirited defences of democracy. Sharing quotations from speeches on the night, she told her readers that one Lutheran minister from Philadelphia had 'admitted the movement was Fascist', when he informed his audience: 'There is no line to be drawn between democracy and fascism. It is between communism and fascism. There is no in-between.'[63] Democracy was not an option in the Bund's version of 'one hundred per cent Americanism'.

* * *

On 13 May 1939, the ocean liner *St. Louis* set sail from Hamburg, Germany, with 937 passengers on board. Nearly all of them were Jews fleeing the Holocaust; most were Germans; a few were stateless. They were en route to Havana, Cuba, hoping eventually to find safe harbour in the United States, where many of them had applied for entry visas. None of the passengers knew that, just as they sailed, Cuba had invalidated most of their landing certificates. Cuba would only allow twenty-eight passengers to disembark when they arrived on 27 May, twenty-two of whom were Jewish and already held US visas. The other six were Spanish and Cuban, and had entry papers. One passenger attempted to commit suicide and was hospitalised. The rest continued to hope for US visas.

But they did not receive American papers, and Cuba would not receive the refugees, ordering them to depart Cuban waters. With nowhere else to go, they set sail for Florida, and when they were near enough to see the lights of Miami passengers sent telegrams to the president, pleading with him to let them enter. Roosevelt did not respond. A State Department official sent a cable informing the refugees they would have to get on a waiting list with everyone else.

The 1924 Johnson–Reed anti-immigration laws were still in force, and the quotas for German immigrants had long been filled;

nor did Roosevelt's administration invoke the special measures necessary to override them. The *St. Louis* was forced to return to Europe, where eventually the refugees were distributed among Britain, France, Belgium and the Netherlands. Half survived the Holocaust; the other half perished.

The *St. Louis* was far from the only ship of Jewish refugees to be turned away from the Americas and forced to return to Europe, but it became the most infamous, symbolising the plight of so many stranded, imperilled people. In a grim little historical irony, twelve years after the *Spirit of St. Louis* had bridged the distance between the United States and Europe, the spirit of St Louis had become decidedly less unifying – a divisiveness that would soon be voiced by none other than the pilot of the *Spirit of St. Louis* himself, Charles Lindbergh, who was about to make his own isolationist views widely known.

Before Lindbergh spoke up, however, yet another callous spirit was evinced on behalf of St Louis. In August 1939, a letter was sent to the *St. Louis Star and Times* urging the US to turn away 20,000 refugee children in the name of 'America First': 'I agree with "American",' a previous correspondent, it began. 'How can we take care of 20,000 refugee children when we can't take care of our own poor and needy?'

Disputing another previous correspondent, the anonymous writer added: '"Humanitarian" says the United States was once known for its kindness and friendliness to refugees, which is true, but why shouldn't we help our own people first? Bringing in 20,000 refugees

> "Humanitarian" says the United States was once known for its kindness and friendliness to refugees. which is true, but why shouldn't we help our own people first? Bringing in 20,000 refugees to add to those who already have entered will only make it that much harder for our own children to get work later on.
>
> **AMERICA FIRST.**

to add to those who already have entered will only make it that much harder for our own children to get work later on. – America First.'[64]

'Uncle Sam was the goat for England and France in the last war,' wrote a citizen of Rochester, New York. 'Let England and France stand on their own feet and not hide behind the Stars and Stripes. America first, last, and always.'[65] A correspondent from Alabama had the virtue, at least, of honesty: '"America first" may sound selfish, but it is a pretty good slogan in a selfish world,' he contended; the justification was reprinted around the country.[66]

Editorials also conceded selfishness in order to extenuate it. 'We, too, think selfishly. We think: "America First!",' announced the *Miami News*, rejecting 'foreign entanglement'. 'America is civilization's rear guard, its reserve. It serves best by strengthening those whom a less happy fortune has placed in the battle front. Never again an army abroad! England stands for England first, France for France first. We strengthen England or France only if that serves America first. Don't be sentimental. America first!'[67]

By the end of the year, Congress had passed its fourth Neutrality Act since 1935. When the 1939 Neutrality Act was debated, isolationists once again argued that 'we of America owe a responsibility: to America first'.[68]

Observers began to point out that America first isolationism was difficult to distinguish from Hitler's German nationalism (just as comparisons between 'America first' and 'Deutschland über Alles' had noted twenty years earlier). A Hawaii editorial compared it to *Mein Kampf*, noting that Hitler had written: 'The National Socialist movement does not want to be the defender of other nations, but the champion Vorkaempfer of its own nation – this means that National Socialism is not the champion of the general idea of nationalism, or of some right belonging to other nations or races; it serves only its own nationalism and its own rights.' This echoed, stated the leader, 'to a degree, our own isolationists … It is quite outspoken in the slogan, "America First."'[69]

Increasingly, they also recognised the association of isolationism with the rise of pro-fascist organisations, many of which claimed 'America first' as their slogans. A Cincinnati editorial titled 'An Ugly Picture Unfolds', reprinted around the country, believed it 'genuinely disturbing' how many extreme right-wing organisations were gathering in the United States: 'the Bund, the Silver Shirts, the Knights of the White something-or-other, America First, Incorporated – these and many other rackets preying on ignorance and intolerance have ceased to be mere shell games designed to part yokels from their money. They have become an intrenched [sic] bloc serving the common end of destroying democracy and supplanting it with a tyranny which they will not call Fascism until it succeeds. All, of course, are "patriotic" and "Christian"!'[70]

On 1 September 1939, Hitler invaded Poland. Two days later, Britain and France declared war on Germany, and the Second World War commenced. Three days after war began in Europe, Dorothy Thompson let her exasperation sound in a radio broadcast. 'I think it is one of the most incredible stories in history, that a man could sit down and write in advance' – in *Mein Kampf* – 'exactly what he intended to do; and then, step by step, begin to put his plan into operation. And that the statesmen of the world should continue to say to themselves: "He doesn't really mean it! It doesn't make sense!"'[71]

13

AMERICA FIRST AND THE AMERICAN
DREAM 1939–1941:
Americans! Wake Up!

It was during the Second World War that the long-standing, implicit friction between the principles of 'America first' nativist isolationism, and the 'American dream' of tolerance and equality, finally ignited into open conflict. And they did so in part due to the intervention of Charles Lindbergh, spokesman for the most famous iteration of all the various America first movements, which would become known as the America First Committee.

Two weeks after Germany invaded Poland, Lindbergh delivered his first national radio broadcast. Over the next two years, in a series of speeches, essays and broadcasts, he urged the United States to stay out of the conflict. Instead of fighting in Europe, he argued, America should defend – and dominate – the Western Hemisphere.

After the kidnapping and murder of their infant son, Lindbergh and his wife Anne had fled the American media circus that ensued in 1935. While living in England and then in France, they travelled throughout Europe, including several trips to Germany at the invitation of the Nazis, to survey German air power. The transparency of Hitler's attempts to use Lindbergh to intimidate the United States was obvious to many, but not, apparently, to Lindbergh, who was duly impressed by his few, carefully staged – and, history would show, carefully misleading – visits. Lindbergh accepted the Distinguished Service Cross of the German Eagle from Hermann Goering, Hitler's second in command, in 1938.

Isolationism was one thing, accepting a Nazi medal quite another. The decision was widely denounced in the American press, which raised sharp questions about Lindbergh's loyalty, even accusing him directly of being a Nazi sympathiser. The 'charitable explanation', wrote an Alabama editorial in typical terms, would assume that Lindbergh was 'much embarrassed by the honor'. But 'it seemed like a betrayal of our own country's best European friends ... It was as if he had been going around Europe getting confidential knowledge of military aviation in the various countries and then using it for the benefit of the Nazis.' If Lindbergh had been 'misrepresented', the item added, 'he should take the trouble to explain publicly'.¹ He didn't.

A year later, as the blitzkrieg was exploding across Europe, Lindbergh began a series of radio broadcasts urging America not to take arms against Hitler, insisting that Nazi air power was overwhelming.

Lindbergh could envision only one rationale for joining a European conflict: to defend 'the white races' against 'foreign invasion'. In his first broadcast, he argued that America should stay out of the war because the 'white race' was not under threat. 'These wars in Europe are not wars in which our civilization is defending itself against some Asiatic intruder,' he maintained. 'There is no Genghis Khan or Zerzes marching against our Western nations. This is not a question of banding together to defend the White race against foreign invasion.' As this war was merely a fight between 'white races', America could leave two equal foes to battle it out.

A month later, Lindbergh repeated the logic, saying again that America's only obligation was to preserve 'the white race'. 'This is a war over the balance of power in Europe, a war brought about by the desire for strength on the part of Germany and the fear of strength on the part of England and France ... Our bond with Europe is a bond of race and not of political ideology ... It is the European race we must preserve ... If the white race is ever seriously threatened, it may then be time for us to take our part in its protection, to

fight side by side with the English, French, and Germans, but not
with one against the other for our mutual destruction.' Only 'racial'
allegiance mattered, not political principles or democratic values,
let alone sympathy with the victimised.

By 1939, Hitler's savage persecution of minority groups,
especially the Jews, was all but universally recognised. If few yet
realised the extent of the atrocities taking place at the concentration
camps, everyone was well aware of their existence; the Nazis had
been ceremoniously opening them since 1933. Reports of mass
arrests and deportations, vigilantism and torture, the murder of
wholesale groups of people, as on Kristallnacht only a year earlier,
were ubiquitous in the American press.

Take just a few, deliberately arbitrary, examples from 1938. That
autumn, two thousand people in Cincinnati gathered to 'protest
against the Hitler government's persecution of Jews', at which 'a
clergyman's unexpected demand that the United States break off all
trade relations with Nazi Germany drew tumultuous cheers'.[2] In a
Christmas review of the key events of 1938, the *Brooklyn Daily Eagle*
singled out 'Jews Persecution'. 'Hitler shocked the world with his
revolting treatment of the jews [*sic*] in Germany.'[3] The *Pittsburgh Press*
argued: 'The same class of reactionary financiers and industrialists
who are behind Hitler's barbaric persecution of Jews and Catholics
in Germany are at work in this country.'[4] In December the *Daily
Times* in Davenport, Iowa, commented on 'the outrage to humanity
of the Hitler government's treatment of the Jews … It has for some
time been plain that it was not "purity of blood" – the Hitler Aryan
myth – that dictated the oppression of Jews, but a plan to seize their
wealth to bolster a faltering national economy.'[5]

For months it seemed that everyone in the United States, with
the marked exception of Charles Lindbergh, had been talking
about Hitler's brutality towards the Jews. Lindbergh had not a
word of condemnation for Hitler's violence, insisting that there
was aggression on both sides, and both sides were simply bent on
preserving their own power. Indeed, he all but said in so many words

that as long as some 'white race' was left in undisputed dominion over Europe, he didn't much care which 'white race' it was.

In a widely syndicated article for *Reader's Digest* in November 1939, Lindbergh spelled out his views a little more clearly, although still veiled behind careful euphemisms. As a European war would 'reduce the strength and destroy the treasures of the White race', the West must unite against 'foreign races', 'turn from our quarrels and build our White ramparts again'. Lindbergh warned against 'our heritage' being 'engulfed in a limitless foreign sea' of 'Mongol and Persian and Moor', calling only for defence against 'either a Genghis Khan or the infiltration of inferior blood'. British, German, French and American should stand together, he insisted, and the implication was clear: if that meant submitting to German aggression, so be it.

Lindbergh's argument was markedly eugenicist, contending that white people must 'band together to preserve that most priceless possession, our inheritance of European blood', to 'guard ourselves against attack by foreign armies and dilution by foreign races'. In his diaries, Lindbergh was more explicit about which people he feared were doing the diluting. 'We must limit to a reasonable amount the Jewish influence,' he mused, to prevent the problems created when 'the Jewish percentage of total population becomes too high'.

The logic of the one-drop rule raised its ugly head once more, as people continued to dole out humanity to other people in percentages.

* * *

Although Lindbergh was not yet invoking 'America first' in the name of his isolationist arguments, plenty of other people were. 'This writer,' announced a citizen in Pennsylvania, 'believes that the inventions and gifts of our good old USA, and even the hated Germany, could match all of Britain's gifts and have plenty left over. I suppose this makes me a Fifth Columnist, for unfortunately those who are not Anglophiles and who think in terms of America First, Last, and Always, are called Nazis, etc., etc. Some day the real Fifth

Columnists will be smoked out and the American people may learn the truth … America First.'[6]

'Why not work for the reorganization of our high schools,' asked a letter writer in Ohio, 'and give our future generation a vocational college education free, instead of trying to send them over to Europe to be killed. – America First.'[7]

'Let's clean our own house of an increasing national debt, unemployment and thousands of sharecroppers, who are not much more than slaves, before we tell the rest of the world how to live,' suggested a reader in St Louis. 'Let's arm to the teeth and mind our business. – America First.'[8]

Three weeks into the European war, Dorothy Thompson responded to Lindbergh's first radio address by declaring that 'Lindbergh's inclination toward Fascism is well known to his friends', before adding: '"Pity, sentiment and personal sympathy" play a small part in his life. On the other hand he has a passion for mechanics and a tendency to judge the world and society purely from a technical and mechanical standpoint. The humanities, which are at the very center and core of the democratic idea, do not interest him, and he is completely indifferent to political philosophy.'[9] The implication was clear: Lindbergh was bound to find an affinity with what was already known as 'the Nazi machine'.

Walter Lippmann also spoke out against Lindbergh's broadcast in his column, condemning the 'deplorable' implication that the United States should dominate the Western hemisphere, and warning 'against the spread of such imperialist ideas in this country and the repercussions among all our neighbors in this hemisphere'.[10]

Even Eleanor Roosevelt jumped into the fray in her own nationally syndicated column. 'Mrs. Roosevelt Says He Has Nazi Tendencies,' read a Pennsylvania headline quoting her column, in which Mrs Roosevelt spoke of the great 'interest' aroused nationally by both Lippmann and Thompson, who 'sensed in Colonel Lindbergh's speech a sympathy with Nazi ideals which I thought existed but could not bring myself to believe was really there'.[11]

Many Americans found Lindbergh's arguments increasingly persuasive, however, while those sympathetic to business interests were often inclined to see in Nazism simply a hyper-efficient corporation, as Thompson had pointed out the previous year. (This was also how Nazis liked to view themselves, as Adolf Eichmann would notoriously make clear at his trial twenty years later, his complacent view of himself as a good company man prompting Hannah Arendt to identify 'the banality of evil'.)

After Lindbergh's first broadcast, acquaintances of Dorothy Thompson's with ties to Wall Street spoke up in favour of American neutrality, defending the corporate nature of fascism. She lost her temper, and was heard to shout, 'God damn it, they've discovered that Hitler is a good Republican!'[12]

Thompson went on to publish more than a dozen articles denouncing Lindbergh and the policies he represented – at least as many columns as he gave speeches and broadcasts. Just as she had become one of the most prominent voices arguing against fascism, so Lindbergh rapidly became the spokesman for American isolationism, and the battle was joined.

In January 1940, Thompson wrote a column attacking Father Coughlin's 'Christian Front' as fascist. Ten days later, in response to demands that she defend the charge, she drily noted that it was Fritz Kuhn who had named the Christian Front as a 'sympathetic' organisation cooperating with the Bund, along with the Christian Mobilizers, the Christian Crusaders, the Social Justice society, the Silver Shirt Legion of America and the Knights of the White Camellia. Many other fascist 'fellow travelers', she noted, were 'camouflaged under the names of "Christian" or "patriotic" or "American"'.[13]

The affinity between European fascism and American white nationalism was becoming ever clearer. In July 1940, a Confederate memorial in Danville, Virginia, was draped in a swastika, a recognition that they were equivalent symbols of intimidation and terror; both were on the side of white supremacy, like calling to like.[14]

Swastika Shows Up In Danville

Danville, Va., had a "whodunit" on its hands when this swastika was discovered hanging across the entrance of the public library, which as the last capitol of the Southern Confederacy, is a Confederate memorial.

'Government by agitator-led masses is not American democracy,' Thompson wrote that summer. It didn't matter whether a movement like 'America first' isolationism was widespread; that didn't make it right. 'The concept that there is some sacred wisdom inherent in majorities, however ignorant, is not American democracy,' she insisted, echoing, whether consciously or not, Walter Lippmann's criticism of what he called the American dream twenty-five years earlier.[15]

'Everywhere power has been divorced from responsibility,' she warned. 'We have been living for a generation on unearned increment, wasting and abusing the liberties which our ancestors won for us in blood; mortgaging our children's patrimony to pay today's bills, which are our own. Born in liberty, we have forgotten the stern fact of liberty – namely, that it involves the highest degree of personal and group responsibility. Freedom without responsibility means anarchy.

'We do not need to abandon democracy,' she ended, 'we need to go back to it – to go back to its moral and intellectual foundations and build on them again.'[16]

Seeking a way to distinguish those democratic foundations, ideas of ordered democracy and individual and collective responsibility for its liberties, the nation found an axiom ready to hand: the 'American dream' of democratic equality and justice.

For example, an extraordinary editorial from Louisville, Kentucky, in June 1940, shared around the country, began by announcing that Lindbergh's tacit acceptance of anti-Semitism was fundamentally opposed to the American dream, before it went on to indict American racism as well. 'Colonel Lindbergh is still worried about our meddling in Europe. He does not mention the ways in which Hitler's Europe meddles with us,' the item began. 'A wicked and deadly example is the Nazi promotion in our midst of anti-Semitism.'

Just as Hitler had explained outright in *Mein Kampf* that people who would reject a small lie as absurd will accept an enormous lie precisely because of its outrageousness ('They cannot believe possible so vast an impudence. Even after being enlightened they will long continue to doubt and waver, and will still believe there must be some truth behind it somewhere'), so, the editorial explained, Hitler had since taught the world 'a lesson even more sinister', namely, 'that a big crime will numb and bewilder the people who would fight against smaller iniquities'.[17]

The sheer scale of the atrocities in Europe was desensitising Americans to it, the writer charged: 'our minds close at the thought of half the Jews in Europe being crucified. If we could bear to face the enormous horror we would find in Nazi anti-Semitism the true symbol of totalitarian might.'[18] Chaos could perversely be used to normalise what once would have seemed outrageous, as it was difficult for ordinary citizens to know where to direct their resistance.

Although in retrospect some have defended Lindbergh and other America first isolationists on the basis that they could not have predicted the range and depth of Nazi savagery, this editorial alone shows that many Americans were quite aware, at least in broad terms, of the persecutions taking place under Hitler. A local editor in Louisville knew by the summer of 1940 that 'half the Jews in Europe' were 'being crucified', and clearly assumed that all his readers knew it, too. It required neither extraordinary insight nor hindsight to make this basic fact clear.

But the Louisville editorial was not finished with America. 'It is not an accident,' it went on, 'that every enemy of the American dream is an anti-Semite. Here is our Achilles heel. Whoever hates America and all she stands for has only to persuade us to this one villainy, and America is dead.'[19]

The American dream was of democratic justice, of equality under the law. The country made a promise to the world, and wrote it on the Statue of Liberty, the editorial observed. That promise had not been met. 'We have failed. We have failed miserably; but we have not yet denied the dream. Even with the Negro, where our failure has been most base, we still hope and we still slowly improve. Failure can be redeemed so long as it is not excused. There is no cause for despair until man boasts of his sin, and recommends it as a virtue,' it ended. 'Anti-Semitism is the entering wedge for racism. And racism once accepted, America becomes an impossibility.'[20]

What a nation should do once it was led by men who boasted of their sins and recommended them as virtues – apart from despair – the writer unfortunately did not reveal.

* * *

Although the Louisville editorial was surely one of the most prescient and trenchant appeals to the American dream as a corrective to America first bigotries, it was not the only one. A St Louis leader argued in similar terms (redeeming the spirit of St Louis) that the American dream was specifically an image of how to create a harmonious society, one that took into account injustice and the struggles of 'suppressed minorities' to create a government 'for the people' that did not divide groups in rancour against each other. The American republic would not survive 'through hysterical suppression of minorities', or 'reaction which can serve only to deepen group antagonism and class consciousness'. The nation needed instead to 'transform into present-day reality the ideals of the freedom and equality of men which are the heart of the American dream. If government of and by the people is not to perish from the earth, it must continue to function as government for the people.'[21]

A widely reprinted article called 'Intolerance in America' shared the warning of Louis Adamic, a celebrated immigrant writer, that intolerance would 'turn the American dream into a nightmare'. 'There is increasing anti-Semitism,' Adamic wrote. 'There is also a new scorn for aliens and for naturalized immigrants. The scorn includes even their American-born children. This sort of thing does not protect democracy and Americanism.' Instead, Americans were treating their hard-won democracy with complacency and disregard. 'The drive against our civil liberties and cherished ideals is given an entering wedge by our own neglect and abuse of them.'[22]

A Wisconsin editorial predicted that totalitarian regimes would find their greatest satisfaction in a divided America. In the vitriolic upcoming US election foreign powers would find malicious gratification. 'There is, in the present contest, the seed of just such division, and it is an evil thing. The campaign tends to blot out, if only for the moment, the essential unity of the American people.'

Americans were together, the editorial insisted, 'as we have not been for years, in our devotion to our free institutions, standing as they do mountain-high above any president, any administration'.

Presidents come and go, but Americans must be 'united in our determination to evolve a better social order, one that will come nearer to fulfilling the American dream of men and women free economically and politically to seek their individual destinies. Our unities are infinitely more compelling than our divisions.'[23]

'Now we must have teamwork of a sort that has never been necessary before,' an essay in *Harper's* magazine exhorted its readers.

> Hitler and his spokesmen say with contempt that we cannot get it and retain democracy; that the strong and competent will not work for and with the weak and incompetent. The strong and competent will decide, both for the present and for the future. If they withhold

the full measure of their energy and skill now or later, our American dream will be over. With armies and navies we can doubtless stop Hitler, but not Hitlerism; for in the long run there will be only one way to give him and his henchmen the lie: by making our democracy fulfill its promises of freedom and plenty for all.[24]

How to protect democracy from fascism in the long run – that was the question. But the American dream – still not fixed in its meanings – was not only used to support liberal democracy, although that seems to have been by far its most common meaning at the time. Its connotations could also lead to exceptionalist arguments on behalf of isolationism, as in a letter to the *Hartford Courant*: 'It would appear that the interventionist element is losing its enthusiasm for the crusade to propagate peace and democracy by means of bombs and is coming to the realization that here in America the American dream of a perfected democracy must finally be consummated.'[25]

Such reasoning led to rebuttals against isolationism that returned to the meaning of 'dream' as illusion. The *Minneapolis Star* retorted: 'The "great American dream" was a pipe-dream, if by the term is meant a unique aloofness in the world.' America could not be uniquely detached from a global world that was 'inextricably bound together through improved means of transportation and communication'. All nations, including America, 'must learn to live and share its life through co-operation. That we have partly failed so far is due partly to our own ineptitude and the failure of all peoples to understand the nature of twentieth century society.'[26]

A Pennsylvania editorial agreed that the American dream might once have been isolationist, but bluntly told the country to grow up. 'Isolation is part of the American dream,' it thought, because the vast majority of immigrants who had arrived since 1607 'came to get away from something', again associating isolationism with ideas of exceptionalism. But the United States could no longer 'achieve a destiny separate and unique in an interlaced world … if it ever could'.

Retreating into a 'dream of childhood' was as impossible for a nation as it was for a person. 'We are grown up now, and the world, from which we might have liked to withdraw, is on our doorstep. We must play our part in that world, and play it like free men and women.'[27]

Dorothy Thompson also used the 'American dream' more than once in her fight against fascism. In the summer of 1940, she proposed 'An American Platform', a credo for all Americans. The column was a composite of phrases from letters she had received from readers around the world. Its language echoed the pledges during the First World War to bring the American dream to Europe in the shape of democratic liberty, promising that all Americans would fight so that 'the American dream of freedom, of equality and of happiness may be realized by us and through us for mankind', throughout the world, appealing to the same logic that would drive American policies during the Cold War.[28]

A few months later, returning to the idea that Nazi corporatism was dangerously reflected in American corporate oligarchies, Thompson argued that the American dream was viscerally opposed to such systems. 'The concepts and values cultivated by monopolistic big business lead logically to the Nazi form of world order. The American dream rejects it with the spontaneity with which a healthy organism vomits poison.'[29] Not only did Thompson hold that the American dream had nothing to do with economic aspiration; she maintained that it was fundamentally allergic to corporate capitalism.

* * *

In April 1940, Hitler let fly the blitzkrieg, as his army stormed into Denmark and Norway. Within weeks, the Nazis had overpowered Holland and Belgium, invaded France, and trapped the British expeditionary forces and their French Allies at Dunkirk, in northern France. Western Europe had all but fallen, six months into the war. Only Britain stood.

In May 1940, Walter Lippmann, by now the most influential columnist in America, responded to the British evacuation at Dunkirk in a column called, simply and devastatingly, 'America First'.

With the Allied army and the British fleet both imperilled in northern France and Flanders, Lippmann warned, unless Hitler was stopped he would 'master' the Atlantic as well as Europe. 'Let no one delude himself and others into thinking that this is just another and more exciting chapter in the long debate of the past two years as to whether the United States should help the allies a little, a lot, or not at all ... The questions which we shall now have to decide will be forced upon us by the others – by the action of the Japanese and the Italians.'

It was time for American politicians to put partisan differences aside, Lippmann maintained, and unite to decide what was in the nation's best interest. 'If in such a moment as this we cannot count unhesitatingly upon our leaders to put the country above their party and to put their conscience above their ambitions and their prejudices, then all the defenses for which we may appropriate money will not defend America.'[30]

Even as Republican leaders were being urged to include an 'America first' isolationist plank in their platform for the 1940 national convention, an Oregon paper offered its readers a salutary little history lesson, listing five memorable events from 'Twenty Years Ago Today – June 9, 1920. (It was Tuesday)'. The first incident from 1920 was a Republican presidential candidate from Illinois who'd said: 'Let's end our own woes first, and then Europe's.' The third was a similar reminder: '"America First" is keynote of Republican convention. Sen. Lodge in first talk says "defeat of Woodrow Wilson dynasty, and all it stands for, transcends all other issues along with the restoration of fundamental ideals trampled on while war raged."'

The next noteworthy event from 1920 was 'New reichstag near in Germany'.[31] The 1920 German election had established the first Reichstag of the Weimar democracy, when the governing Weimar Coalition lost its parliamentary majority and a weak minority government was formed, paving the way for the rise of the far right, including the Nazi Party, in the 1924 elections. In other words, the apparently whimsical list of memorable events from 1920 was in fact sharply pointed, associating 'America first' historically with the rise of German fascism, and exposing their correlations.

Meanwhile Lindbergh kept making speeches, prompting responses such as a letter headlined 'Heil Lindbergh' in the Kansas *Iola Register*, as its author observed that the few cents the Nazi medal had cost Hitler to give Lindbergh was 'paying big dividends'. In his most recent broadcast, Lindbergh 'practically invited Hitler to take us over'. Americans had better start practising the Nazi salute, the correspondent recommended, and 'learning to say Heil Lindbergh correctly or we may find ourselves in one of the concentration camps that Lindbergh and the Bund are probably preparing right now'.[32]

It was not until the summer of 1940 that the America First Committee, which so many people now identify as the origin of the slogan 'America First', was actually established.[33] Originally started by students at Yale University as an anti-war movement, the coalition brought together pacifists, socialists and conscientious objectors with libertarians, nativists and fascists.

In September 1940, the unofficial student movement was taken up by far more powerful proponents in Chicago, quickly becoming America's primary non-interventionist organisation, categorically opposed to any American involvement in the European conflict. At its peak it had more than 800,000 members from across the political spectrum, including Walt Disney, Frank Lloyd Wright, E. E. Cummings, Lillian Gish and Henry Ford, as well as young students including Gore Vidal and Gerald Ford. Isolationism made for some very strange bedfellows, uniting left-wing socialists like Norman Thomas with reactionary industrialists like Colonel Robert R. McCormick, who owned the *Chicago Tribune* and was one of the AFC's founders. Sargent Shriver, the future director of the Peace Corps, and socialite Alice Roosevelt Longworth were rubbing shoulders with Father Coughlin; Democrat Senator Burton K. Wheeler joined along with Republican Senator Gerald P. Nye.

The number of industrialists on the board made many Americans ask precisely whose interests were being served; rumours that powerful Americans were financing Hitler began to circulate (and never died). In addition to Henry Ford, the committee's president was the head of Sears, Roebuck, the treasurer was vice president of the Central Republic Bank of Chicago, and the board included former members of the American Legion, itself long called a 'fascist' organisation by some. The anti-war sentiments of the students who founded it soon became abrogated by other motives and policies; Lindbergh, however, did not immediately join.

The AFC saw themselves as anti-imperialists, many equating the British Empire with Nazi Germany and the Japanese Empire in arguments that were all but indistinguishable from those made by the America Firsters of the First World War. That summer, Lindbergh had invoked the old 'foreign entanglements' shibboleth. 'We have by no means escaped the foreign entanglements and favoritisms that Washington warned us against when he passed the guidance of our nation's destiny to the hands of future generations … Our accusations of aggression and barbarism on the part of Germany, simply bring back echoes of hypocrisy and Versailles.'[34]

In December 1940, Dorothy Thompson took direct aim at the America First Committee. 'We are beginning to see a concerted move, backed by a great deal of money, supported by one section of the press and one section of congress, and assisted by a high-pressure advertising campaign,' she charged, with but one purpose: to 'collaborate for a Hitler peace'. They would claim that blocking supplies and aid to Britain was simply 'protecting America first', she warned, thus bringing about a Hitler victory with high-minded calls for armistice. 'The movement, already well under way, is "100 per cent American," and it follows to a "t" the line being promoted by the Nazi propaganda.'[35]

The America first movement was backed 'enthusiastically', she observed, by the German-American Bund. The 'Nazification of the United States', Thompson wrote, was also sought by 'personally ambitious' extremists, including Lawrence Dennis, author of *The*

Coming American Fascism, whose object was 'despotic power based on mass seduction'. 'First to be removed are the "articulate 10 per cent," and they are silenced by calumny, terrorization and economic pressure. The new elite of brain-trusters steps in to rationalize the new order as socialism for the masses, and security for the classes. Thus, if it ends, will end Jefferson's and Lincoln's dream.'[36]

Suddenly America was facing a world, Thompson noted, 'where tyranny is young again, and Democracy old'.[37]

In February 1941, she described what she saw as the blueprint of 'native fascism'. 'American Fascism, while preaching isolation from Europe, is designing a program of American imperialism which is a copy of Hitler's continental imperialism. The outlines of it are most clearly discernible in the speeches of Colonel Charles A. Lindbergh. It consists of giving Europe to Hitler and Asia to Japan and Russia, in return for a new Monroe Doctrine ... We are to be the Master Folk of the Western Hemisphere.'[38]

This idea made her remember, she said, something that Huey Long had once told her. 'American Fascism would never emerge as a Fascist but as a 100 per cent American movement; it would not duplicate the German method of coming to power but would only have to get the right President and Cabinet.' Moreover, Long had added, 'it would be quite unnecessary to suppress the press. A couple of powerful newspaper chains and two or three papers with practical monopolies of certain fields would go out to smear, calumniate and blackmail opponents into silence, and ruthlessly to eliminate competitors.' When American fascism came to power, 'it would be war on neighbors, war on liberals, war on racial minorities, militarism ...'[39]

All it would take was one powerful news organisation to support it.

That same month Thompson also responded to Henry Luce's influential column 'The American Century', in which he argued that the twentieth century would be either the American century or the Nazi century. Her rebuttal ended by castigating 'the floundering timidity that has cursed our policy ever since the last war. If we had been doing our part in the world this war would not have happened. Now we must do it or take a back seat in history. This will either be an American century or it will be the beginning of the decline and fall of the American dream.'[40]

A few weeks earlier, President Roosevelt had delivered a State of the Union address in which he called for 'a world founded upon four essential freedoms' that distilled the principles of democracy: freedom of speech, freedom of worship, freedom from want and freedom from fear. 'That is no vision of a distant millennium. It is a definite basis for a kind of world attainable in our own time and generation. That kind of world is the very antithesis of the so-called new order of tyranny which the dictators seek to create with the crash of a bomb.'

Within a few months, Roosevelt's four freedoms were converging with the American dream, as in a series of discussions at the University of Iowa that summer, which announced that their 'text' was the 'Four Freedoms', and began from the premise that 'democracy is now meeting its greatest challenge since 1776'. 'The University of Iowa's plan is to counter totalitarian attacks on the democratic philosophy' by analysing 'the so-called "American Dream" and what is meant by democracy in American terms'.[41] An organisation called the Council for Democracy took out advertisements that featured the US Capitol as the nation's 'symbol of democracy, power behind the powerhouse of freedom. Our American conscience, our American dream, our American devotion to the Four Freedoms.'[42]

Editorials responded to criticisms that it was 'impractical to spread the four freedoms about the world' by urging America to recognise that an ideal world was 'a world which needs our work', and 'the response to the need has quickened the old American dream of work ... We shall cherish the world's needs; it is the only way of filling our own.'[43]

The America First Committee declared that Roosevelt was seeking to impose the four freedoms by tyrannical force. Republican Senator Henrik Shipstead gave a radio address sponsored by the

AFC, in which he demanded: 'Does it seem sensible to depose dictators and impose upon foreign peoples, dictators according to our own liking, who will force the four freedoms upon their people who have never heard of the four freedoms?'[44]

* * *

Charles Lindbergh officially joined the America First Committee in April 1941, travelling around the country speaking before audiences of thousands, often in front of a symbolic picture of George Washington, as America First rapidly gained in strength and popularity.

Thompson responded instantly, and bluntly, to Lindbergh's joining the AFC in a column called 'Lindbergh and the Nazi Program'. Not pulling any punches, she announced: 'I think that Colonel Lindbergh is pro-Nazi. I think that he envisages America as part of Hitler's "new order" and himself as playing a leading role in the American end of that new order ... In the Chicago speech, which had the full support of the German-American alliance to the traitorous bund, he advocated a "treaty" with the dominant power of Europe, as the only way of securing peace.'[45]

That spring *Liberty* magazine reported that a nightclub song had recently gained popularity in Nazi Germany.

> Heil Lindbergh, Fuehrer of America
> Who will destroy plutocratic democracy,
> The Jews and Freemasonry
> In the United States.[46]

Maybe it scans better in German. Or maybe it was concocted. But regardless, the story circulated around the country, suggesting widespread unease at Lindbergh's apparent Nazi sympathies.

A week later, Thompson attacked Lindbergh's 'grotesque crusade' to persuade America to make a non-aggression pact with Germany, accusing him of collaborating by likening him to the complicitous leader of Nazi-occupied Norway. 'This is not Hitlerism, it is Quislingism,' she alleged, 'the last and most grotesque form of Fascism.'[47]

At such times, Thompson added, '"America first" takes on a really ominous significance — ominous, but somehow ridiculous'.[48] Many Americans agreed. 'Pathetic to see Lindy voicing views of Nazis,' read one letter to the *Pittsburgh Press*, 'delivering lurid speeches nicely calculated to further terrify the already craven-hearted America Firsters.'[49]

In practice, Thompson repeatedly wrote, at best America First meant appeasement; at worst, it was simply surrendering to fascism. 'Tell me what American pacifists, America First members, American communists, socialists, labor leaders, and anti-imperialists are saying today, and I can write you Hitler's speech for tomorrow. He knows that democracies can best be destroyed by democracy's own slogans. Their destruction is his sole aim and the sole purpose of his propaganda.'[50]

Although Thompson was certainly one of Lindbergh's most public critics, she was by no means the only prominent one. In a 1941 speech before the Jewish National Workers Alliance of America, Secretary of the Interior Harold Ickes called Lindbergh 'the No. 1 U.S. Nazi Fellow Traveler', saying baldly, 'he wants Germany to win … It would seem that he prefers fascism to democracy; that he is indifferent to liberty … and condones, if he does not actually applaud, the brutalities of which the Nazi ideology has already been guilty.' Refusing to call them the America First Committee, Ickes referred to them instead as 'the America Next committee', adding that they were all 'Nazi fellow travelers' and Hitler's 'dupes'.[51]

That summer a series of anti-isolationist cartoons were reprinted around the country, including several denouncing America First as Nazi sympathisers, drawn by Theodore Seuss Geisel, better known as Dr Seuss.

Although the *Chicago Tribune* supported the movement in its editorials, other papers condemned the AFC as 'the Fascist Front in America', listing some of the individuals associated with the movement, among them the various leaders of the Bund, the KKK, the Christian Front and Christian Mobilizer and the American Destiny Party, as well as Lawrence Dennis (Fascist 'theoretician').[52] 'All of these organizations are recognized to be pro-Nazi appeasement agencies which have united upon Lindbergh' as leader, wrote an Iowa paper; under the pretext of peace, they were joined in 'doing the work of Hitler in America'.[53]

They continued to be supported by Americans around the country, however, sending letters under the headings or signatures of 'America First'. 'America must come first! We positively cannot afford to fight Hitler on his own terms ... Is the question before us to save England and imperialism, or is it to save ourselves?'[54]

'Wake up, Americans, and fight for your rights!' pronounced one citizen signed 'An American'. 'Keep our money at home ... Look up the history of England and you'll find that she got her land by the same method Hitler is now getting his. I am for America first, and only for America.'[55] Another 'America First' correspondent warned that entering the war on the side of Great Britain would mean the United States would finish the war having become a British colony again.[56]

> I predict that, if we enter this war, we will return to Great Britain as her prodigal colony. I want this country to be a real democracy where the people can decide on war or peace, and do not relish becoming a dependency of Great Britain or Russia. AMERICA FIRST.

In May 1941, it had suddenly been announced that Sinclair Lewis had joined the America First Committee; by that point he and Dorothy Thompson had quietly separated.[57] According to Lewis's biographer, he was 'at that time vigorously opposed to American intervention in the European war and was quite cool toward Franklin D. Roosevelt, his sympathies with the America First people'. It may also have been more personally motivated; as their marriage was unravelling, Lewis was said to have vowed: 'If Dorothy comes out for war, I'll take Madison Square Garden and come out against war.'[58]

That spring Walter Lippmann, too, had spoken up once more against America first, with considerably less amusement than he had directed at Hearst seven years earlier. Lippmann forcefully argued that isolationism made no sense as a policy of appeasement, because isolation would leave America alone, either to fight or to surrender: 'surely it cannot be argued that standing alone in the last ditch against a world of enemies is a desirable situation, that it is anything but an appallingly dangerous one which a sane people will, while it still can, do all in its power to avert'.[59]

Unsurprisingly, the America First Committee also claimed the American dream, again uniting isolationism with exceptionalism. 'Americans! Wake Up!' the AFC exhorted in an advertisement, urging everyone to write to the president demanding America stay out of the war. 'In 1776 three million Americans dared to sign a Declaration of Independence, unsupported by any foreign navy, unafraid of any foreign economy. And the "American Dream" was born.' Americans must insist 'you *will not* out of fear countenance KILLING and SLAUGHTERING in "many and varied terrains" in the so-called "defense of this country"'.[60]

The argument was not universally accepted. 'What has happened to you, America First?' demanded an opposing advertisement taken out by Fight For Freedom, Inc., which called for 'immediate unrelenting action to crush Hitlerism'. 'You claim you are trying to think of America first, but can't you think a little more clearly?'[61]

As it became more evident that pro-fascist sympathies were aligning themselves with the supposedly pacifist AFC, Lindbergh was widely criticised for having 'rebuffed repeated efforts' to publicly reject the 'fascist elements' attached to the organisation.[62] A spokesman for the Veterans of Foreign Wars denounced the 'sinister support from Bundist, Fascist, and Silvershirt organizations', calling 'upon the America First Committee to purge itself of these treacherous elements'.[63] But they did not.

* * *

On 11 September 1941, Lindbergh travelled to Des Moines, Iowa. Although his appearance made the front page of the *Des Moines Register* that morning, he was not necessarily welcomed with open arms. 'His Most Appreciative Audience,' read the caption of a front-page cartoon depicting Lindbergh speaking to a rapturously applauding Hitler, Mussolini and Hirohito, while a small man in the corner labelled 'U.S. Public' grabs his hat and heads 'out', with an arrow showing the way.

In his Des Moines speech, Lindbergh claimed that it was in the best interests not only of the British but of the Jews to drag the US into the European conflict. Their interests were not America's interests, he insisted, while Jews' (supposed) control of the nation's media, films, businesses and government posed a threat to the country.

It is not difficult to understand why Jewish people desire the overthrow of Nazi Germany. The persecution they suffered in

Germany would be sufficient to make bitter enemies of any race. No person with a sense of the dignity of mankind can condone the persecution of the Jewish race in Germany. But no person of honesty and vision can look on their pro-war policy here today without seeing the dangers involved in such a policy both for us and for them. Instead of agitating for war, the Jewish groups in this country should be opposing it in every possible way, for they will be among the first to feel its consequences. Tolerance is a virtue that depends upon peace and strength. History shows that it cannot survive war and devastations. A few far-sighted Jewish people realize this and stand opposed to intervention. But the majority still do not. Their greatest dangers to this country lie in their large ownership and influence in our motion pictures, our press, our radio, and our government.

His language strongly recalled the argument made by Fritz Kuhn before the German-American Bund in 1938, when he complained that 'the American press and radio were controlled by Jews "who are trying to smash this country even as they tried to ruin Germany"', the old conspiracy theories of a Jewish cabal controlling global media and finance circulated in *The Protocols of the Elders of Zion* – which was also, of course, the pretext that had been offered by the Nazis.[64]

Father Coughlin had made similar claims about Jews' control of finance and media, but Lindbergh went too far. The dog whistle was too loud; codes don't work if what is supposed to be covert becomes overt. The Des Moines speech prompted a national outcry.

Iowa papers declared that Lindbergh's 'resort to racial and political prejudice' had brought forth 'unanimous protest from the press, the church and political leaders'.[65] The *Kansas City Journal* announced: 'Lindbergh's interest in Hitlerism is now thinly concealed.'[66] The *New York Herald Tribune* denounced the 'dark forces of prejudice and intolerance', especially the anti-Semitism, that the speech marshalled.[67] The *Chicago Herald Examiner* declared: 'the assertion that the Jews are pressing this country into war is unwise, unpatriotic and un-American',[68] while the *Omaha World Herald* deplored the speech's 'slimy weapons of hate and prejudice', which were 'as un-American as the swastika, as venomous as a rattlesnake'. 'The voice is the voice of Lindbergh,' wrote the *San Francisco Chronicle*, 'but the words are the words of Hitler.'[69]

In a widely reprinted editorial, *Liberty* magazine called Lindbergh 'the most dangerous man in America'. Revealing 'the sincerity of the witch burner', he had given anti-Semitism a platform, which until then 'was a back-alley business' in the US, led by 'shoddy little crooks and fanatics sending scurrilous circulars through the mails. There were many of them, it is true, but none was important.' Now Lindbergh had legitimised their views, issuing 'a summons to the pogrom'. Lindbergh was not only 'America's number one Nazi'; he was 'the forerunner of Hitler, ambassador of the Antichrist, Fuehrer of the forces of hell'.[70]

In response to the outrage, the AFC fanned the flames further by issuing a clumsy statement saying they deplored the 'injection' of 'race issues' into the debate over the war – but then claiming that the interventionists had done the injecting, not them, as if protesting against Lindbergh's anti-Semitism was what made anti-Semitism an issue.

The claim that there was intolerance on many sides provoked sarcastic outrage: it was like saying the war 'was started by Poland's treacherous assault on Germany'.[71]

In an editorial headlined 'The Un-American Way', the *New York Times* called the Des Moines speech 'completely un-American', demolishing the AFC's attempt to blame interventionists for 'the injection of the race issue' into the debate. Pointing out the racism inherent in this supposed defence by demanding 'whether a religious group whose members come from almost every civilized country and speak almost every Western language can be called a "race"', the *Times* then turned to Lindbergh's words and their 'clear echo' of 'Nazi propaganda in Germany'.[72]

Noting that the America First Committee's refusal to 'disown one syllable of these statements' meant that it 'associates itself with them', the editorial went on to argue that 'the most sinister aspect' of the speech was not its 'appeal to anti-Semitism, however obvious the intent to make that shameful appeal may be'. America would never condone anti-Semitism, it insisted. 'What is being attacked is the tolerance and brotherhood without which our liberties will not survive. What is being exposed to derision and contempt is Americanism itself.'[73]

As people called for Lindbergh's name to be removed from streets, bridges and his home town's water tower, even Hearst ran an editorial denouncing the speech, giving wide coverage throughout his papers to criticism of Lindbergh's words. 'Mr. Lindbergh has made an un-American speech,' the editorial concurred. 'The assertion that the Jews are pressing this country into war is unwise, unpatriotic, and un-American', while his claim that they controlled the media 'sounds exactly like things that Hitler said', it added.[74] Roosevelt's press secretary Stephen Early also publicly noted 'a striking similarity' between Lindbergh's speech and recent 'outpourings of Berlin'.[75]

Dorothy Thompson accused Lindbergh of trying to 'blackmail' Jewish Americans; others saw in his language a clear threat. William Allen White maintained it was 'moral treason', adding: 'Shame on you, Charles Lindbergh, for injecting the Nazi race issue into American politics.[76] The *Des Moines Register* called it 'a "smear" speech', 'so intemperate, so unfair, so dangerous in its implications' that it 'disqualifies [Lindbergh] for any pretensions of leadership of this republic in policy-making'.[77] The AFC stopped inviting Lindbergh to speak, and sought belatedly to distance themselves from him.

In November 1941, Thompson gave an outspoken interview to *Look* magazine, headlined 'What Lindbergh *Really* Wants', widely quoted from in the press. She was 'absolutely certain in [her] mind that Lindbergh is pro-Nazi', she stated; he intended to 'be President of the United States, with a new party along Nazi lines behind him'.

'Lindbergh thinks that America will enter the war, and he thinks that America will lose it. He will then emerge as the one who said "I told you so."' Pressed on how she knew this about him, she explained: 'I recognize the manner, the attitude, the behavior of the crowds, the nature of Lindbergh's following, the equivocal speech, the sentiments that are played to, the line of reasoning that is no reasoning. I knew from his very first speech, a speech that on the face of it was harmless, that in a few months he would come out openly against the Jews.'

He was the kind of person she had long predicted would seek 'the Nazification of America', although she hadn't known that person's identity. Whoever it was would be, as Lindbergh was, followed by 'rabidly disgruntled Republicans – especially industrialists – neglected politicians, frustrated socialists, Ku Klux Klanners – whether they call themselves Christian Mobilizers or what – and a number of neurotic women. He would preach the purification of American life and he would have a slight martyr complex. Most of his followers would be completely ignorant of his real program.'[78]

Lindbergh's followers revealed the true nature of his politics, she held. 'He has attracted to himself every outright Fascist sympathizer and agitator in the country.' The mere fact that the Klan supported him ought to give everyone pause, she maintained, noting that he was also supported by all the anti-Semitic groups of 'Jew-baiters' who styled themselves the 'Christian' this or that. Those were reason enough to discredit him.

'The whole crowd of them consider Lindbergh their leader,' Thompson said. 'They are his shock troops, and he has never made an unequivocal break with their ideas ... The whole setup is Hitlerian. These boys are violent. They use free speech to stir up violence.'[79]

It was a matter of understanding how to read fascism, she insisted. 'I know the handwriting. This man has a notion to be our Fuehrer.'

* * *

Two weeks later, on 7 December 1941, the Japanese bombed Pearl Harbor, and the United States entered the Second World War. Four days after that, the America First Committee officially disbanded and pledged its support to the American war effort.

Thompson responded to Pearl Harbor with a column not about Lindbergh or fascism but about the debasement of the American dream. The attack had happened, she believed, because America had contented itself for decades with a degraded ideal, a dream of just getting by. 'For a whole generation the American ideal has been to get as much as it could for as little effort,' she charged. 'For a whole generation the American motto has been, "I guess it's good enough."'

'We have admired success, and success has been measured in money ... The question has not been "How well is it done?" but "How much does it pay?" And mediocrity – in high places and low – has been the American dream ... to "get by with things," to make pleasure and leisure the aim of life, to indulge in fatuous optimism, to be certain that in some way "everything will turn out all right," and to run screaming after a scapegoat if it didn't.'

The American dream had become a sense of complacent entitlement, one that quickly turned resentful when easy promises weren't fulfilled.

Thompson urged her readers to remember 'the eternal American – the American who did not "buy" independence but wrenched it from fate with blood. The American who did not "sell" an idea but thought it and created it ... That American is still here, under all the lax habits, fretful under them, struggling through bonds of luxury toward greater cleanness and hardness. Had you forgotten, Americans, that luxury can be the worst bondage of all?'

It was no good just blaming the fascists, she concluded. 'I accuse us. I accuse the twentieth century American. I accuse me.'[80]

EPILOGUE 1945–2017:
Still America Firsting

The Second World War came to an end in the summer of 1945. In the summer of 1946, Fred C. Trump had a son named Donald. Seventy years later, he would become the forty-fifth president of the United States, promising in his campaign and inaugural speeches to put 'America first' because 'sadly, the American dream is dead'.

What happened to the American dream in the intervening seventy years would take many more volumes to recount properly – but volumes have been written. After the Second World War, the 'American dream' was retooled as shiny middle-class comfort and ease, a tale of upward social mobility and infinite generational progress – the 'fatuous optimism' Dorothy Thompson had railed against in her Pearl Harbor column, warning it would always demand a scapegoat when things went wrong.

'America first' had sunk rapidly into obscurity. Although there were a few half-hearted attempts to revive the motto – in 1942, one newspaper reported that a handful of people were 'Still America Firsting' – it seemed discredited beyond survival, as did the word 'isolationist', which became similarly disreputable.[1]

In 1947, the same year that the title of Walter Lippmann's eighteenth book made the 'Cold War' a household phrase, President Harry S. Truman delivered a speech at Baylor University in Waco, Texas – less than a mile from where Jesse Washington had been publicly burned to death a little over thirty years earlier. In it, Truman revised Roosevelt's four freedoms, speaking instead of three essential forms of freedom. Freedom of speech and religion remained, but Truman replaced the final two – freedom from want and fear – with a promise of 'freedom of enterprise'.

It was an alteration with profound symbolic consequence, as Truman insisted that the 'first two of these freedoms are related to the third'. Capitalism was being enshrined as an essential freedom, central to American concepts of democracy: American notions of freedom would never more be disentangled from free markets.

Substituting freedom of enterprise for freedom from want and fear meant replacing social democracy with capitalism, as historians have noted.[2] It was a rhetorical shift that reflected a cultural shift, as freedom of enterprise became intertwined with the American dream from that point forward. Ever since, freedom of enterprise has been viewed by virtually all Americans as a fundamental American right, the foundation of all other American freedoms. Truman did not single-handedly create that cultural shift, as this history has already shown – but his speech legitimised and codified it.

Roosevelt's establishment of 'freedom from fear' as a human right had been an attempt to end the 'fear economy' that Walter Lippmann had named as the product of unchecked capitalism. Replacing freedom from fear with freedom of enterprise effectively returned America to the fear economy, and it's been in charge ever since.

By the 1950s, the American dream had shrugged off all sense of moral disquiet, becoming a triumphalist patriotic assertion. The Cold War ensured that a new wave of internationalism and interventionism swept through American politics, becoming the norm. What Hearst and his followers had long feared did indeed shape American policy for decades: as the military-industrial complex took hold, America formed permanent – or, at least, enduring – alliances with Western Europe, and continued to wage war. The American dream of spreading the American way of life became the principle (or pretext, depending on your perspective) driving US foreign policy. With the coming of globalisation, a protectionist, isolationist America seemed even further away.

The American dream became a key rhetorical weapon in the Cold War, in which US post-war prosperity was held up, in quasi-Calvinist terms once more, as evidence that American society was morally superior, that its values led to security and comfort. Part of the internationalist campaign of soft power was the American dream as a vision of democracy upheld by individual consumerist prosperity.

* * *

As part of America's post-war recovery, the Federal Housing Administration offered loans to incentivise the development of housing projects. Developers were encouraged to keep neighbourhoods racially 'homogeneous', a code word we've seen many times before.[3] One of the investors taking advantage of the housing loans was Fred C. Trump, who began using federal funds to develop residences around the New York area.

The singer-songwriter Woody Guthrie lived in one of Fred Trump's Brooklyn housing projects for two years in the early 1950s. Guthrie was so outraged by what he saw as the overt racism of Trump's policies as a landlord that he wrote a song about 'Old Man Trump', who 'knows just how much racial hate / He stirred up'. In 'Trump's Tower … no black folks come to roam'.

Fred Trump was investigated in 1954 by a US Senate Committee for 'profiteering off public contracts' in his housing developments. Under oath, he admitted having 'wildly overstated the costs of a development to obtain a larger mortgage from the government'.[4] Some might call it fraud.

* * *

Throughout the 1950s, the cause of civil rights was gaining real legal and political traction. In 1955, Justice Hugo Black joined the unanimous Supreme Court decision in *Brown* v. *Board of Education*, the landmark civil rights case that declared the segregation of American schools unconstitutional. To the surprise of many, Black was in fact distinguishing himself as a remarkably liberal member of the bench.

In 1963, the American dream as it was first imagined – a dream of democratic and economic equality – was powerfully revived by Martin Luther King Jr, who invoked the American dream to suggest that it has never been extended to black people in the United States.

'I still have a dream,' King proclaimed at the March on Washington for Jobs and Freedom. 'It is a dream deeply rooted in the American dream. I have a dream that one day this nation will rise up and live out the true meaning of its creed: "We hold these truths to be self-evident, that all men are created equal."' It is something of a truism among civil rights historians that King's 'dream' was a 'subversive', even 'prophetic' repurposing of the Founding Fathers' ideas in connecting civil rights to the nation's founding promises of democratic equality, a promise from which the framers had specifically excluded black Americans. (King could 'see things the rest of the nation [couldn't] make out', as one expert on King told the *Huffington Post* in 2013.)[5] But whether King was aware of it or not, he was in fact far from the first to suggest that the 'American dream' of equality had a principle of civil rights built into it, as we have seen. While no one would deny the force and influence of King's vision, it was not unique to him.

The Second Klan had disbanded in 1944, but the civil rights movement of the 1960s provoked a white supremacist backlash: local Klans re-formed across the South, inflicting violence against black and white activists alike. In 1965, President Lyndon B. Johnson publicly condemned the Klan, the same year that the Johnson–Reed Act of 1924 was finally reversed by the Immigration Act of 1965, as part of the domestic programme of liberal civil reform known as Johnson's Great Society.

Through the 1960s and 70s, 'America first' remained a slogan of the underground Klan, emblazoned on insignia such as a commemorative coin struck in 1965.[6]

The American fascist movement reared its ugly head again as well, primarily in the form of George Lincoln Rockwell's American Nazi Party, which grabbed some headlines between its founding in 1958 and Rockwell's assassination by a disgruntled member of a splinter group in 1967. The National States' Rights Party was also established in 1958, which opposed racial integration in the South using Nazi slogans and insignias. The affinity between fascists and the Klan remained clear.

Fred Trump handed the management of his property development business to his son Donald in 1973. That year the US Department of Justice sued Trump Management for racial discrimination: by 1967, New York State investigators had established that of approximately 3,700 apartments in Coney Island's Trump Village, just seven were rented to African-Americans. Complaining that the government was trying to force him to rent to 'welfare recipients', Donald countersued for defamation, hiring Roy Cohn, Joseph McCarthy's lawyer, to represent him. He ultimately signed a consent decree, with pages of stipulations designed to ensure the desegregation of Trump properties. In 1978, the Trumps were accused of violating the consent decree, and continuing their racially discriminatory policies.

In the 1970s, a Klansman named David Duke campaigned for senator in Louisiana; he would run for president in 1988. He had joined the Klan in 1967, and as a student at Louisiana State University had established a neo-Nazi group called the White Youth Alliance, which was associated with the American Nazi Party. In 1974, Duke founded the Knights of the Ku Klux Klan.

In 1989, five young black men were wrongfully convicted of raping a white woman in Central Park, New York. Donald Trump took out signed full-page advertisements in four of the city's newspapers calling for the death penalty. Thirteen years after their convictions another man confessed to the crime; DNA confirmed his guilt, and the convictions were vacated. Far from apologising, Trump wrote an opinion piece for the *New York Daily News* calling the acquittal of the Central Park Five 'the heist of the century'.

* * *

'America first' suddenly returned to the headlines in 1992, thanks to the presidential campaign of Pat Buchanan, widely recognised as representing the values of the paleo-conservatives of the early twentieth century. He announced his candidacy with a speech declaring that America must not lose its 'sovereignty' in response to the economic challenges 'presented by the rise of a European super state'. Calling for 'a new patriotism' and 'a new nationalism', he promised to 'put the needs of Americans first'.

Buchanan's opponents 'would put America's wealth and power at the service of some vague New World Order', he charged. 'We will put America first.' Buchanan's campaign was unsuccessful, his xenophobic platform generally viewed as having backfired and ultimately benefitting Bill Clinton's candidacy.

In October 1999, Buchanan announced he would run on a newly created 'Reform Party' ticket in the 2000 presidential campaign, and Donald Trump declared his intention to challenge Buchanan for the Reform Party nomination.

'I really believe the Republicans are just too crazy right,' Trump said, explaining why he was withdrawing his Republican registration. He went on to call Buchanan 'a Hitler lover'. 'I guess he's an anti-Semite,' Trump added. 'He doesn't like the blacks. He doesn't like the gays … It's just incredible that anybody could embrace this guy.' But then, Trump observed, it was obvious that Buchanan was going after the 'really staunch right wacko vote'.[7]

In the end, Trump didn't run, and in 2000 he left the Reform Party, issuing a statement that said: 'The Reform Party now includes a Klansman, Mr. Duke, a neo-Nazi, Mr. Buchanan, and a communist, Ms. [Lenora] Fulani. This is not company I wish to keep.'[8] A spokesman for the Reform Party responded that Trump was merely a 'hustler' who had pretended to have political aspirations to promote a book: it was all just 'a serious hustle of the media'.[9] A few days later Trump repeated the rejection. 'Well, you've got David Duke just joined – a bigot, a racist, a problem. I mean, this is not exactly the people you want in your party.'[10] It was ten years after a *Vanity Fair* profile had revealed that Trump kept a collection of Hitler's speeches in his office.

Sixteen years later, Trump launched his campaign as a Republican nominee. 'I'm not an isolationist,' he announced on the campaign trail in 2016, 'but I am '"America First,"' he said. 'So I like the expression. I'm "America First."'[11]

The phrase was taken up by his supporters, many of whom were most likely unaware of its history.

But not all of them were. In February 2016, David Duke said he supported Donald Trump for president of the United States. 'I'm overjoyed to see Donald Trump and most Americans embrace most of the issues that I've championed for years. My slogan remains America first.'[12]

Asked to disavow Duke's support, Trump said: 'David Duke endorsed me? Okay, all right. I disavow, okay?'[13] Two days later, pressed to repudiate Duke more forcefully, he tried to sidestep. 'I would disavow if I thought there was something wrong ... But you may have groups in there that are totally fine, and it would be very unfair. So, give me a list of the groups, and I will let you know.' Told that the only people in question were the Ku Klux Klan and David Duke, he responded: 'I don't know David Duke. I don't believe I have ever met him ... And I just don't know anything about him.'[14]

Trump's non-committal replies cost him neither the nomination nor the election.

* * *

If history is to the nation as memory is to the individual, Arthur Schlesinger Jr once observed, then all history is contemporary history.

In August 2017, seven months into Trump's presidency, American fascists staged a rally in Charlottesville, Virginia. Many American citizens who were outraged at the sudden upsurge of so-called 'alt-right' fascism under Trump went to protest. When a car ploughed into anti-fascist protesters, nineteen were injured and one, Heather Heyer, was murdered.

In the following days, Trump declined to condemn unreservedly either the alt-right rally or the fascist attack on peaceful protesters. It came as a shock to many observers that the Klan and neo-Nazis could stage a march in modern America, shouting, 'Jews will not replace us.' It came as an even bigger shock to them that Trump refused to denounce extreme right-wing violence, issuing instead a boilerplate condemnation of 'hate from many sides' that was clearly calculated to suggest that the protesters – the ones there to object to fascism and white supremacy – were also 'haters'. Trump claimed there were 'many fine' people on both sides, when one side was made up entirely of neo-Nazis, Klansmen and white nationalists.

'Alternative right' had been adopted as an early-twenty-first-century euphemism, rebranding 'neo-Nazi' in more socially acceptable terms. The Unite the Right movement in Charlottesville insisted they were not Nazis, all the while shouting bona fide Nazi slogans like 'Blood and Soil'. As Dorothy Thompson warned, no one ever forms the Dictator Party.

The alt-right movement had joined forces with a loose faction of other far-right groups, including conspiracy-minded libertarians who feared the rise of an internationalist new world order run by a shadowy cabal of powerful elites (who may or may not be Jewish); armed militias who cast themselves as freedom fighters against an oppressive (usually socialist) state; the Tea Party movement and its most prominent spokesperson, Sarah Palin; the right-wing politicians and pundits who deliberately stoked post-9/11 xenophobic fears of Muslim terrorism and the rise of Islamic State; and evangelicals who had, with increasing success, driven what had recently been viewed as extremist agendas into the Republican mainstream.

These disparate but sympathetically minded groups, who found a national outlet in Fox News, which served to normalise their views and communicate them to conservatives around the country, all united around a common enemy when Barack Obama became president in 2008. The election of the first African-American president incited a racist backlash across the country.

Trump's rise as a politician was profoundly intertwined with Obama's presidency. He gained political purchase by spreading the nativist 'birther' conspiracy theory that Obama was foreign-born, and thus disqualified for the presidency. The bottom line was the effort to delegitimise the first black president. When Obama retaliated by mocking Trump at the 2011 White House Correspondents dinner, Trump's rage was visible; many observers concluded that his entire presidential campaign was provoked by his affront at being publicly humiliated by a black man.

Trump's accommodationist response to the violence in Charlottesville therefore did not come as a shock to everyone. During the campaign Trump had circulated anti-Semitic and neo-Nazi symbols and tropes on social media, and incited violence at his largely white rallies against protesters, many of whom were black. Despite the clear racial lines being drawn, Trump and his supporters insisted their concerns were economic, and that any racism was being injected into the discussion by their critics — much as the America First Committee had blamed their critics for objecting to Lindbergh's anti-Semitism in 1941. While denying that the contest was driven by racial politics, Trump relentlessly focused his campaign on the resentments of white people, just as Hiram Evans had done when defending the Klan back in 1926.

When he was inaugurated, Trump promised to put 'America first' by 'transferring power from Washington' and 'giving it back to you, the people'. Those people – his followers and voters – were overwhelmingly white. Immediately following his inauguration Trump installed outspoken white nationalists in his administration, including Steve Bannon and Stephen Miller, as well as bringing in Sebastian Gorka (whose membership of the Hungarian Nazi Party journalists had firmly established, although Gorka denied it) as an adviser.[15]

In January 2018, Trump made international headlines when he demanded during discussions of immigration from Haiti and African nations why he would want 'all these people from shithole countries', adding that he thought the United States should 'admit more people from places like Norway'.[16] Although most commentators saw that Norway is ethnically white, others were puzzled by what seemed an arbitrary white country to name. 'Why Norway?' asked a *Houston Chronicle* report, highlighting the 'racialism' of the choice; it added that the neo-fascist website *Daily Stormer* had approved Trump's remarks, saying they showed that 'Trump is more or less on the same page as us'.[17] The *Chronicle* did not, however, mention that followers of the page in question continue to support Nordicism per se as a racial ideal for America.[18]

It was all, as Dorothy Thompson said of Charles Lindbergh, 'old stuff'. Meanwhile summary violence against black people escalates, as unarmed black Americans continue to be shot in cold blood with impunity by white police officers, a national scourge of executions that have been described, with good reason, as lynchings.

* * *

The signals – dog whistles – of white nationalism were everywhere, and converged with a history of accusations of systemic racism against Trump and his father.

When the story emerged during the 2016 campaign that Trump's father had been arrested in 1927 at what was often erroneously described as a 'Klan rally', Trump at first denied that the Fred Trump in question was his father, saying they'd never lived at the address named in the newspaper reports, 175–24 [*sic*] Devonshire Road, in Queens. But as other newspaper reports verify, although Donald never lived there, the Trump family did.

There is no evidence that Fred C. Trump was at the 1927 Memorial Day parade to support the Klan. What is remarkable is that of the parade's 20,000 spectators, only seven were arrested, and one instantly released. The other six were five 'avowed Klansmen', and Fred Trump.

Donald has spoken often, and proudly, of having inherited the world view of his father, whom he idolised. 'My legacy has its roots in my father's legacy,' he stated in 2015.

An important aspect of that legacy, according to at least one of Trump's biographers, is eugenicism. 'The family subscribes to a racehorse theory of human development,' the biographer said. 'They believe that there are superior people and that if you put together the genes of a superior woman and a superior man, you get a superior offspring.'[19]

Trump himself endorsed a garbled version of eugenics (without appearing able to recall the word), when he explained in a 2010 interview with CNN: 'Well I think I was born with the drive for success because I have a certain gene. I'm a gene believer.' His example could have come straight from the 1922 *Saturday Evening Post* article on Nordicism that compared people to horses: 'Hey, when you connect two race horses, you usually end up with a fast horse. I had a good gene pool from the standpoint of that.'[20]

In October 2017, Trump was widely ridiculed for his reply to reports that his Secretary of State, Rex Tillerson, had referred to him as 'a fucking moron'. Trump responded: 'I think it's fake news. But if he did [say] that, I guess we'll have to compare IQ tests. And I can tell you who is going to win.'[21] Although presumably Trump is unaware of the eugenicist theories behind IQ tests that Walter Lippmann denounced back in 1923, his faith that they will show him to be a genius is not unrelated.

The world view Fred Trump bequeathed to his son came from a eugenicist America in which Klan members marched, 1,400 strong, down the street where he lived, loudly proclaiming that they were for one hundred per cent Americanism and America first. It was a world of nativism and the one-drop rule, in which being one hundred per cent American meant being one hundred per cent white. It was a world in which self-styled American fascists fought on the streets with anti-fascists. It was a world in which the German-American Bund drew a crowd of 20,000 Americans to a Nazi rally in Madison Square Garden in 1939. (There are unsubstantiated rumours that the German-American Fred Trump was a member of the Bund, but no evidence has yet surfaced to support this claim.)

And while it is true that no one knows why Fred Trump was arrested along with five self-identified members of the Klan at the Memorial Day parade riots in Queens in 1927, it is also true that his later record would not suggest he was there to protest against the Klan.

Maybe it was all just a coincidence.

* * *

But this story has been full of coincidences, which is another name for the patterns created by hindsight, which is another name for history. Indeed, this book was motivated by such patterns of resemblance, and they kept appearing.

Take Trump's political resemblance to many of this story's figures, including William Randolph Hearst, the 'America first' tycoon who became the model for Charles Foster Kane in the 1941 film *Citizen Kane*. When Trump accepted the Republican nomination in 2016, he did so in front of a giant image of himself that quoted almost exactly the visuals of Kane's political rally – and cult of personality – in the film. Trump once told an interviewer that *Citizen Kane* was his favourite film, adding that he identified with Kane. Whether Trump realised that Orson Welles was deliberately likening Charles Foster Kane to fascists – and that Welles himself was visually referring to Leni Riefenstahl's images from *Triumph of the Will* – is a different question.

Hearst's efforts to keep America from fighting fascism in Europe were, for people like Welles, indistinguishable from supporting fascism. In the opening scene of *Citizen Kane*, Welles invokes Hearst's 1934 visit to Hitler: Kane declares there will be no world war, and then the voiceover adds that Kane would often support and then denounce a given world figure, showing Kane on a balcony with Hitler.

Kane's authoritarianism may not be why Trump liked *Citizen Kane*, but he certainly realised the political power that Hearst's newspaper chain gave him, for he told the *Guardian* in 2012 that social media worked for him like owning a newspaper.

> My Twitter has more followers than the New York Times has readers. I have a newspaper – I literally have my own newspaper and it's called @iamdonaldtrump. Literally. Now when someone

attacks me, I attack them right back. I used to have to make
speeches to attack people, now I don't even have to do that.[22]

(As the interviewer noted, this was not 'literally' the name of his
Twitter account, which Trump narcissistically misnamed.)

Introducing the phrase 'America first' to the world in 1915,
Woodrow Wilson had also warned that the forces of propaganda
were creating 'fake news', a phrase that became a hallmark of
Trump's political career (undergoing a remarkable reversal from
a charge levied against him for his brazen lies, distortions and
fabrications, to a complaint he turned on his accusers, claiming that
any unflattering fact about him was just 'fake news').

Then there is Sinclair Lewis's President Windrip, preening
himself on how successful his media appearances are and the
loyalty of his crowds in terms that sound eerily like Trump. 'You
forget that I myself, personally, made a special radio address to that
particular section of the country last week! And I got a wonderful
reaction. The Middle Westerners are absolutely loyal to me. They
appreciate what I've been trying to do!' Or the fact that Lewis uses
the word 'deplorable' – controversially used by Hillary Clinton
to characterise Trump's followers – to describe a conflict on the
Mexican border, where Trump notoriously promised to build a wall
during his campaign.

And let us not forget Warren G. Harding, who ran on an
'America first' platform, insisted being a president would be so
easy, and promised to run America like a business before actually
running it like a disorganised crime syndicate. The 'birther'
conspiracy surrounding Harding proved an uncanny reverse
image of the one against Obama that Trump used so despicably
to launch his own national political career. (The claims of 'black
blood' continued to follow Harding's descendants, and were not
finally disproven until they did a DNA test in 2015; one of them
'confessed to a little disappointment. "I was hoping for black
blood," he said.')[23]

Then there is the fact that press coverage of Trump accepted rationalisations disturbingly similar to those used by Imperial Wizard Hiram Evans to defend the Klan in 1926: the 'economic distress' of Klan members ninety years ago was almost identical to the 'economic anxiety' obsessively held by the media to have motivated Trump's voters, rather than racial resentment. Likewise, Evans explicitly called for 'a return to power' ('We are demanding, and we expect to win, a return of power into the hands of the everyday, not highly cultured, not overly intellectualized, but entirely unspoiled and not de-Americanized, average citizen of the old stock'), just as white supremacists would later chant in Charlottesville: 'Jews will not replace us.'

These symmetries go beyond Trump himself, extending to members of his administration. 'Economic nationalism', the phrase appropriated by his campaign manager and chief adviser Steve Bannon, emerged from the 'America first' debates over internationalism and the Versailles Treaty. The outcry that met the confirmation of Hugo Black following his history as a Klansman mirrored that which greeted the confirmation of Jefferson Beauregard Sessions as Attorney General in 2016 despite his well-documented opposition to civil rights, down to their shared home state of Alabama, and Dorothy Thompson's sarcastic reference to Black's inability to 'recall' his racist past, an inability that Sessions also repeatedly demonstrated in his testimony before Congress in 2017.

Sessions had also praised the Johnson–Reed Act during a 2015 radio interview with Steve Bannon. 'In seven years we'll have the highest percentage of Americans, non-native born, since the founding of the Republic … It's a radical change. When the numbers reached about this high in 1924, the president and congress changed the policy, and it slowed down immigration significantly. We then assimilated through the 1965 [Immigration Act] and created really the solid middle class of America, with assimilated immigrants, and it was good for America. We passed a law that went far beyond what anybody realized in 1965, and we're on a path to surge far past what the situation was in 1924.'[24] He sounded remarkably like the 1923 *Chicago Tribune* editorial arguing that assimilation could only occur 'without a perpetual flux of new elements' if the country were to achieve racial 'homogeneity': once again, old immigrants were in, new immigrants out.

In October 2017, the *New York Times* reported that on Stephen Miller's high school yearbook page he quoted Theodore Roosevelt on 'one hundred per cent Americanism'. 'There can be no fifty-fifty Americanism in this country. There is room here for only 100 percent Americanism, only for those who are Americans and nothing else.'[25] Unsurprisingly, the quotation was taken out of context.

The parallels go on and on. Seventy-five years before the Unite the Right movement would march on Charlottesville and kill Heather Heyer, there was a 'Union Party' in 1941 that brought together white supremacist groups. In 1940 Americans were hanging swastikas on Confederate monuments in Virginia. The 2017 rally at Charlottesville had been staged in protest at the planned removal of a Confederate monument, a statue of Robert E. Lee.

The myth of the Confederate Lost Cause, an act of deeply revisionist history, had been disavowing for 150 years the idea that slavery had anything to do with Southerners' reasons for the Civil War. The Confederacy was motivated by states' rights, Northern aggression, the Unionists' perfidy, anything but the savage protection of a white privilege that owed its existence to the bloody inheritances of slavery.

This deliberate separation of the Confederacy from the institutional slavery it was established to preserve led to defenders of Lee's statue even insisting that Robert E. Lee wasn't a white supremacist, either. His decision to lead the Confederate army to war in order to defend slavery and the white supremacy it upheld was apparently just another coincidence. Ironically, few have ascribed the South's secession to 'economic anxiety', although the threat of losing plantation slavery and the capital it concentrated had indeed created profound economic anxiety in white Southerners. It's why they waged war against their fellow Americans – to protect their entitlements to the profits created by the labour of the black people they brutalised.

* * *

Most Americans today assume that Confederate statues were put up after the Civil War in simple white supremacist pride, or fury, by people who didn't realise how history would one day judge them. For some of the statues, that is indeed the case – but not all.

Almost exactly a hundred years before Trump was elected, a debate arose in the South about whether to put up a white supremacist statue – a debate framed precisely in terms of how history would judge them.

In September 1916 the novelist Thomas W. Dixon tried to erect a statue in North Carolina, in honour of the uncle who was the inspiration for the hero ('the little Colonel') of *The Clansman*, the novel that inspired *The Birth of a Nation*. Dixon wanted Colonel McAfee's statue clothed in the robes of the Ku Klux Klan, but a newspaper in nearby Charlotte objected, arguing that the colonel should be wearing a Confederate uniform.

The *Charlotte Observer*'s leader maintained that, while a statue of Dixon's uncle in Confederate uniform would meet 'unquestioned acceptance', to put him in the robes of the Klan was an entirely different matter.

'It would be hard to conceive of a statue more grotesquely treated,' the editorial protested. 'It is history that belongs to the past, that should be of record and stored in the archives as a sealed book … The erection of a statue of the class proposed would impose upon the people of this and succeeding generations the duty of perpetual explanation and defense, a duty that might become irksome with the passing of the years and that might in the end be repudiated.'[26]

To be sure, there were no doubts expressed about commemorating the Confederate cause; on the contrary. The *Observer* concluded that it would be fine to memorialise Colonel McAfee 'as a Confederate officer, in which role for all ages there would be none to give his name other than acclaim'.

So they were only drawing the line at the Klan: but they did draw that line. And even as they told themselves that a Confederate statue would meet nothing but acclaim through the ages, they also admitted that any paean to white supremacism might in the end be 'repudiated'.

The controversy made it to the pages of the *New York Times*, where it appeared next to an (unrelated) article about 'America First'. The *Times* began with a counter-editorial written by the *Advertiser*, in Montgomery, Alabama, who called the *Observer*'s position 'ridiculous', arguing that if McAfee was famous for organising the Klan, that's what he should be memorialised for.

The American paper of record then weighed in, saying that where Southerners disagreed, Northerners might 'express opinions'. The *New York Times*'s opinion? 'It was with the better part of the Klan's history, its fight for the preservation of civilization in the South, that this soldier was connected,' it declared, endorsing the Lost Cause myth that the Klan fought for something other – 'better' – than white supremacy. 'If he is to be honored by a statue, it should be one that will recall his real work. It was, as the Advertiser says, a phase of Southern civilization which has passed.'

'The Observer is perhaps too touchy,' it concluded.[27]

Perhaps.

* * *

We have achieved Scott Fitzgerald's ironic vision in 'The Swimmers' of a country that thinks it can dispense with history altogether, as if it is a handicap weighing us down, when in fact it is the common ground upon which we walk. Historical amnesia is certainly liberating, in one sense – but a knowledge of history can be emancipatory, too.

CODA

These comparisons only take us so far, of course. The world of 1916 is not the same as the world of 2016. Such parallels do not end the story: rather, they begin to enlighten us about the shared meanings of America.

History is not a question of surface resemblances, and people are not generally defined by a single choice. Take just one example: Hugo Black was a member of the Ku Klux Klan, before becoming a notably liberal Supreme Court Justice. But if people should not be defined by one choice or one position, it is also worth demanding, as the *Pittsburgh Post-Gazette* did in its exposé of Black, whether certain choices are unforgivable, disqualifying. And it is also worth asking, as Dorothy Thompson did, what the cost of pure political expediency is to any society. If you are not defined by one choice, that doesn't mean you won't be judged by one – especially by history.

For just as we must be alert to the differences between past and present, so we should also see the continuities. One thing this history demonstrates is that democracy depends upon good faith. That's what Dorothy Thompson was insisting upon, as was Walter Lippmann, over and over. Individuals operating in bad faith are nothing new, but the system must work in good faith if it is to prevail.

It turns out our idealism was there to protect our ideals. 'Common decency', after all, means not only basic decency, but a decency that is held in common. The struggle between common decency and common crooks will never end: common decency won't triumph on its own.

The American dream did not have to come true to shape the history of the nation: it merely needed to be reiterated to keep the ideal alive. When the dream changed from a collective ideal of democracy, variously defined and vigorously debated, to an individual desire for success that was rarely questioned, it altered the character of the nation. We were all better for the dreaming, as the 1914 Virginia editorial had observed.

It might fairly be said that every era invented its own American dream – not that the American dream kept failing, but rather that it kept successfully adapting to new conditions. The Progressive Era inspired an American dream of social justice and economic equality; the First World War aroused an American dream of international democracy; the jazz age excited an American dream of endless riches; the Depression precipitated an American dream of social democracy; the Second World War enflamed an American dream of liberal democracy; post-war prosperity advanced an American dream of upward mobility and democratic capitalism; the civil rights movement reclaimed an American dream of democratic equality.

But if each era has its own American dream, which one do we have today?

The meaning of the American dream has stopped being debated by each generation, only the reality of it is debated now; and maybe that's all James Truslow Adams meant when he said that every generation must fight for it anew.

Instead, for all the noisy shouting about the American dream, as a concept it went inert, fossilising into something static and flat. The American dream ceased to adapt – not to changing economic conditions, but to changing ethical imperatives.

Today America has inherited a story that diminishes it, obscuring the fact that once it dreamed more expansively. If even your dreams are ungenerous, then surely you have lost your way. This rich, complex, difficult dream that was a birthright was forgotten in a gold rush, a land grab in the post-war era. That this dream might be abandoned in a race for wealth is precisely what F. Scott Fitzgerald,

Sinclair Lewis, Dorothy Thompson and all the others were warning against.

Loving democracy is not a bromide, and it is not sentimental. Americans have acted as if democracy could survive anything thrown at it. Now the time has come again, seventy-five years after the last, for another 'titanic resistance' to the forces of authoritarianism that have always existed within American life. The American dream did once serve to unite Americans in times of national crisis, before eventually changing course and dividing them.

The truth is always uglier than any meliorist ideal. As this chronicle has shown (both implicitly and explicitly), America routinely shields itself from the horrors of its own history. The facts are vastly less heroic than the myths America tells itself, and the world. But the myths and the facts are not entirely distinct, either, for – as this account has also shown – the myths have helped shape the facts.

In the wake of Trump's election, many of the commentators writing columns about the 'death' of the American dream did so to point out that what once had been a national ideal of larger spiritual aspiration had shrivelled into mere materialism.[1] And to be sure that shrinking of individual aspiration did indeed occur over the post-war era.

But it isn't simply the case that individual Americans once had a broader definition of personal success, as James Truslow Adams argued. The point is that the American dream was once a collective ideal, not an individualist one. Then it was reduced from a political dream of egalitarian democracy to an individual dream of opportunity, and then that further devolved into mere materialism. Our elegies to the death of the American dream only begin at the point of cremation, as if its ashes were all we'd lost.

Perhaps even more important is that the principles of social democracy the American dream once symbolised are now proclaimed by so many self-styled experts on American culture to be *antithetical* to it. On the contrary: ideas of social democracy and social justice are at the root of the expression, which derives from a conversation about progressivism, social democracy and inequality. Those are the forces that gave birth to the term: the efforts to control unbridled capitalism, to secure the well-being of all Americans, not just the wealthy and powerful.

Although some people think the American dream can only refer to free-market capitalism, and assert that social democracy is inherently anti-American, history is not on their side. The facts say something else about what Americans have always thought the American dream might mean. At the very least, no one can accurately claim the American dream *must only* mean capitalism and individual economic aspiration. Nor is it true, as some have also contended, that the American dream was invented as a fig leaf to protect white privilege, to obscure the racist foundations of the capitalist system in institutional slavery. It certainly has been used to do that, in recent years probably more often than not; but when it emerged, the American dream worked as an exhortation, urging all Americans to do better, to be fairer, to combat bigotry and inequality, and strive for a republic of equals. That the dream wasn't realised – that it didn't come close – doesn't mean that the dream was corrupt. It does mean that people are.

None of this is to deny the legitimacy of the way we use the 'American dream' now. Language is collective, and protean; it evolves. Clearly the American dream means now what people use it to mean, including individual prosperity. And equality of opportunity has indeed always been embedded in the idea – the phrase has simply changed course on what it suggested to the country about how to achieve that equality of opportunity.

The point is less to pass a moral judgement on the way the term is now used, than to challenge claims that this is how it has always been used, or that the way it is now used is the only thing it has ever meant, or can ever mean again.

Nor is my argument a version of what's known as 'originalism', the doctrine holding that the earliest meaning of a word or document is correct by virtue of being the original meaning – as if older definitions of the American dream must be correct because they are older. I don't prefer the American dream of democracy over the American dream of materialism because it came first. I prefer it because it is better.

Idealism is not inexhaustible; neither is democracy. We have to renew them, as so many of these writers warned. Our ideals are not always the same as theirs, but they are supposed to be founded on shared principles. This is a story about old-fashioned intangibles: about ethics, morals and character – and we dismiss them as old-fashioned at our peril. Without them, we are left with some very concrete tangibles: corruption, kleptocracy, swindling. Those are old-fashioned, too. So is white supremacism, in all its nationalist malevolence.

Americans need to restore belief in the social contract, our sense of society as a moral economy, and there is much good reason to do so in the name of a reclaimed American dream. There is no good reason to do so in the name of America first.

There is no progress without aspiration. But not all aspirations are created equal.

* * *

In August 1941, Dorothy Thompson wrote an article for *Harper's* magazine, called 'Who Goes Nazi?', in which she recommended a 'somewhat macabre parlor game' for social gatherings, 'to speculate who in a showdown would go Nazi'.[2] Fascism was a disease of modern man, she observed, of someone who 'has been fed vitamins and filled with energies that are beyond the capacity of his intellect to discipline. He has been treated to forms of education which have released him from inhibitions. His body is vigorous. His mind is childish. His soul has been almost completely neglected.'

Identifying various groups of people around the room – 'the born Nazis, the Nazis whom democracy itself has created, the certain-to-be fellow-travelers', and 'those who never, under any conceivable circumstances, would become Nazi' — Thompson notes that Nazism is not a matter of nationality but rather of 'a certain type of mind'. She describes Person A, Person B, and so on, predicting each one's potential for fascism, before arriving at 'D.', who is, Thompson declares, 'the only *born* Nazi in the room'.

D. is 'the spoiled son' of a doting mother; he has

never been crossed in his life. He spends his time at the game of seeing what he can get away with. He is constantly arrested for speeding and his mother pays the fines. He has been ruthless toward two wives and his mother pays the alimony. His life is spent in sensation-seeking and theatricality. He is utterly inconsiderate of everybody. He is very good-looking, in a vacuous, cavalier way, and inordinately vain. He would certainly fancy himself in a uniform that gave him a chance to swagger and lord it over others.

There is also a young immigrant in the room. Although 'his English is flawed — he learned it only five years ago', he has 'devoured volumes of American history, knows Whitman by heart, wonders why so few Americans have ever really read the Federalist papers'.

The other people in the room 'think he is not an American, but he is more American than almost any of them. He has discovered America and his spirit is the spirit of the pioneers. He is furious with America because it does not realize its strength and beauty and power.'

Along with the Americans who understand their own values — one of which is generosity — the immigrant is the greatest opponent of fascism in the room.

Only together, history shows, can they defeat the forces of D. Only together can they keep renewing the effort towards some commonweal, one that presses against us all.

SC, Chicago and London, 2017

NOTES

INTRODUCTION

1 See, for example, Peggy Noonan, 'What's Become of the American Dream?', *Wall Street Journal*, 6 April 2017.

2 Carol Graham, 'Is the American Dream Really Dead?', *Guardian*, 20 June 2017.

3 See, for example, Robert J. Shiller, 'The Transformation of the "American Dream"', *New York Times*, 4 August 2017.

4 'Taking Bad Ideas Seriously: How to Read Hitler and Ilyin?', interview with Timothy Snyder, *Eurozine*, 28 August 2017.

5 Dorothy Thompson, 'What Lindbergh *Really* Wants', *Look*, 18 November 1941, pp. 13–14; original emphasis.

6 Women and people of colour were not held to have written novels of the American dream, of course, as their stories were never judged suitably universal.

PROLOGUE

1 *Tribune*, Seymour, IN, 31 May 1927.

2 *Los Angeles Times*, 31 May 1927.

3 Ibid.

4 *Ithaca Journal-News*, Ithaca, NY, 3 November 1927.

5 *New York Times*, 31 May 1927.

6 *Brooklyn Daily Eagle*, 31 May 1927.

7 *Philadelphia Inquirer*, 1 June 1927.

8 *Brooklyn Daily Eagle*, 4 June 1927.

9 Ibid, 9 June 1927.

10 *Daily Messenger*, Canandaigua, NY, 31 May 1927.

11 *Brooklyn Daily Eagle*, 31 May 1927.

12 Fred Trump is not named in all the reports, some of which only identify six arrests: five 'avowed Klansmen' and the unfortunate man

whose foot was run over (*Brooklyn Daily Eagle*, 31 May 1927). The *New York Times*, however, identified seven men arrested 'in the near-riot of the parade', who were arraigned in Jamaica Court, including 'Fred Trump of 175–24 Devonshire Road, Jamaica', who 'was discharged', *New York Times*, 1 June 1927.

I THE SPIRIT OF AMERICAN DREAMS

1   *Semi-Weekly Messenger*, Wilmington, NC, 4 December 1900.
2   Ibid.
3   *Brooklyn Daily Eagle*, 16 December 1877.
4   *New Orleans Bulletin*, 13 July 1875.
5   *Corvallis Gazette*, Corvallis, OR, 20 February 1880.
6   *Goodwin's Weekly*, Salt Lake City, UT, 9 May 1903.
7   'Bastard dream', *St. Louis Republic*, 23 September 1900; 'Pan-American dream', *San Francisco Call*, 12 June 1900.
8   *Minneapolis Journal*, 29 September 1906.
9   *Times-Leader, Evening News*, Wilkes-Barre, PA, 24 March 1916.
10 *Manchester Guardian*, 20 December 1922.
11 Cyril Ghosh, *The Politics of the American Dream: Democratic Inclusion in Contemporary American Culture*, New York: Palgrave Macmillan, 2013, p. 30.
12 *Record-Union*, Sacramento, CA, 30 October 1899.
13 *New York Evening Post*, New York, 17 January 1845; original emphasis.
14 *Sunday Inter Ocean,* Chicago, IL, 28 April 1895.
15 *Brooklyn Daily Eagle*, 9 October 1899.
16 *Leavenworth Times*, Leavenworth, KS, 14 July 1908.
17 Grover Cleveland, Second Inaugural Address, delivered 4 March 1893.
18 Frank Parsons, *The City for the People, or, The Municipalization of the City Government and of Local Franchises*, Philadelphia: C. F. Taylor, 1900, p. 9.
19 *Philadelphia Times*, 22 April 1900.
20 *Duluth Labor World*, Duluth, MN, 21 September 1901.
21 *Manchester Guardian*, 29 March 1910.
22 David Graham Phillips, *Susan Lenox: Her Fall and Rise*, New York: D. Appleton & Company, 1917, Vol. I, p. 439.
23 Ibid., Vol. II, p. 553.
24 *Chicago Tribune*, 14 December 1912.
25 For example, in a 2011 PhD dissertation on the American dream, James E. Ayers wrote: 'The American dream makes its debut in print discourse

in 1914 in journalist and political commentator Walter Lippmann's book, *Drift and Mastery* ... This is, historically, the first printed use of the term at all.' James E. Ayers, '"The Colossal Vitality of His Illusion": The Myth of the American Dream in the Modern American Novel', *LSU Doctoral Dissertations*, 2767, p. 20. http://digitalcommons.lsu.edu/gradschool_dissertations/2767. See also: John Kenneth White and Sandra L. Hanson, eds, *The Making and Persistence of the American Dream*, Philadelphia: Temple University Press, 2011; and Demetri Lallas, '"From the People, by the People, to the People": The American Dream(s) Debut', *Journal of American Culture*, Vol. 37, No. 2, June 2014.

26 Walter Lippmann, *Drift and Mastery: An Attempt to Diagnose the Current Unrest*, New York: Mitchell Kennerley, 1914, p. 211.

27 *Federalist* No. 51, *Independent Journal*, 6 February 1788.

28 Walter Lippmann, *Drift and Mastery: An Attempt to Diagnose the Current Unrest*, New York: Mitchell Kennerley, 1914, p. 177.

29 Ibid.

30 Ibid., p. 146.

31 John Locke, *An Essay Concerning Human Understanding*, 24th edn, London: W. Baynes & Son, 1823 (1689), p. 196.

32 Sherwood Anderson, *Windy McPherson's Son*, Book III, New York: John Lane, p. 257.

33 Ibid., p. 258.

34 *Times-Dispatch*, Richmond, VA, 20 August 1914.

2 PURE AMERICANISM AGAINST THE UNIVERSE

1   *Tribune*, Union, MO, 1 February 1889.

2   *New York Times*, 19 June 1891.

3   *Morning News*, Wilmington, DE, 13 November 1894.

4   *Advocate*, Topeka, KS, 14 February 1894.

5   *Centralia Enterprise and Tribune*, Centralia, WI, 2 December 1899.

6   *News-Journal*, Mansfield, OH, 1 December 1914.

7   *Baltimore Sun*, 21 April 1915.

8   Ibid.

9   John Brisben Walker, 'Woodrow Wilson: Has He Been for "America First?"' Address given at Cooper Union, 18 November 1915.

10 *Chicago Tribune*, 2 June 1889.

11 *New York Times*, 14 September 1889.

12 *Minneapolis Star Tribune*, Minneapolis, MN, 14 April 1912.

13 See, for example: *Baltimore Sun*, 14 October 1892; and *Natchez Democrat*, Natchez, MS, 13 October 1916. 'Mercenary minded – money mad', 'unmergeable', 'alien and unassimilable' from H. W. Evans, 'The Menace of Modern Immigration', Knights of the Ku Klux Klan, pamphlet, 1924, p. 24.

14 *New York Times*, 13 October 1915.

15 Ibid.

16 *Lawrence Daily Journal-World*, Lawrence, KS, 19 October 1915.

17 *Palladium-Item*, Richmond, IN, 29 October 1915.

18 *New York Times*, 14 June 1916.

19 Ibid., 10 October 1916.

20 *Cincinnati Enquirer*, 8 June 1916, p. 2.

21 *Scranton Republican*, Scranton, PA, 7 November 1916.

22 *Allentown Leader*, Allentown, PA, 26 January 1916.

23 *Washington Post*, 26 April 1916.

24 *North American Review*, Vol. 204, No. 731, October 1916, p. 514; original emphasis.

25 *Altoona Tribune*, Altoona, PA, 25 October 1916.

26 *Los Angeles Times*, 2 January 1916.

27 *Farmer and Mechanic*, Raleigh, NC, 3 November 1903.

28 *Weekly Journal-Miner*, Prescott, AZ, 6 June 1917.

29 *Arizona Republic*, Phoenix, AZ, 28 June 1916.

30 *Wichita Daily Eagle*, Wichita, KS, 28 November 1915.

31 *Reno Gazette-Journal*, Reno, NV, 2 August 1917.

32 *New York Tribune,* 30 September 1917.

33 *Hardin County Ledger*, Eldora, IA, 15 February 1917.

34 Quoted in John Milton Cooper, Jr., *Woodrow Wilson: A Biography*, New York: Alfred A. Knopf, 2009, p. 585.

35 *New York Times*, 19 July 1918.

36 Ibid., 20 December 1915.

37 Ibid., 27 June 1916.

38 *Topeka State Journal*, Topeka, KS, 31 May 1916.

39 Roosevelt's position on race was complicated. While he shared many of the eugenicist assumptions of white superiority of his time, he also believed in racial 'uplift' and progress, that black people could advance, and in 1901 he was the first president to invite a black person, his friend, adviser and former slave Booker T. Washington, to dine at the White House, a decision that shifted the national conversation on race, and made him the target of a deluge of racist vitriol. For a fuller examination of Roosevelt's perspectives on race,

see Thomas G. Dyer, *Theodore Roosevelt and the Idea of Race*, Baton Rouge: Louisiana State University Press, 1980.

40 *Portsmouth Herald*, Portsmouth, NH, 1 June 1918.

41 *Argus-Leader*, Sioux Falls, SD, 1 July 1918.

42 Ibid., 21 April 1917.

43 *San Francisco Chronicle*, 9 February 1919.

44 Ibid.

45 *Cincinnati Enquirer*, 1 May 1923.

46 Madison Grant, *The Passing of the Great Race*, New York: Charles Scribner's Sons, 1916, p. 198.

47 Ibid., p. 98. There is an enormous literature on scientific racism and its relation to Americanism. See, for example, Ewa Barbara Luczak, *Breeding and Eugenics in the American Literary Imagination: Heredity Rules in the Twentieth Century*, New York: Palgrave Macmillan, 2015, p. 164: 'The reference to the nordic race quickly grew to embody the doctrine of the superiority of the American descendants of North European immigrants and came to be identified with Americanism'.

48 *Greensboro Daily News*, Greensboro, NC, 17 October 1920.

49 *Wichita Daily Eagle*, Wichita, KS, 1 March 1918.

50 *Ocala Evening Star*, Ocala, FL, 5 April 1918.

51 *Liberator*, Boston, MA, 26 September 1835.

52 *Anti-Slavery Bugle*, Lisbon, OH, 24 November 1855.

53 *New York Times*, 10 February 1859.

54 Ibid., 13 November 1914.

55 *Henderson Gold Leaf*, Henderson, NC, 27 February 1902.

56 Hernán Vera and Andrew M. Gordon, *Screen Saviors: Hollywood Fictions of Whiteness*, New York: Rowman & Littlefield, 2003, p. 20.

57 The number was widely circulated in 1922, including in a full-page advertisement the NAACP took out in the *New York Times*, while local papers around the country reported: '3436 victims have been lynched by mobs since 1889. Only 17 per cent of them were accused of assaulting women. Lynched victims included 64 women.' *Richmond Item*, Richmond, IN, 13 January 1922.

3 WHAT DO YOU CALL THAT BUT SOCIALISM?

1 *Oregon Daily Journal*, Portland, OR, 27 March 1918.

2 *Burlington Free Press*, Burlington, VT, 10 December 1915.

3 *Chicago Tribune*, 7 February 1916.

4 *Evening World*, New York, NY, 26 February 1917.

5   Ibid.

6   *Chicago Tribune*, 18 January 1917.

7   *Baltimore Sun*, 7 January 1917, p. 6; *Washington Post*, Washington DC, 15 July 1919.

8   *Daily Times*, Davenport, IA, 5 September 1917.

9   *Chicago Tribune*, 29 October 1917, p. 8.

10 Ibid., 8 April 1918.

11 *Walnut Valley Times*, El Dorado, KS, 25 April 1918.

12 *Nebraska State Journal*, Lincoln, NE, 7 November 1918.

13 *San Bernardino County Sun*, San Bernardino, CA, 25 June 1919.

14 *Reading Times*, Reading, PA, 4 November 1919.

15 *Nebraska State Journal*, Lincoln, NE, 1 January 1920.

16 *Chattanooga News*, Chattanooga, TN, 5 January 1918.

17 Theodore Dreiser, *Twelve Men*, Philadelphia: University of Pennsylvania Press, 1998 (1919), p. 219.

18 George Barr McCutcheon, *West Wind Drift*, New York: A.L. Burt Company, 1920, pp. 292–3.

19 Ibid., p. 294.

20 Ibid.

4 WE HAVE EMERGED FROM DREAMLAND

1   *Greensboro Daily News*, Greensboro, NC, 25 July 1916.

2   *Buffalo Commercial*, Buffalo, NY, 17 February 1917.

3   *Washington Times*, 29 August 1917.

4   *Los Angeles Times*, 4 April 1918.

5   Ronald Steel, *Walter Lippmann and the American Century*, New York: Little, Brown, 1980, pp. 158–9.

6   *New York Herald*, 27 January 1919.

7   *St. Louis Post-Dispatch*, 20 November 1918.

8   *New York Tribune*, 1 March 1920.

9   *Washington Times*, 8 February 1920.

10 *Scranton Republican*, Scranton, PA, 26 July 1919.

11 *Burlington Free Press*, Burlington, VT, 28 May 1920.

12 *New York Times*, 29 February 1920.

13 Ibid., 15 February 1920.

14 Ibid., 10 March 1920.

15 *Times-Dispatch*, Richmond, VA, 10 March 1920.

16 Ibid.

17 *Brooklyn Daily Eagle*, 13 February 1920.

18 *New York Times*, 20 March 1920.

19 Ibid., 13 June 1920.

20 *Courier*, Asheboro, NC, 5 August 1920.

21 *Indianapolis Journal*, 23 December 1895.

22 *Albany-Decatur Daily*, Albany, AL, 8 June 1920.

23 *Fayetteville Observer*, Fayetteville, NC, 1 July 1920.

24 *Kinsley Mercury*, Kinsley, KS, 1 July 1920.

25 *Winston-Salem Journal*, Winston-Salem, NC, 2 July 1920.

26 *El Paso Herald*, El Paso, TX, 3 July 1920.

27 *New York Times*, 25 July 1920.

28 Ibid., 1 September 1920.

29 *Pittsburgh Daily Post*, 1 July 1920.

30 Ibid.

31 *New York Times*, 19 October 1920.

32 Warren G. Harding, 'Address to Foreign Born', Marion, OH, 18 September 1920.

33 *New York Times*, 25 October 1920.

34 Ibid., 31 October 1920.

35 Ibid., 18 October 1920.

36 Ibid., 4 November 1920.

37 Ibid., 14 November 1920.

38 Ibid., 28 November 1920.

39 *Indianapolis Star*, 23 February 1920.

40 *News and Observer*, Raleigh, NC, 5 July 1919.

41 *New York Tribune*, 2 February 1920.

42 *Washington Progress*, Washington, NC, 22 July 1920.

43 'Economic competition between the negroes and the "poor whites" is a source of trouble … The Southern "cracker" is the bitterest enemy of the negro, and he leads and composes a large part of the lynching parties', *Courier-Journal*, Louisville, KT, 10 May 1903.

44 *North Platte Semi-Weekly Tribune*, North Platte, NE, 23 November 1920.

45 *Dallas Express*, 17 January 1920.

46 *Santa Ana Register*, Santa Ana, CA, 10 December 1920.

47 *Dallas Express*, 17 January 1920.

48 *New York Herald*, October 1920.

49 *Lincoln Star*, Lincoln, NE, 28 October 1920.

50 Quoted in *Public Ledger*, Maysville, KY, 30 October 1920.

51 *Daily Arkansas Gazette*, Little Rock, AR, 31 October 1920, p. 24.

52   Ibid.

53   *St. Louis Post-Dispatch*, 31 October 1920.

54   William Allen White to Ray Stannard Baker, 8 December 1920,
     Walter Johnson, ed., *Selected Letters of William Allen White*, New York:
     Henry Holt, 1947, p. 213.

5 SALESMEN OF PROSPERITY

1   Steel, *Walter Lippmann and the American Century*, p. 190.

2   *Pittsburgh Press*, 6 January 1922.

3   *Akron Beacon Journal*, Akron, OH, 11 January 1922.

4   Sinclair Lewis, *Babbitt*, New York: Harcourt, Brace, 1922, p. 13.

5   Ibid., p. 25.

6   Ibid., p. 391.

7   Ibid.

8   Ibid., p. 392.

9   James Truslow Adams, *The Epic of America*, New York: Little, Brown,
     1947 (1931), p. 191.

10   Rupert Brooke, *Letters from America*, New York: Beaufort, 1988
     (1916), p. 68.

11   *New York Times*, 16 October 1922.

12   *Oregon Daily Journal*, Portland, OR, 2 July 1922.

13   *Chicago Tribune*, 27 March 1923.

14   While most historians start the genealogy of the 'American dream'
     in 1931, some do trace it back to Lippmann in 1923 and fewer to
     his Drift and Mastery in 1914. While I was pursuing this research, I
     published journalism that used each date as I discovered them. That
     information has since been superseded by my subsequent research
     here. See, for example, Scott A. Sandage, *Born Losers: A History of Failure
     in America*, Cambridge, MA: Harvard University Press, 2005, p. 337.

15   Walter Lippmann, 'The Mental Age of Americans: II. The Mystery of
     the "A" Men', *New Republic* 32, No. 413 (1 November 1922), 246–8.

16   Ibid., No. 417 (29 November 1922), 9–11.

17   *Hartford Courant*, Hartford, CT, 2 May 1918, p. 14.

18   Phil A. Kinsley, '*The Vegetable* Proves Bird When Right Post Is Found',
     Philadelphia Record, 13 May 1923. In Jackson Bryer, ed., *F. Scott
     Fitzgerald: The Critical Reception*, New York: Burt Franklin & Co.,
     1978, p. 172.

19   *Chicago Tribune*, 1 July 1923.

20   *Harrisburg Telegraph*, Harrisburg, PA, 20 July 1923.

6 THE SIMPLICITY OF GOVERNMENT

1   Warren G. Harding, *Our Common Country: Mutual GoodWill in America*, Columbia: University of Missouri Press, 2003 (1921), p. 18.

2   *Baltimore Sun*, 19 December 1920.

3   *Salt Lake Herald-Republican*, Salt Lake City, UT, 1 February 1920; *Washington Herald*, Washington DC, 19 April 1920.

4   *New York Times*, 22 January 1921.

5   Harding, *Our Common Country*, p. 73.

6   Ibid., p. 8.

7   Ibid., p. 18.

8   Ibid.

9   *Charlotte News*, Charlotte, NC, 25 June 1921.

10 Ibid.

11 See, for example, the *Courier-Journal*, Louisville, KT, 10 January 1920: 'The Socialist party ... stands discredited and its members are shunned by every 100 per cent American ... One hundred per cent Americanism means the destruction of I.W.W.-ism, Boolshevism [*sic*] and Socialism ... Should the "unexpected happen" and the three alien enemies arrested in Louisville on immigration warrants escape deportation by immigration authorities, officials declared last night that there are "two other steps" that can be taken leading to their deportation ... Volunteer informers are coming ... every day, explaining activities of person with radical tendencies. L.A. Hickman, attorney ... said yesterday he was just as desirous as every other 100 per cent American to "see the 'Reds' get what is their due".'

12 *Cincinnati Enquirer*, 12 November 1919.

13 Upton Sinclair, *100%: The Story of a Patriot*, The Floating Press, 2013 (1920), p. 133.

14 Ibid., p. 319.

15 Ibid., p. 262.

16 Walter Lippmann, *Men of Destiny*, New York: Macmillan, 1927, p. 8.

17 *Tampa Bay Times*, St Petersburg, FL, 6 July 1921.

18 *Evening Star*, Washington DC, 25 February 1922.

19 *Marion Star*, Marion, OH, 5 March 1921.

20 *Brooklyn Daily Eagle*, 16 January 1921.

21 *St. Louis Star and Times*, 5 March 1921.

22 *New York Times*, 14 November 1921.

23 *Harrisburg Telegraph*, Harrisburg, PA, 8 August 1921.

24 *Wilmington Morning Star*, Wilmington, NC, 4 March 1921.

25 *Des Moines Register*, 16 July 1921.

26 *Capital Times*, Madison, WI, 21 March 1921; original emphasis.

27 Calvin Coolidge, 'Whose Country Is This?', *Good Housekeeping*, February 1921, Vol. 72, No. 2, pp. 13, 14, 106, 109.

28 *Pittsburgh Daily Post*, 27 January 1922.

29 *Muncie Evening Press*, Muncie, IN, 14 February 1921.

30 *New York Tribune*, 28 January 1921.

31 *Palm Beach Post*, West Palm Beach, FL, 28 January 1921.

32 *Honolulu Star-Bulletin*, 21 July 1921.

33 *Evening World*, New York, 6 September 1921.

34 Frederick Lewis Allen, *Only Yesterday: An Informal History of the 1920s*, New York: Harper & Row, 1931, p. 54.

35 *Evening World*, New York, September 1921.

36 Nancy K. MacLean, *Behind the Mask of Chivalry: The Making of the Second Ku Klux Klan*, Oxford: Oxford University Press, 1995, pp. 8–9.

37 Knights of the Ku Klux Klan, *Kloran*, Ku Klux Press, 1918, p. 5.

38 *Salina Evening Journal*, Salina, KS, 31 October 1922.

39 Reprinted in *Los Angeles Times*, 9 October 1921. Klan historian Nancy MacLean, for example, would write in 1995: 'Much more than American historians have realized, in fact, Klan ideology shared common features with its Nazi contemporary', *Behind the Mask of Chivalry*, p. 180. Historians may later have lost sight of this resemblance, but the Americans who lived through both phenomena did not.

40 *Morning Register*, Eugene, OR, 1 January 1922.

41 *Town Talk*, Alexandria, LA, 30 January 1922.

42 *McKinney Courier-Gazette*, McKinney, TX, 17 August 1922.

43 *New York Times*, 24 November 1922.

44 Ibid., 25 November 1922.

45 Ibid., 6 November 1922.

46 Ibid., 13 February 1923 and 22 June 1923.

47 *Brooklyn Daily Eagle*, 1 February 1921.

48 *Great Falls Tribune*, Great Falls, MT, 29 May 1921.

49 *Tampa Times*, 12 December 1922.

50 *Appeal*, St Paul, MN, 9 December 1922.

51 *Minneapolis Star Tribune*, Minneapolis, MN, 1 August 1921.

52 *Philadelphia Inquirer*, 5 August 1922.

53 *New York Tribune*, 12 November 1922.

54 *Great Falls Tribune*, Great Falls, MT, 5 November 1922.

55 *New York Times,* 21 November 1922.
56 Ibid.
57 *Brooklyn Daily Eagle,* 1 April 1923.
58 Ibid., 22 November 1923.
59 *Des Moines Register,* 9 August 1923.
60 *News Leader,* Staunton, VA, 27 September 1923.
61 *Washington Times,* Washington DC, 17 November 1922.
62 *Appeal,* St Paul, MN, 23 December 1922.
63 Ibid.
64 *Baltimore Sun,* 30 December 1922.
65 *Des Moines Register,* 21 January 1923.
66 *St. Louis Post-Dispatch,* 31 May 1923.
67 *Independent Record,* Helena, MT, 14 May 1923.
68 *El Paso Herald,* 13 December 1922.
69 Ibid.
70 *Chicago Tribune,* 18 November 1922.
71 *St. Louis Post-Dispatch,* 6 May 1923.
72 *Star Press,* Muncie, IN, 12 November 1922.
73 *Wichita Daily Times,* Wichita Falls, TX, 3 January 1922.
74 *Buffalo American,* Buffalo, NY, 29 July 1920.
75 Ibid., 19 January 1922.
76 *Dallas Express,* 16 December 1922.
77 *Brooklyn Daily Eagle,* 30 September 1923.
78 Ibid.
79 *Baltimore Sun,* 22 March 1923.
80 *El Paso Herald,* 10 April 1923.
81 *New York Times,* 3 May 1923.
82 *Baltimore Sun,* 22 March 1923, p. 26.
83 Ibid.
84 *Santa Ana Register,* Santa Ana, CA, 20 March 1923.
85 *Nebraska State Journal,* Lincoln, NE, 23 March 1923.

7 A WILLINGNESS OF THE HEART

1 F. Scott Fitzgerald, *The Great Gatsby,* Oxford University Press, 1998 (1925), p. 14.
2 Ibid., p. 99.
3 Ibid., p. 143.
4 Ibid., pp. 143–4.

5   Ibid., p. 79.
6   Bruce Barton, *The Man Nobody Knows: A Discovery of the Real Jesus*, New York: Grosset & Dunlap, 1924, 1925, pp. iv, 32, 23.
7   Ibid., p. iv.
8   Ibid., p. 107.
9   Ibid., p. 140.
10 Ibid., pp. 159–63; original emphasis.
11 *Racine Journal-Times*, Racine, WI, 19 January 1925.
12 Calvin Coolidge, 'Have Faith in Massachusetts: Massachusetts Senate President Acceptance Speech', 7 January 1914.
13 *Daily Republican*, Monongahela, PA, 3 September 1925.
14 *Los Angeles Times*, 29 January 1926; *Daily Times*, Davenport, IA, 29 January 1926.
15 *Brooklyn Daily Eagle*, 12 June 1927.
16 *Philadelphia Inquirer*, 17 October 1925.
17 *Ironwood Daily Globe*, Ironwood, MI, 1 Oct 1927.
18 *Morning Herald*, Uniontown, PA, 17 September 1925; *Ithaca Journal*, Ithaca, NY, 16 November 1929.
19 *Los Angeles Times*, 6 July 1925.
20 *St. Louis Post-Dispatch*, 18 March 1928.
21 *Miami News*, 8 April 1927.
22 *Los Angeles Times*, 12 August 1928.
23 Fitzgerald, 'The Swimmers', *Saturday Evening Post*, 19 October 1929, p. 13.
24 Ibid., p. 152.
25 Ibid., p. 150.
26 Ibid., p. 154.

8 A SUPER PATRIOT, PATRIOT

1   *Philadelphia Inquirer*, 2 July 1923.
2   *Chicago Tribune*, 12 December 1923.
3   Ibid., 15 December 1923.
4   *Baltimore Sun*, 14 September 1923.
5   H. W. Evans, 'The Menace of Modern Immigration', Knights of the Ku Klux Klan, pamphlet, 1924, pp. 6–8.
6   *New York Times*, 18 November 1923.
7   Ibid.
8   Ibid.
9   Ibid.

10   Ibid., 30 January 1924.

11   *St. Louis Post-Dispatch*, 17 May 1924.

12   *New York Times*, 25 September 1924.

13   *Press and Sun-Bulletin*, Binghamton, NY, 23 June 1924.

14   See, for example, Thomas Pegram, *One Hundred Percent American: The Rebirth & Decline of the Ku Klux Klan in the 1920s*, Chicago: Ivar R. Dee, 2011, on estimating membership numbers. Pegram concludes: 'Reasonable estimates of Klan membership range from about two million members to four or even five million Klansmen at the peak of the movement,' p. 26. Nancy Maclean writes that by the mid-1920s 'the total reached perhaps as high as five million, distributed through nearly four thousand local chapters. Yet the numbers barely suggest the reach of the Klan's tentacles.' *Behind the Mask of Chivalry*, p. 10.

15   *Age*, Melbourne, Australia, 14 February 1924.

16   *Mail Tribune*, Medford, OR, 29 December 1924.

17   Ibid.

18   *New York Times*, 11 August 1980.

19   *New York Times*, 21 June 1924.

20   Kenneth L. Roberts, 'Shutting the Sea Gates', *Saturday Evening Post*, 28 January 1922, p. 51.

21   *Minneapolis Star Tribune*, Minneapolis, MN, 3 July 1922.

22   Ibid.

23   Ibid.

24   *Vardaman's Weekly,* Jackson, MI, 10 May 1923.

25   *Marion Democrat*, Marion, AL, 10 April 1907.

26   *Philadelphia Inquirer*, 13 April 1924.

27   *New York Times*, 17 October 1924.

28   *Detroit Free Press*, 27 October 1924.

29   *Asbury Park Press*, Asbury Park, NJ, 6 October 1925.

30   *Freeport Journal-Standard*, Freeport, IL, 22 April 1921.

31   *Buffalo American*, Buffalo, NY, 19 November 1925.

32   *North American Review (1821–1940)*, 1 March 1926, Vol. CCXXIII, No. 830, p. 52.

33   *Manchester Guardian*, 9 November 1926.

34   *Minneapolis Star Tribune*, 2 February 1928.

35   *St. Louis Post-Dispatch,* 30 October 1927.

36   *New York Times*, 6 November 1927.

37   *Chicago Tribune*, 5 April 1928.

38 *St. Joseph Observer*, St Joseph, MO, 7 October 1927, p. 1.
39 Ibid.
40 Ibid.
41 Ibid.

9 DAS DOLLARLAND

1 Allan Nevins, *James Truslow Adams: Historian of the American Dream*, Chicago: University of Illinois Press, 1968, p. 68.
2 Adams, *The Epic of America*, p. viii.
3 Ibid., p. 172.
4 Ibid., p. 173.
5 Ibid., p. 216.
6 Ibid., p. 71.
7 Ibid., p. 192.
8 Ibid., p. 427.
9 Ibid.
10 Garet Garrett, 'America Can't Come Back', *Saturday Evening Post*, 23 January 1932.
11 *Noblesville Ledger*, Noblesville, IN, 1 January 1929.
12 Allen, *Only Yesterday*, p. 146.
13 James Truslow Adams, *A Searchlight on America*, New York: Routledge 1930, p. 143.
14 *New York Times*, 9 April 1933.
15 Ibid.
16 Ibid., 13 May 1934.
17 Ibid., 20 January 1935.
18 John Dewey, 'Tomorrow May Be Too Late', *Good Housekeeping,* 20–1 March 1934.
19 *Pantagraph,* Bloomington, IL, 30 January 1934.
20 *Decatur Daily Review*, Decatur, IL, 11 November 1934.
21 *New York Times*, 13 January 1934.
22 *Brooklyn Daily Eagle*, 26 June 1932.
23 *New York Times*, 27 May 1932.
24 Ibid., 6 November 1932.
25 Nevins, *Adams*, p. 198.
26 *New York Times*, 14 May 1933.
27 Ibid.

10 THE OFFICIAL RECOGNITION OF REALITY

1   *Chicago Tribune*, 21 March 1933.
2   Dorothy Thompson, *I Saw Hitler*, New York: Farrar & Rinehart, 1932, p. 14.
3   Ibid., p. 32.
4   Ibid., p. 4; original emphasis.
5   *Daily Press*, Newport News, VA, 3 May 1933.
6   Dorothy Thompson, *Saturday Evening Post*, 'Back to Blood and Iron', 6 May 1933, and 'Room to Breathe In', 24 June 1933.
7   *New York Times*, 21 February 1926.
8   MacLean, *Behind the Mask of Chivalry*, p. 178.
9   *Altoona Mirror*, Altoona, PA, 19 July 1930.
10 *Baltimore Sun*, 12 September 1930.
11 *Dixon Evening Telegraph*, Dixon, IL, 27 August 1930.
12 *Baltimore Sun*, 12 September 1930.
13 *Oshkosh Northwestern*, Oshkosh, WI, 2 September 1930.
14 *Oakland Tribune*, Oakland, CA, 18 May 1930.
15 *Pittsburgh Courier*, 31 May 1930.
16 *Muncie Evening Press*, Muncie, IN, 8 August 1930.
17 *New Yorker*, 8 September 1934, p. 26.
18 *New York Times*, 28 October 1934.
19 Quoted in Dora Apel, *Imagery of Lynching: Black Men, White Women, and the Mob*, New Brunswick, NJ: Rutgers University Press, 2004, p. 137.
20 Ibid.
21 *Tampa Bay Times*, St Petersburg, FL, 23 October 2011.
22 *Times*, Shreveport, LA, 3 March 1930.
23 *Decatur Herald*, Decatur, IL, 10 October 1930.
24 *Sandusky Register*, Sandusky, OH, 14 October 1930.
25 *Detroit Free Press*, 27 April 1930; *Ludington Daily News*, Ludington, MI, 10 August 1930.
26 *New York Times*, 31 December 1931.
27 *Millard County Chronicle*, Delta, UT, 29 February 1930.
28 *New York Times*, 3 January 1932.
29 *Lincoln Journal Star*, Lincoln, NE, 8 January 1932.
30 Ibid.
31 *Quad-City Times*, Davenport, IA, 19 January 1932.
32 *New York Times*, 17 January 1932.

33   Ibid., 23 February 1933.

34   Ibid., 27 July 1933.

35   *New Castle News*, New Castle, PA, 7 July 1933.

36   *Kentucky Advocate*, Danville, KY, 8 July 1933.

37   *Oakland Tribune,* Oakland, CA, 25 April 1933.

38   Ibid.

39   *Morning News,* Wilmington, DE, 7 October 1933.

40   *New York Times*, 29 January 1933.

41   Ibid.

42   *Akron Beacon Journal*, Akron, OH, 20 December 1933.

43   *Miami News*, 28 August 1933.

44   *Morning Call*, Allentown, PA, 19 May 1934.

45   *Brooklyn Daily Eagle*, 18 May 1934.

46   *Chicago Tribune*, 18 May 1934.

47   *New York Times*, 18 May 1934.

48   Ibid., 31 March 1934.

49   *Brooklyn Daily Eagle*, 13 August 1934.

50   *New York Times*, 10 September 1934.

51   *Scranton Republican*, Scranton, PA, 9 September 1934.

52   *New York Times*, 17 September 1934.

53   Ibid., 15 October 1934.

54   Ibid., 4 November 1934.

55   *Times Herald*, Port Huron, MI, 28 November 1934.

56   *Press and Sun-Bulletin*, Binghamton, NY, 25 September 1934.

57   *Burlington Free Press*, Burlington, VT, 17 September 1934.

58   *Brooklyn Daily Eagle*, Brooklyn, NY, 30 September 1934.

59   *Burlington Free Press*, Burlington, VT, 17 September 1934.

11   THE PAGEANT OF HISTORY

1   *New York Times*, 9 April 1934.

2   Ibid.

3   *Clovis News-Journal*, Clovis, NM, 29 June 1934.

4   *Shamokin News-Dispatch*, Shamokin, PA, 22 September 1934.

5   *Los Angeles Times*, 8 August 1934.

6   *New York Times*, 7 August 1934.

7   *Asbury Park Press*, Asbury Park, NJ, 18 November 1935.

8   *Courier-Journal*, Louisville, KY, 30 August 1935.

9   *Des Moines Register*, 1 December 1935.

10   *Statesman Journal*, Salem, OR, 13 August 1935.

11   *Lincoln Star*, Lincoln, NE, 2 May 1935.

12   *Lincoln Evening Journal*, Lincoln, NE, 2 May 1935.

13   *Press and Sun-Bulletin*, Binghamton, NY, 1 July 1935.

14   *Ithaca Journal*, Ithaca, NY, 23 November 1935.

15   *Daily Press*, Newport News, VA, 15 June 1935.

16   *Brooklyn Daily Eagle*, 15 September 1935.

17   *Arizona Daily Star*, Tucson, AZ, 22 September 1935.

18   *Des Moines Register*, 13 December 1935.

19   *Eugene Guard*, Eugene, OR, 28 May 1935.

20   John Hyde Preston, 'Searching for Roots in America', *Harper's*, October 1936.

21   *Baltimore Sun*, 14 December 1936.

22   *Pittsburgh Press*, 27 June 1935.

23   Herbert Agar, *What is America?*, London: Eyre Spottiswoode, 1936, pp. 228–9.

24   *New York Times*, 11 June 1936.

25   *Minneapolis Star*, 15 May 1936.

26   Franklin Delano Roosevelt, Address at Madison Square Garden, New York City, 31 October 1936.

27   Quoted in *Lincoln Journal Star*, Lincoln, NE, 26 November 1938.

28   *Salt Lake Tribune*, Salt Lake City, UT, 22 January 1937.

29   *Republic*, Columbus, IN, 20 January 1936.

30   *Greeley Daily Tribune*, Greeley, CO, 20 February 1937.

31   *Ogden Standard-Examiner*, Ogden, UT, 29 December 1937; *Courier News*, Blytheville, AR, 30 December 1937; *Anniston Star*, Anniston, AL, 28 December 1937.

32   *Reading Times*, Reading, PA, 28 April 1938.

33   A 1949 item headlined 'The American Dream' is the earliest association I have seen; it begins: 'The green-shuttered country cottage with a white picket fence around it has become as emblematic of American aspiration as was homemade apple pie a symbol of American soldier hope during the last war.' *Salt Lake Tribune*, Salt Lake City, UT, 1 May 1949.

34   *Brooklyn Daily Eagle*, 29 August 1937.

35   *Courier-News*, Bridgewater, NJ, 15 August 1935.

36   *New York Times*, 3 July 1943.

37   *Times-Leader, Evening News*, Wilkes-Barre, PA, 21 October 1937.

38   *Cincinnati Enquirer*, 26 February 1938.

39   *Pittsburgh Post-Gazette*, 25 February 1939.
40   *Hartford Courant*, Hartford, CT, 3 February 1938.
41   *New York Times*, 30 October 1938, Section 6.
42   *Los Angeles Times*, 24 April 1938.
43   *Denton Journal*, Denton, MD, 16 April 1938.
44   *St. Louis Star and Times*, 4 October 1938.
45   *Lead Daily Call*, Lead, SD, 14 April 1938.
46   Ibid.
47   *Post-Register*, Idaho Falls, ID, 14 April 1938.
48   *Hope Star*, Hope, AR, 16 December 1938.
49   *Nebraska State Journal*, Lincoln, NE, 28 November 1938.
50   Although the earliest example the *OED* offers of the American political usage of 'libertarian' is from 1945, and political scientists date the movement to the early 1950s, the meaning was in use in the US by 1893: 'Society cannot much longer get on upon the old libertarian, competitive, go-as-you-please system to which so many sensible persons seem addicted', *Stark County Democrat*, Canton, OH, 19 October 1893.
51   *Baltimore Sun*, 1 December 1938.
52   *Tennessean*, Nashville, TN, 25 November 1938.
53   *Times*, Shreveport, LA, 27 November 1938.
54   *Cincinnati Enquirer*, 5 May 1939.
55   *Sheboygan Press*, Sheboygan, WI, 31 May 1939.
56   *St. Louis Star and Times*, 13 July 1939.
57   John Steinbeck, *The Grapes of Wrath*, New York: Penguin, 1939, p. 112.
58   Ibid., p. 193.
59   *New York Times*, 19 February 1939.

12   IT CAN HAPPEN HERE

1   *Brooklyn Daily Eagle*, 10 February 1935.
2   Ibid., 13 February 1935.
3   *Pittsburgh Press*, 11 March 1935.
4   *St. Louis Post-Dispatch*, 19 August 1935.
5   See, for example, *Pittsburgh Press*, 30 November 1934.
6   *Hartford Courant*, Hartford, CT, 11 September 1935.
7   Forrest Davis, *Huey Long: A Candid Biography*, New York: Dodge Publishing, 1935, p. 286.
8   *Baltimore Sun*, 3 September 1935.

9   *Cincinnati Enquirer*, 7 October 1935.

10 Letter from Thompson to Sinclair Lewis, 13 March 1933. Quoted in Peter Kurth, *American Cassandra: The Life of Dorothy Thompson*, Boston: Little, Brown, 1990, p. 187.

11 *Cincinnati Enquirer*, 28 May 1936.

12 Ibid.

13 *Oakland Tribune*, Oakland, CA, 3 May 1936.

14 *Christian Century*, Vol. 53, 5 February 1936, p. 245.

15 *Central Home New Jersey Home News*, New Brunswick, NJ, 20 February 1936.

16 *San Bernardino County Sun*, San Bernardino, CA, 26 July 1936.

17 *Morning Call*, Allentown, PA, 21 July 1936.

18 *Corpus Christi Caller-Times*, Corpus Christi, TX, 24 July 1936.

19 W. E. B. Du Bois, *Black Reconstruction in America 1860–1880*, New York: Free Press, 1999 (1935), p. 700.

20 'Jew Shoot', *Time*, 24 August 1936.

21 Ibid.

22 *Wisconsin Jewish Chronicle*, Milwaukee, WI, 28 August 1936.

23 *Independent Record*, Helena, MT, 21 February 1937.

24 *Lincoln Journal Star*, Lincoln, NE, 6 September 1937.

25 *Tampa Tribune*, Tampa, FL, 14 September 1937.

26 *Arizona Daily Star*, Tucson, AZ, 1 August 1937; *Courier*, Waterloo, IA, 1 September 1937.

27 *New York Times*, 17 August 1937.

28 *Pittsburgh Post-Gazette*, 18 September 1937.

29 *St. Louis Post-Dispatch*, 3 October 1937.

30 *Pittsburgh Post-Gazette*, 4 October 1937.

31 *Marion Star*, Marion, OH, 4 October 1937.

32 *Cincinnati Enquirer*, 27 September 1937.

33 *News of the World*, Hollywood, CA, 18 September 1937.

34 *Brooklyn Daily Eagle*, 27 June 1937.

35 *Greenville News*, Greenville, SC, 3 November 1937.

36 *Pittsburgh Post-Gazette*, 11 January 1938.

37 *Brooklyn Daily Eagle*, 6 April 1938.

38 *New York Times*, 12 September 1938.

39 Ibid., 20 November 1938.

40 Ian Mugridge, *The View from Xanadu: William Randolph Hearst and United States Foreign Policy*, Montreal: McGill-Queen's University Press, 1995, p. 113.

41 *Times-Leader, Evening News,* Wilkes-Barre, PA, 2 May 1939.
42 *Argus Leader,* Sioux Falls, SD, 6 May 1939.
43 *Moberly Monitor-Index,* Moberly, MO, 19 November 1938.
44 Ibid.
45 *Star Press,* Muncie, IN, 19 November 1938.
46 Ibid.
47 Kurth, *American Cassandra,* p. 328.
48 *Daily Capital Journal,* Salem, OR, 3 January 1939.
49 *Emporia Gazette,* Emporia, KS, 3 January 1939.
50 *Abilene Reporter-News,* Abilene, TX, 21 October 1939.
51 *Asheville Citizen-Times,* Asheville, NC, 6 September 1939.
52 *Oakland Tribune,* Oakland, CA, 15 February 1939.
53 *Pittsburgh Press,* 27 January 1939.
54 *New York Times,* 13 January 1939.
55 *Daily Press,* Newport News, VA, 17 February 1939.
56 *Decatur Daily Review,* Decatur, IL, 21 February 1939.
57 *Danville Morning News,* Danville, PA, 21 February 1939.
58 'Stupid fools', *Danville Morning News,* Danville, PA, 21 February 1939; 'President Rosenfeld', *San Bernardino County Sun,* San Bernardino, CA, 21 February 1939.
59 *Reading Times,* Reading, PA, 1 March 1939.
60 *Chillicothe Gazette,* Chillicothe, OH, 21 February 1939.
61 *Santa Cruz Sentinel,* Santa Cruz, CA, 21 February 1939.
62 *Greenville News,* Greenville, SC, 21 February 1939.
63 *Cincinnati Enquirer,* 22 February 1939.
64 *St. Louis Star and Times,* 5 August 1939.
65 *Democrat and Chronicle,* Rochester, NY, 7 July 1939.
66 *Indianapolis Star,* 30 March 1939.
67 *Miami News,* 5 March 1939.
68 *New York Times,* 6 October 1939.
69 *Honolulu Star-Bulletin,* 14 October 1939.
70 *Cincinnati Enquirer,* 2 June 1939.
71 Quoted in Kurth, *American Cassandra,* p. 310.

13 AMERICANS! WAKE UP!

1 *Jackson Sun,* Jackson, TN, 13 November 1938.
2 *Cincinnati Enquirer,* 23 November 1938.

3   *Brooklyn Daily Eagle*, 25 December 1938.

4   *Pittsburgh Press*, 10 December 1938.

5   *Daily Times*, Davenport, IO, 19 December 1938.

6   *Times-Leader, Evening News*, Wilkes-Barre, PA, 11 July 1940.

7   *Akron Beacon Journal*, Akron, OH, 11 July 1940.

8   *St. Louis Post-Dispatch*, 8 October 1940.

9   *New York Herald Tribune*, 20 September 1939.

10 *Detroit Free Press*, 19 October 1939.

11 *Plain Speaker*, Hazelton, PA, 20 October 1939.

12 Quoted in Kurth, *American Cassandra*, p. 311.

13 *Salt Lake Tribune*, Salt Lake City, UT, 28 January 1940.

14 *Jackson Sun*, Jackson, TN, 7 July 1940.

15 *Harrisburg Telegraph*, Harrisburg, PA, 3 June 1940.

16 Ibid.

17 *Courier-Journal*, Louisville, KT, 17 June 1940.

18 Ibid.

19 Ibid.

20 Ibid.

21 *St. Louis Post-Dispatch*, 18 August 1940.

22 *Tribune*, Kokomo, IN, 15 March 1940.

23 *Eau Claire Leader*, Eau Claire, WI, 1 November 1940.

24 Guy Greer, 'Arming and Paying for It', *Harper's*, November 1940.

25 *Hartford Courant*, Hartford, CT, 20 June 1941.

26 *Minneapolis Star*, 21 April 1941.

27 *News-Dispatch*, Shamokin, PA, 30 April 1941.

28 *Harrisburg Telegraph*, Harrisburg, PA, 25 June 1940.

29 *Amarillo Globe Times*, Amarillo, TX, 7 October 1940.

30 *Freeport Journal-Standard*, Freeport, IL, 24 May 1940.

31 *Medford Mail Tribune*, Medford, OR, 9 June 1940.

32 *Iola Register*, Iola, KS, 6 August 1940.

33 The claim that the America First Committee of 1940 originated the slogan 'America first' is widespread. See, for example: Louisa Thomas, 'America First, For Charles Lindbergh and Donald Trump', *New Yorker*, 24 July 2016; Eric Rauchway, 'Donald Trump's new favorite slogan was invented for Nazi sympathizers', *Washington Post*, 14 June 2016; Susan Dunn, 'Trump's "America First" has ugly echoes from U.S. history', CNN, 28 April 2016; '"America First": From Charles Lindbergh to President Trump', NPR podcast, 6 February

2017. Historian Timothy Snyder made the same claim in an October 2017 interview, 'Trump and Bannon's idea of "America First" is technically from 1940', from 'Taking Bad Ideas Seriously: How to Read Hitler and Ilyin?', interview with Timothy Snyder, *Eurozine*, 28 August 2017.

34   Lindbergh, 'Our Relationship with Europe', August 1940.

35   *Daily Times*, Davenport, IA, 30 December 1940.

36   Ibid.

37   *Abilene Reporter-News*, Abilene, TX, 24 January 1941.

38   *Cincinnati Enquirer*, 17 February 1941.

39   *Escanaba Daily Press*, Escanaba, MI, 18 February 1941.

40   *Tampa Bay Times*, St Petersburg, FL, 23 February 1941.

41   *Quad-City Times*, Davenport, IA, 17 August 1941.

42   *Sikeston Standard*, Sikeston, MO, 7 November 1941.

43   *St. Louis Star and Times*, 18 October 1941.

44   *Minneapolis Star*, 20 July 1941.

45   *Harrisburg Telegraph*, Harrisburg, PA, 25 April 1941.

46   *Index-Journal*, Greenwood, SC, 28 May 1941.

47   *Nebraska State Journal*, Lincoln, NE, 6 June 1941.

48   *Cincinnati Enquirer*, 4 June 1941.

49   *Pittsburgh Press*, 18 May 1941.

50   *Miami News*, 21 March 1941.

51   *Independent Record*, Helena, MT, 14 April 1941.

52   *Chicago Tribune*, 25 April 1941.

53   *Daily Times*, Davenport, IA, 29 April 1941.

54   *Daily Tar Heel*, Chapel Hill, NC, 29 January 1941.

55   *Akron Beacon Journal*, Akron, OH, 8 March 1941.

56   *St. Louis Star and Times*, 16 August 1941.

57   Ibid., 23 May 1941.

58   Mark Schorer, *Sinclair Lewis: An American Life*, New York: McGraw Hill, 1961, p. 661.

59   *Democrat and Chronicle*, Rochester, NY, 30 April 1941.

60   *Arizona Republic*, Phoenix, AZ, 29 April 1941.

61   *Akron Beacon Journal*, Akron, OH, 13 July 1941.

62   *Star Gazette*, Elmira, NY, 9 June 1941.

63   *Oakland Tribune*, Oakland, CA, 28 June 1941.

64   *Moberly Monitor-Index,* Moberly, MO, 19 November 1938.

65   *Daily Times*, Davenport, IO, 16 September 1941.

66   Quoted in *Des Moines Register*, 14 September 1941.

67   Ibid.

68   *Daily Times*, Davenport, IO, 16 September 1941.

69   Ibid.

70   *News Leader*, Staunton, VA, 20 October 1941.

71   *Minneapolis Star*, 25 September 1941.

72   *New York Times*, 26 September 1941.

73   Ibid.

74   *Weekly Town Talk*, Alexandria, LA, 27 September 1941. Reprint of Hearst editorial from *New York Journal-American*.

75   *Wisconsin Jewish Chronicle*, Milwaukee, WI, 19 September 1941.

76   *Stanberry Headlight*, Stanberry, MO, 16 October 1941.

77   *Des Moines Register*, 13 September 1941.

78   Dorothy Thompson, 'What Lindbergh *Really* Wants', *Look*, 18 November 1941, pp. 13–14.

79   Ibid.

80   *Cincinnati Enquirer*, 17 December 1941.

STILL AMERICA FIRSTING

1   *Star Gazette*, Elmira, NY, 28 January 1942.

2   John Fousek, *To Lead the Free World: American Nationalism and the Cultural Roots of the Cold War*, Chapel Hill, NC: University of North Carolina Press, 2000.

3   Warning against 'the infiltration of inharmonious racial or nationality groups,' the Federal Housing handbook stated that 'a change in social or racial occupancy generally leads to instability and a reduction in values,' the Federal Housing handbook stated. *The Handbook of Social Policy*, James O. Midgley and Michelle Livermore, eds, Thousand Oaks, CA: Sage, 2008, p. 406.

4   *New York Times*, 27 August 2016.

5   This is such a customary view that it is even shared in popular outlets. See for example '"I Have A Dream" Speech's Social Critique Sometimes Lost In Celebrations', *Huffington Post*, 24 August 2013, in which several civil rights historians stress the 'subversive' and 'prophetic' nature of King's speech.

6   The Invisible Empire Token, supposedly commemorating the centennial year of the Ku Klux Klan, Cajun Coins, Mandeville, LA, 1965.

7   Francis X. Clines, 'Trump Quits Grand Old Party for New', *New York Times*, 25 October 1999.

8   *New York Times*, 14 February 2000.

9   Ibid.

10 Glenn Kessler, Fact Checker: 'Donald Trump and David Duke: For the Record', *Washington Post*, 1 March 2016.

11 *Los Angeles Times,* 20 January 2017.

12 'David Duke, former Ku Klux Klan leader, to run for Congress', BBC News, 22 July 2016.

13 *US News &World Report*, 28 February 2016.

14 Ibid.

15 See for example 'Sebastian Gorka and the White House's Questionable Vetting', *Atlantic,* 26 March 2017, and 'Sebastian Gorka: Former Trump Aide Accused of Ties to Nazi Group Heads to Israel', *Newsweek*, 6 September 2017.

16 *New York Times*, 11 January 2018.

17 *Houston Chronicle*, 15 January 2018.

18 See for example websites including Amfirstbooks.com, which recycle the eugenicist theories of Madison Grant and Lothrop Stoddard, and issue warnings such as 'America, Look to Norway, and Look at Yourself and Stop Murdering Nordic Peoples!' They inform their readers that 'the Nordic countries must maintain a certain level of homogeneity to preserve the "Viking traits" that give them an edge in technological innovation and entrepreneurial start-ups.' Their versions of American history also combine Nordicism with Lost Cause myths: 'The real *coup de grace* came with the "King Lincoln" dictatorship during the War of Northern Aggression Against Southern Independence ... By embracing forced racial and ethnic integration, the Federal government smothered Nordic/Celtic entrepreneurial tribal culture and accelerated a de facto Jewish-Catholic dispossession of WASPs from the strategic bases of society. On an ethnic level, the Federal government made its first major foray into the forced racial integration business during the so-called "Reconstruction Era" by installing anti-Southern white carpetbagger regimes in the South ...' Etc.

19 'The Choice 2016', *Frontline*, PBS, Season 35, Episode 1, 27 September 2016.

20 Donald Trump Interview, CNN, Correspondent: Becky Anderson, 10 February 2010.

21 'Trump Challenges Tillerson to "Compare IQ Tests" After Reported "Moron" Dig', *Guardian*, 10 October 2017.

22   Hadley Freeman, 'Donald Trump: It is My Hair and It is an Amazing Thing', *Guardian*, 2 October 2012.

23   Peter Baker, 'DNA Shows Warren Harding Wasn't America's First Black President', *New York Times*, 18 August 2015.

24   Adam Serwer, 'Jeff Sessions's Unqualified Praise for a 1924 Immigration Law', *Atlantic*, 10 January 2017.

25   'Stephen Miller, the Powerful Survivor on the President's Right Flank', quoted in *New York Times*, 9 October 2017.

26   *Charlotte Observer*, Charlotte, NC, 19 September 1916.

27   *New York Times*, 26 September 1916.

CODA

1   See for example: Peggy Noonan, 'What's Become of the American Dream?', *Wall Street Journal*, 6 April 2017.

2   Dorothy Thompson, 'Who Goes Nazi?', *Harper's*, August 1941.

SELECTED BIBLIOGRAPHY

Adams, James Truslow, *A Searchlight on America*, New York: Routledge, 1930.

—— *The Epic of America*, New York: Little, Brown, 1931.

Agar, Herbert, *The Land of the Free*, New York: Houghton Mifflin, 1935.

—— *What is America?: A New Declaration of Independence*, London: Eyre Spottiswoode, 1936.

Allen, Frederick Lewis, *Only Yesterday: An Informal History of the 1920's*, New York: Perennial, 1964 (1931).

Anderson, Sherwood, *Windy McPherson's Son*, New York: John Lane, 1916.

Apel, Dora, *Imagery of Lynching: Black Men, White Women, and the Mob*, New Brunswick, NJ: Rutgers University Press, 2004.

Ayers, James E. '"The Collosal Vitality of His Illusion": the Myth of the American Dream in the Modern American Novel', *LSU Doctoral Dissertations*, 2767.

Barton, Bruce, *The Man Nobody Knows: A Discovery of the Real Jesus*, New York: Grosset & Dunlap, 1924, 1925.

Bouchard, Gerard, *National Myths: Constructed Pasts, Contested Presents*, New York: Routledge, 2013.

Brooke, Rupert, *Letters From America*, New York: Beaufort, 1988 (1916).

Bryer, Jackson, ed., *F. Scott Fitzgerald: The Critical Reception*, New York: Burt Franklin & Co., 1978.

Campbell, Marius Robinson, et. al., *Guidebook of the Western United States*, Washington: Government Printing Office, 1915.

Chandler, Lester V., *America's Greatest Depression, 1929–1941*, New York: Harper & Row, 1970.

Cole, Wayne S, *America First: The Battle Against Intervention, 1940–1941*, Madison, WI: University of Wisconsin Press, 1953.

Coolidge, Calvin, 'Whose Country Is This?', *Good Housekeeping*, February 1921, Vol. 72, No. 2.

Cooper, Jr., John Milton, Jr., *Woodrow Wilson: A Biography*, New York: Alfred A. Knopf, 2009.

Cullen, Jim, *The American Dream: A Short History of an Idea that Shaped a Nation*, Oxford: Oxford University Press, 2004.

Davis, Forrest, *Huey Long: A Candid Biography*, New York: Dodge Publishing, 1935.

Delbanco, Andrew, *The Real American Dream: A Meditation on Hope*, Cambridge, MA: Harvard University Press, 1998.

Dewey, John, 'Tommorrow May Be Too Late', *Good Housekeeping*, 20–1 March, 1934.

Dreiser, Theodore, *Twelve Men*, Philadelphia: University of Pennsylvania Press, 1998 (1919).

Du Bois, W. E. B, *Black Reconstruction in America 1860–1880*, New York: Free Press, 1999 (1935).

Dyer, Thomas G., *Theodore Roosevelt and the Idea of Race*, Baton Rouge: Louisiana State University Press, 1980.

Evans, H. W., 'The Menace of Modern Immigration', Knights of the Ku Klux Klan, pamphlet, 1924.

Faulkner, William, *Absalom, Absalom!*, New York: Random House, 1936.

Fitzgerald, F. Scott, *The Great Gatsby*, Oxford: Oxford University Press, 1998 (1925).

— 'The Swimmers', *Saturday Evening Post*, 19 October 1929.

— *The Vegetable: or from President to Postman*, New York: Charles Scribner's Sons, 1923.

Fousek, John, *To Lead the Free World: American Nationalism & the Cultural roots of the Cold War*, Chapel Hill: University North Carolina Press, 2000.

Garrett, Garet, 'America Can't Come Back', *Saturday Evening Post*, 23 January 1932.

Garrett, Paul Willard, 'The Jazz Age in Finance', *North American Review*, Vol. 229, No. 2 (February 1930).

Ghosh, Cyril, *The Politics of the American Dream: Democratic Inclusion in Contemporary American Culture*, New York: Palgrave Macmillan, 2013.

Gilbert, Felix, *To the Farewell Address: Ideas of Early American Foreign Policy*, Princeton, NJ: Princeton University Press, 1961.

Grant, Madison, *The Passing of the Great Race: or, The Racial Basis of European History*, New York: Charles Scribner's Sons, 1916.

Greer, Guy, 'Arming and Paying For It', *Harper's*, November 1940.

Harding, Warren G., *Our Common Country: Mutual Good Will in America*, Columbia: University of Missouri Press, 2003 (1921).

Herring, George C., *From Colony to Superpower: US Foreign Relations since 1776*, New York: Oxford University Press, 2008.

Hertog, Susan, *Dangerous Ambition: Rebecca West and Dorothy Thompson, New Women in Search of Love and Power*, New York: Ballantine, 2011.

Hewes, Jr., James E., 'Henry Cabot Lodge and the League of Nations', *Proceedings of the American Philosophical Society*, Vol. 114, No. 4 (August 1970).

Hofstadter, Richard, *The Age of Reform: From Bryan to FDR*, New York: Random House, 1988 (1955).

Jenkins, McKay, *The South in Black and White: Race, Sex and Literature in the 1940s*, Chapel Hill: University of North Carolina Press, 1999.

Jillson, Cal, *The American Dream in History, Politics, and Fiction*, Lawrence, KS: University Press of Kansas, 2016.

Katznelson, Ira, *Fear Itself: The New Deal and the Origins of Our Time*, New York: Liveright, 2013.

Kauffman, Bill, *American First!: Its History, Culture and Politics*, Amherst, New York: Prometheus Books, 1995.

Kennedy, David, *Freedom From Fear: The American People in Depression and War, 1929–1945*, Oxford, Oxford University Press, 1999.

Kurth, Peter, *American Cassandra: The Life of Dorothy Thompson*, Boston: Little, Brown, 1990.

Lallas, Demetri. '"From the People, by the People, to the People": The American Dream(s) Debut', *Journal of American Culture*, 2014, 37.

Leuchtenburg, William E., *Franklin D. Roosevelt and the New Deal, 1932–1940*, New York: Harper & Row, 1963.

— *The Perils of Prosperity, 1914–1932*, Chicago: University of Chicago Press, 1993 (1958).

Lewis, Sinclair, *Babbitt*, New York: Harcourt, Brace, 1922.

— *It Can't Happen Here*, New York: Doubleday, 1935.

Lippmann, Walter, *Drift and Mastery: An Attempt to Diagnose the Current Unrest*, New York: Mitchell Kennerley, 1914.

— *The Stakes of Diplomacy*, New York: Henry Holt, 1915.

— 'Education and the White Collar Class', *Vanity Fair*, July 1923.

— *Men of Destiny*, New York: Macmillan, 1927.

— *Public Opinion*, New York: BN Publishing, 2008.

Littell, Robert, *Read American First*, Freeport, New York: Books for Libraries Press, 1968 (1926).

Locke, John, 'An Essay Concerning Human Understanding', London: W. Baynes & Son, 1823 (1689), 24th edn.

Luczak, Ewa Barbar, *Breeding and Eugenics in the American Literary Imagination: Heredity Rules in the Twentieth Century*, New York: Palgrave Macmillan, 2015.

McCutcheon, George Barr, *West Wind Drift*, New York: A.L. Burt Company, 1920.

MacLean, Nancy K., *Behind the Mask of Chivalry: The Making of the Second Ku Klux Klan*, Oxford: Oxford University Press, 1995.

Manela, Ezra, *Wilsonian Moment: Self-Determination and the International Origins of Anticolonial Nationalism*, New York: Oxford University Press, 2007.

Marchand, Roland, *Advertising the American Dream: Making Way for Modernity, 1920–1940*, Berkeley, CA: University of California Press, 1985.

Midgley James O., and Livermore, Michelle, eds, *The Handbook of Social Policy*, Thousand Oaks, CA: Sage, 2008.

Mugridge, Ian, *The View from Xanadu: William Randolph Hearst and United States Foreign Policy*, Montreal: McGill-Queen's University Press, 1995.

Nevins, Allan, *James Truslow Adams: Historian of the American Dream*, Chicago: University of Illinois Press, 1968.

Olson, Lynne, *Those Angry Days: Roosevelt, Lindbergh, and America's Fight Over World War II, 1929–1941*, New York: Random House, 2013.

Parsons, Frank, *The City for the People: Or, The Municipalization of the City Government and of Local Franchises*, Philadelphia: C. F. Taylor, 1900.

Pegram, Thomas, *One Hundred Percent American: The Rebirth & Decline of the Ku Klux Klan in the 1920s*, Chicago: Ivar R. Dee, 2011.

Phillips, David Graham, *Susan Lenox: Her Fall and Rise*, New York: D. Appleton & Company, 1917.

Procter, Ben, *William Randolph Hearst: The Later Years, 1911–1951*, Oxford: Oxford University Press, 2007.

Ravage, Marcus Eli, *An American in the Making*, New York: Harper & Brothers, 1917.

Rawlings, William, *The Second Coming of the Invisible Empire: The KKK of the 1920s*, Macon, GA: Mercer University Press, 2016.

Rieder, Jonathan, *Gospel of Freedom: Martin Luther King, Jr.'s Letter from Birmingham Jail and the Struggle that Changed a Nation*, New York: Bloomsbury, 2013.

Roberts, Kenneth L., 'Shutting the Sea Gates', *Saturday Evening Post*, 28 January 1922.

Rosenberg, Emily S., *Spreading the American Dream: American Economic and Cultural Expansion, 1890–1945*, New York: Farrar, Straus and Giroux, 1982.

Samuel, Lawrence R., *The American Dream: A Cultural History*, Syracuse, NY: Syracuse University Press, 2012.

Sandage, Scott A., *Born Losers: A History of Failure in America*, Cambridge, MA: Harvard University Press, 2005.

Sarles, Ruth, *A Story of America First: The Men and Women Who Opposed American Intervention in World War II* (ed. Bill Kauffman), Santa Barbara, CA: Praeger, 2003.

Schorer, Mark, *Sinclair Lewis: An American Life*, New York: McGraw Hill, 1961.

Sinclair, Upton, *100%: The Story of a Patriot*, Auckland, New Zealand: The Floating Press, 2013 (1920).

Sirkin, Gerald, 'The Stock Market of 1929 Revisited: A Note', *Business History Review*, Vol. 49, No. 2 (Summer 1975).

Steel, Ronald, *Walter Lippmann and the American Century*, New York: Little, Brown, 1980.

Steinbeck, John, *Of Mice and Men*, New York, Covici-Friede, 1937.

— *The Grapes of the Wrath*, New York: Penguin, 1939.

Thompson, Dorothy, *I Saw Hitler*, New York: Farrar & Rinehart, 1932.

— 'Back to Blood and Iron', *Saturday Evening Post*, 6 May 1933.

— 'Back to Blood and Iron', *Saturday Evening Post*, 6 May 1933.

— 'Room to Breathe In', *Saturday Evening Post*, 24 June 1933.

— 'Who Goes Nazi?', *Harper's*, August 1941.

— 'What Lindbergh Really Wants', *Look*, 18 November 1941.

Vera Hernán, and Gordon, Andrew M., *Screen Saviors: Hollywood Fictions of Whiteness*, New York: Rowman & Littlefield, 2003.

Wall, Wendy L., *Inventing the 'American Way': The Politics of Consensus from the New Deal to the Civil Rights Movement*, Oxford: Oxford University Press, 2008.

Wheelock, David C., 'Regulation and Bank Failures: New Evidence from the Agricultural Collapse of the 1920s', *Journal of Economic History*, Vol. 52, No. 4 (December 1992).

White, Eugene N., 'The Stock Market Boom and Crash of 1929 Revisited', *Journal of Economic Perspectives*, Vol. 4, No. 2 (Spring 1990).

White, John Kenneth and Hanson, Sandra L., eds, *The Making and Persistence of the American Dream*, Philadelphia: Temple University Press, 2011.

White, William Allen, *Selected Letters of William Allen White 1899–1943*, Walter Johnson, ed., New York: Henry Holt, 1947.

ACKNOWLEDGEMENTS

This was not a book I planned to write; it emerged all but serendipitously from a convergence between an idea I'd been pursuing – the rhetorical history of the American dream – and the rise of populist nationalism in western democracies. It took shape when Donald Trump became the global face for those movements in 2016, and succeeded in gaining the US presidency with his slogan 'America First'.

After the publication of my last book, on F. Scott Fitzgerald and *The Great Gatsby*, I was invited to speak on the American dream at the Hay Festival's London Library Lecture. During the course of my research into the American newspapers of the 1920s and 1930s, which underpinned that book, I had noticed that discussions in the 1930s of the American dream seemed to imply something rather different than our standard understanding. The eventual lecture, 'The Secret History of the American Dream', initiated the course of thinking and research that would result in this book, and so my first thanks go to Peter Florence at Hay, and to the London Library, for that invitation.

Over the course of the next few years, that research and thinking continued to evolve; some earlier versions of the ideas in this book appeared as journalism in the *London Library* magazine, the *Telegraph*, the *Guardian*, the *New Statesman* and the *Financial Times*, as well as at lectures and seminars around the UK. One of those, in the spring of 2016, was at the Bristol Festival of Ideas, where I first brought Donald Trump into the context of this story. On the morning after the 2016 election, I found myself rewriting a piece for the *Financial Times* on the outcome, with reference to Fitzgerald's 'The Swimmers', which also fed into this book; thanks to Jonathan Derbyshire for his kindness that morning.

In February 2017, I gave a lecture at the Institute of English Studies at the University of London, in association with the Princeton Alumni of the UK, that laid out all of this thinking for the first time. My thanks to the organisers and audience for encouraging me to continue pursuing these ideas, and to my colleagues at the IES and the School of Advanced Study for their support and flexibility, without which this book could not have been finished.

A few weeks later, BBC Radio 4 commissioned a documentary about the American dream and America first; thanks to Mohit Bakaya, Penny Murphy and Shabnam Grewal for their work on that documentary, and to Kevin Kruse, Darryl Pinckney, Andrew Ross Sorkin, Thomas Sugrue and Leslie Vinjamuri for their brilliant and generous contributions to it in interviews, all of which helped shape my thinking.

Not long after that, I found myself talking to Alexis Kirschbaum at Bloomsbury, who somewhat to my surprise believed there was a book to be written about this, and has fought for it every step. Her faith in this project has been surpassed only by the brilliance of her editing, and I'm extremely grateful for both, as well as her friendship; I'll tell her the rest over a glass of champagne. Thanks to Angelique Tran Van Sang for her patience and clarity, to Katherine Fry for meticulous copy-editing of a fiddly book, and to Greg Heinimann for a superb jacket design.

I wouldn't have been able to finish this book in time without the superlative aid of Sadaf Betts, research assistant extraordinaire, who tracked down the answers to any number of questions, as well as seriously getting into the spirit of this endeavour. Jane Robertson, Lyndsey Stonebridge and Erica Wagner read early drafts and offered wise suggestions and encouragement. Suzannah Lipscomb, in the final stages of finishing her own book, made the time to go through an early draft with precision and rigour, hugely improving the analysis and argument; while Andrew Rudalevige liberally gave the benefit of his expertise in improving the book's historical and political contexts.

When I started writing this book in earnest, I was in the middle of a book about Henry James, which I began in 2015 with the extremely generous support of the Eccles British Library Writer's Award. The Eccles Centre for American Studies has been an invaluable resource for my work, and they were characteristically gracious when I told them I had interrupted the James project to pursue this one. My gratitude to everyone there, especially Catherine Eccles and Philip Davies, for their championing and encouragement of my work.

Thanks as ever to my agent and dear friend, Peter Robinson, for always having my back, as we say at home. I wish David Miller could have read this. My family, especially my parents, gifted me a belief in the importance of knowledge, and a love of American history and its values, without which I would be immeasurably lessened. This is dedicated to Wyndham for everything, but mostly for caring as deeply as I about what this book is trying to do.

INDEX

A NOTE ON THE TYPE

The text of this book is set in Perpetua. This typeface is an adaptation of a style of letter that had been popularised for monumental work in stone by Eric Gill. Large scale drawings by Gill were given to Charles Malin, a Parisian punch-cutter, and his hand-cut punches were the basis for the font issued by Monotype. First used in a private translation called 'The Passion of Perpetua and Felicity', the italic was originally called Felicity.